All In the Timing

From Operating Room to Board Room

•◆•

A Small Town Boy Climbs the Ladder

•◆•

Charles Hatcher, Jr., M.D.

with Joshua Malin

With a foreword by J. Willis Hurst, M.D.

authorHOUSE®

AuthorHouse™
1663 Liberty Drive
Bloomington, IN 47403
www.authorhouse.com
Phone: 1-800-839-8640

For information contact:
Charles Hatcher, Jr., M.D.
1440 Clifton Road, Suite 318-B
Atlanta, Georgia 30322

First published by AuthorHouse   3/15/2011

ISBN: 978-1-4567-4459-5 (e)
ISBN: 978-1-4567-4460-1 (dj)
ISBN: 978-1-4567-4461-8 (sc)

Library of Congress Control Number: 2011902645
Printed in the United States of America

Any people depicted in stock imagery provided by Thinkstock are models,
and such images are being used for illustrative purposes only.
Certain stock imagery © Thinkstock.

This book is printed on acid-free paper.

Front and back cover photography: Emory University Archives and
Danny Acres Photography (www.dannyacres.com)
Jacket Design by Danny Acres and Kelley Johnson
Back Cover Biography adapted from Sylvia Wrobel, Emory University
Inside Cover Article adapted from Michelle Boone, Emory University
Photo Credits: Emory University Photography Archives, Johns Hopkins Medical Institutions'
Alan Mason Chesney Medical Archives, Cloister photography, Portrait Craft

This book is dedicated to my loving wife Phyllis for her encouragement and devotion; to my children, Marian and Charles, III for their steadfast love and understanding in good times and bad; and finally to Phyllis's children, Andrea, Tom, and Holly for allowing me to be their extra dad.

Contents

Foreword

IT IS WITH GREAT PLEASURE that I write the foreword to Charles Ross Hatcher's autobiography. I learned a great deal from the manuscript that he permitted me to read. I not only learned what made him tick – why he was so successful – but learned about tobacco farming in South Georgia, as well as the damage produced by atom bombs!

Charles tells it all with the bark off. His parents were smart enough to let him develop as he wished. From the beginning, he was a self-starter. He was a natural high-achiever in the classroom, on the basketball court, in the operating room, and in administration.

He attended the University of Georgia and the Medical College of Georgia where he received excellent grades. He then chose to go to the Johns Hopkins for his internship and residency in surgery. He dreamed of being a cardiac surgeon and wanted to work under Dr. Alfred Blalock at Hopkins and Dr. Frannie Moore at the Brigham. He did both. His stories of his work in the intense training programs and about his colleagues make great reading. Charles achieved his goals in the developing field of cardiac surgery. Confidence in his own ability and his capacity for hard work made him draft number one in universities who wished to develop cardiac surgery.

My first encounter with Dr. Hatcher was a bit unusual. Let me restate that sentence. My first encounter with Dr. Hatcher was like no other. Dr. J.D. Martin, who was Professor and Chairman of the Department of Surgery at Emory University, asked me to interview Dr. Hatcher whom he was hoping to recruit for cardiac surgery. I was at that time Professor and Chairman of the Department of Medicine at Emory, and greatly interested in the development of cardiology. I was a patient in the hospital at the time. Dr. Martin had performed a hemorrhoidectomy on me. I was happy to see

Dr. Hatcher in my hospital room. Just before the scheduled time for me to see Dr. Hatcher, I had an acute need to take a sitz bath to ease the pain that accompanies such an operation. So, there I was, sitting in a tub of hot water when Dr. Hatcher arrived. I covered myself with towels and said, "Come in Dr. Hatcher." We had a good talk and I urged him to come to Emory, which he eventually did.

Hatcher, in time, became head of cardiac surgery at Emory. He recruited great cardiac surgeons and became nationally recognized as an accomplished surgeon who had developed a team of surgeons that were second to none. He also trained cardiac surgeons who, in turn, made their name in many hospitals.

Hatcher proved himself to be a great organizer, and this lead to his appointment as Director of the Emory Clinic. The clinic thrived under his direction. His success there led to his selection as Director of the entire Woodruff Health Sciences Center.

His ability to think quickly, speak clearly, and negotiate skillfully was easily seen, so he was quite successful in a difficult position. He played a key role in developing the Rollins School of Public Health which became, in a very few years, one of the best schools in the country. He also played a major role in pulling together the pediatric facilities of the City of Atlanta, making Emory an outstanding place to train pediatricians. He was also able to withstand the tough blow associated with closing the Emory Dental School.

All of these achievements are discussed in this book and make interesting reading. A man with less ability and less confidence in himself could not have achieved half as much as Charles Ross Hatcher. It was my good luck to work with him for several decades. We managed patients together – we taught together – I wish we could do it all again.

J. Willis Hurst, M.D.
Charles Howard Candler Professor Emeritus
Chairman Emeritus, Department of Medicine, Emory University

Acknowledgements: Indispensable Support

IN ORDER FOR ANY ADMINISTRATION of an academic health sciences center to be successful, the CEO must be assisted by a dedicated and talented staff. I was particularly fortunate in having such a loyal and capable staff.

Shortly after my arrival at The Emory Clinic in 1962, I was given the opportunity to interview five potential medical secretaries. I chose a young lady who had just graduated from Agnes Scott College in Decatur with no office experience. Mr. Chisholm, the business manager of the clinic, queried me about my choice.

"Dr. Hatcher," he asked, "I just wondered why you picked the one young lady without experience, when all of the other four were experienced secretaries who have worked at the clinic for some time?"

"Barney, I chose her because I am sure that she can handle the work, and the two of us can learn how to run an office together."

Miss Alice Maxwell, later to become Mrs. Wilber Scott, became my first secretary, and remained with me until my retirement from the clinic nearly forty years later. We occupied a small office on the lowest level of the clinic, but I think we both realized that there would be larger and more impressive offices in our future. Mrs. Scott remained as my personal secretary when I became the Chief of the Cardiovascular Surgical Service, when I became the Director and CEO of The Emory Clinic, and initially after I became Vice President for Health Affairs of Emory University. She returned to The Emory Clinic in 1990 and worked there until her retirement. Alice was most helpful with Marian and Charlie when they were kids, and they remain very fond of her today.

When I became the Vice President for Health Affairs, and director of the Woodruff Health Sciences Center at Emory University, I had frequent contact with the office and staff of President James Laney. I was particularly impressed by his executive administrative assistant, Mrs. Ruth Fincher. Dr. Laney treasured her as well. But just about the time I realized I would have to have an administrative assistant dedicated to each of my major positions, Mrs. Fincher resigned from Emory to accompany her husband, a corporate attorney, who was being transferred to North Carolina. Shortly after their arrival in North Carolina, the company which had retained Mr. Fincher was bought out by another company, which terminated his position.

When Mr. Fincher returned to Atlanta for interviews, Mrs. Fincher came with him and stopped by to visit President Laney. I happened to be in President Laney's office for a meeting that day, and was delighted to see her again, and more delighted when I learned that she and her husband were going to return to Atlanta. Dr. Laney had found a suitable replacement for Ruth, and I therefore offered her a job on the spot.

Mrs. Fincher managed my office at the health sciences center from 1990 until my retirement. She has continued to assist me on a part-time basis in the years since retirement. In all these years, I have never known Ruth to raise her voice or become irritated with any caller, and as my assistant at the health sciences center Ruth proved to be extremely adept at handling a wide range of calls and visitors to the office, including trustees, major donors, and friends of Emory.

I cannot visualize a career that didn't depend in large part on the services of Mrs. Scott and Mrs. Fincher.

•◆•

Soon after I was elected the Director of The Emory Clinic I began to work closely with the senior staff of the clinic's business office. The founding Business Manager and still the Business Manager at that time was Mr. Barney Chisholm. Mr. Chisholm was an excellent and very conservative businessman who tempered many of my wilder financial impulses. Working for Mr. Chisholm were several young accountants and junior financial executives. Among these, Mr. Roy Townsend particularly impressed me. I pointed this out to Mr. Chisholm, and indicated that I would like Roy to be brought along in the organization as rapidly as Mr. Chisholm felt appropriate. He was not certain how others in the business office would react if Roy were fast-tracked to a more responsible position. I then explained to Mr. Chisholm that he should take his time with the training and positioning of Roy, but that within five years I wanted him to be in position to take over for Mr. Chisholm upon his retirement.

This was accomplished, and Mr. Townsend functioned for many years as an effective business manager for me and for my replacement as clinic director, Dr. Garland Perdue. With the establishment of Emory Healthcare, the demands on his position increased significantly, and he moved over to assume the management of the Emory-Grady Foundation, remaining in that position until his retirement. I have never had a more loyal and talented associate than Roy Townsend, and he remains a very close friend and business confidante.

Mr. William J. Todd was the business manager of the Eye Center and Department of Ophthalmology. I interviewed Bill in my recruitment of a senior administrative assistant for the office of Vice President for Health Affairs and Director of The Robert W. Woodruff Health Sciences Center. Bill was a Georgia Tech graduate who functioned beautifully in this position. During this period we became quite involved in the move of the American Cancer Society headquarters from New York to a location on our medical campus across from the Centers for Disease Control. The Cancer Society asked if Bill Todd would be the project manager for the construction of their headquarters building, and he ultimately brought this project in on time and under budget.

When the Georgia Research Alliance was established as a public/private partnership of the major research universities of Georgia, Bill Todd was brought up as a candidate for the top position in that organization. Though reluctant to lose his outstanding services to me and to Emory, I realized this would be a wonderful career opportunity and advancement for Mr. Todd. Bill Todd led the Georgia Research Alliance through its initial years with tact and diplomacy. During this period he became known to many of the movers and shakers of Georgia, and now heads the Georgia Cancer Coalition, directing the expenditure of state tobacco settlement funds in the statewide fight against cancer. Bill has properly been awarded a number of civic and professional recognitions, and I have been personally very proud of his outstanding career.

With the departure of Mr. Todd I was fortunate to recruit for that position the business manager of the department of medicine, Mr. Ronnie Jowers. Mr. Jowers proved to be an excellent choice and functioned very effectively as the CFO of the health sciences center. Mr. Jowers continues to serve Emory University as Vice President for Health Affairs and CFO of the Woodruff Health Sciences Center. Joining him on our administrative team was Mr. Gary Teal, whose responsibilities grew into those of the Chief of Staff of the health sciences center. Mr. Teal continues to serve at Emory

University as Senior Associate Vice President for Administration and Chief of Staff to the CEO of the Woodruff Health Sciences Center.

I worked very closely with these two outstanding young men for several years. When my successor, Dr. Michael M. E. Johns, arrived on campus I explained their value to me and ultimately to him, and asked that he do himself a favor and make no decision about replacing either of these individuals for the first six months of his tenure. He promised me that he would do so, and he kept that promise. Now as Dr. Johns is replaced by Dr. Fred Sanfilippo, these two talented individuals continue in their positions and render invaluable service to Dr. Sanfilippo and the entire health sciences center. I consider myself most fortunate to have had their assistance, and to have had them as professional colleagues and personal friends.

With my appointment as Vice President for Health Affairs and Director of the health sciences center, I realized that I needed significant hospital expertise in dealing with the hospitals, which were divisions of the institution and the several hospitals in the Atlanta communities who were strongly affiliated with the institution. At that time, Mr. Daniel Barker was the administrator and CEO of what was then the Crawford W. Long Hospital of Emory University. I considered him to be a remarkably talented hospital administrator, and I was anxious to add him to the senior administrative staff of the health sciences center as director of hospitals. There is a built in conflict between an academic institution and its hospitals. The hospital administration justifiably seeks to protect their bottom line and financial viability, and is therefore hesitant to assume fiscal responsibility for any portions of an academic program. I felt that it was my job to determine the maximum support the hospitals could provide for the academic mission without compromise to their fiscal integrity, and to ascertain this with accuracy would require the services of Mr. Barker. I spoke to him about the change in his status at Crawford W. Long Hospital, and subsequently obtained the permission of Dr. Wadley Glenn, the medical director at Crawford Long and longtime university trustee. With his permission and approval, I approached Mr. Barker who accepted my offer. Mr. Barker proved invaluable in guiding us through many of the tumultuous changes that took place in healthcare and the medical marketplace. These activities resulted in the creation of The Emory University System of Health Care. I had the privilege of serving as the founding chairman and CEO of this new healthcare system. This organization was renamed Emory Healthcare a year or so later.

When I came to the health sciences center, Mr. Paul Hofmann was the administrator and CEO of Emory University Hospital. Shortly thereafter,

Mr. Hofmann resigned from that position to assume an administrative position in health care in California. His associate director had been Mr. Don Wells. I had known Mr. Wells for several years during my clinical experience with cardiothoracic surgery and as Director of The Emory Clinic. Upon the advice of Mr. Barker, Mr. Wells was elevated to the top administrative position at Emory University Hospital. At Crawford Long Hospital, Mr. Barker's associate director had been Mr. John Henry. Through my work at the Carlyle Fraser Heart Center, I had come to know and admire Mr. Henry, and recommended his promotion to the top spot at Crawford Long to the Woodruff Board of Trustees. As we sought to increase the efficiency and decrease the costs of our hospital operations, it seemed appropriate to merge the two hospitals into an operational unit. I had noted that Mr. Wells had extremely good relationships with the administration of hospitals throughout Georgia, and I asked him to concentrate on our affiliate hospital relationships and to assist in the development of a well thought out network of hospitals to include Emory University, but not to be dominated by it. Mr. Wells was very effective in this assignment. As the CEO of both of the combined hospitals, I recommended Mr. John Henry. There were many advantages to having a single hospital administration rather than having a separate and often duplicative administration for each of the two major hospitals. Subsequently, Mr. Henry in turn recommended Mr. Bob Bachman as COO of Emory University Hospital, and Mr. Al Blackwelder as COO of Emory Crawford Long Hospital. Mr. Barker and I undertook the renegotiation of all contracts between vendors and our hospitals. In each instance in which the contracts were different with the two hospitals we required the vendor to extend the more favorable contract to the combined entity. Several hundreds of thousands of dollars were saved just by expanding the more favored contract to the combined institutions. Mr. John Henry functioned quite effectively until his retirement, and I regard him as one of the most successful hands on hospital administrators I have ever known.

Personally, I have been well taken care of by my medical colleagues at The Emory Clinic. Dr. Donald Davis has been my primary care physician for many years, and Dr. Stephen Clements has been my cardiologist. In 1990, Dr. Clements was joined by Dr. John Douglas, an interventional cardiologist, who performed a PTCA for an obstructive lesion in the right coronary artery. In 1999, Dr. Spencer King performed a PTCA on the left anterior descending coronary artery. No other obstructions were noted at that time, but I am fortunate to have Dr. Clements maintain his excellent follow-up to the present.

In 2005 I experienced an isolated episode of hematuria, and Dr. Fray

Marshall, who joined my team of physicians, performed a cystoscopy which confirmed a transitional cell carcinoma of the bladder which he subsequently removed. Dr. Marshall has maintained a schedule of repeat cystoscopies since this surgery, and to date has noted no evidence of recurrence.

I am very grateful to all of these wonderful physicians who continue to provide excellent care for my several medical problems.

During my years at Emory I have related to four Emory University presidents: Dr. S. Walter Martin, Dr. Sanford Atwood, Dr. James T. Laney, and Dr. William Chace. During my tenure the medical school had five deans: Dr. Arthur Richardson, Dr. James Glenn, Dr. Richard Krause, Dr. Jeffrey Houpt, and Dr. Thomas Lawley. The school of public health has had two deans: Dr. Ray Greenberg and Dr. James Curran. The school of nursing has had five deans: Dr. Ada Fort, Dr. Edna Grexton, Dr. Clair Martin, Dr. Dyanne Affonso, and Dr. Marla Salmon. All of these professionals are truly remarkable individuals, and I consider myself having been most fortunate to relate to all of them in many meaningful ways.

I cannot forget the many friends and associates who helped produce this book. Many thanks to Dr. Neil Shulman for prodding me to write this manuscript. Without him I would never have likely put pen to paper. Thanks to Dr. Willis Hurst for reviewing the text for accuracy and making pertinent suggestions, and to Drs. Willis Williams and Robert Guyton for their invaluable input into the authentic details of this project. My sincere appreciation to Rhonda Mullen, Carol Pinto and Karon Schindler with Health Sciences Publications who digitized all of our valuable photographs and excerpted this project so beautifully in Emory Health. Thank you to Joshua Malin for his assistance assembling materials for the first drafts and his nimble fingers and talent for finding the right word. Thank you Marijan Pejic for producing an outstanding website, (www.charleshatchermd.com) and archiving my many photographs. My autobiography also benefited from Kelley Johnson's management and design skills to shepherd the project into fruition, and Sylvia Wrobel's ability to "get the word out" to my friends and colleagues. And finally to my editor, Lindy Chaffin Start for her priceless contributions to the refinement and organization of a work that is near and dear to my heart. And to all those wonderful people I may have forgotten, thank you for your countless contributions and tireless support of a life less ordinary.

WITH APPRECIATION

With particular appreciation to Mr. Robert W. Woodruff,
whose vision and support made possible
the Robert W. Woodruff Health Sciences Center.

Introduction: Rooted in the South

ATTAPULGUS! A MUSKOGEE INDIAN WORD and the name of the little town in Southwest Georgia where I grew up. Later, in Baltimore, Washington, or Boston, when people asked me where I was from, and I told them, they would look at me as if I were from Mars.

"My God, where's that?" they would exclaim.

So, for years, I thought it a handicap to come from such a small town with such a peculiar name. I would only realize years later how fortunate I was to grow up in this special community.

• ◆ •

I've lived in Atlanta for nearly forty years, and the story of my life, and my time at Emory University, is also a story about Atlanta. In order to understand Atlanta you need to understand that it is a city defined by its roads and rails, and of course its airstrips. Atlanta is a city without a creation myth; so instead, I'll give you the facts. In 1836, the Georgia General Assembly chartered the Western Atlantic Railroad. The land where central Atlanta sits today would serve as the terminal, and a new city named Terminus sprouted up where the tracks ended. The city was known as Marthasville for a while, named after the Governor's daughter, but then in 1845, the General Assembly renamed the city Atlanta. Sherman marched through nineteen years later, burning everything but the churches to the ground. Ironically, by the end of the Civil War, Atlanta's population had doubled. The city was quickly rebuilt, giving rise to the Phoenix seal and the motto *Resurgens*.

The Capital of *The New South* was born and since then the only constant in Atlanta has been unceasing growth. Its population exploded and the skyscrapers grew up and the highways grew out, and a single-runway field just south of the city grew to become the busiest airport in the world.

• ◆ •

It's a long way from Atlanta to Attapulgus. If you stand by a window in Emory University Hospital Midtown, or in Grady Memorial Hospital a dozen blocks to the south, you can see all sixteen lanes of the downtown connector. If you follow the expressway south, the concrete/asphalt eventually splits, and when it does you keep to the right, on I-85, driving past the airport. The airport butts up against I-285, the perimeter, and if you keep on driving, you'll pass under a series of soaring concrete spans. Billboards and fast food restaurants litter the sprawling, suburban landscape. You take a spur down to Columbus, and an hour or so later, depending on the traffic, you'll reach Fort Benning. There the expressway dead-ends at U.S. Highway 27.

When I was a young doctor at Emory I would drive up and down this highway a few times a year, and aside from an extra set of lanes in most parts, the sights you see now aren't so different than the ones I glimpsed a half-century ago. The farther south you drive, the more the present melts into the past. The tall bare-trunk pines line the asphalt like curtains. A few dozen miles later the farmers pull the curtains back, revealing their rolling cotton fields. Every twenty minutes or so you come up on another dot on the roadmap; old homes line the road, Spanish moss hanging from the trees. Some of these rows of houses are regal and proud, but southwest Georgia is a poor place and you see that driving down 27. Junked cars sit on cement blocks amidst overgrown weeds. The wood-framed houses look one storm away from collapsing in on themselves.

Men in suits in government offices in Atlanta plot to turn the road into a major transportation corridor, hoping to alleviate the gridlock on I-75. The cars and trucks haven't come yet; just look around and you'll see that the advertisers haven't arrived with their oversized billboards. Instead you drive through the unspoiled country. The bugs splatter on your windshield, and the asphalt is so worn in many stretches that it has turned white, and the kudzu crawls, and that's the landscape you see, six miles from the Florida State Line, when you pull into a little town that time seems to have forgotten, a little town called Attapulgus.

Section One: Couture and Culture: Growing a Man

A Personal Word

I was a young boy during the Great Depression. Talk about timing, I was conceived the month the stock market crashed and was born amidst the country's epic slide into the Great Depression. As a boy I worked on a local tobacco plantation and quickly realized how little money my fellow workers earned. I didn't want to grow up to be a tobacco farmer. My parents emphasized a strong work ethic, consideration and respect for other people, black or white, honesty and integrity, and performance consistent with my abilities. Though my first ten years were marked by the Great Depression and the next five by World War II, my memories are happy ones.

The Conception and The Crash

ABOUT 400 PEOPLE LIVE IN Attapulgus now, and about 400 people lived there in 1930, the year I was born. Back then, forty or fifty shade tobacco plantations encircled the little town, and they defined the culture of the community. The only other business in town was a Fuller's earth mine. Fuller's earth is clay similar to kaolin. The clay mined in Attapulgus is called Attapulgite, after the town. The clay is used in the refining of petroleum, in face powder and other cosmetics, and up until recently, it was the active ingredient in Kaopectate. The mine is still active today. The tobacco fields of the plantations have long since grown over.

Shade tobacco was a lucrative crop prior to World War II, but then cigarettes replaced cigars as the smoke of choice for most Americans. Shade tobacco was used to wrap hand-rolled cigars, and up until World War II it was one of the most profitable agricultural products in the country. Another reason that shade tobacco fell out of favor is that production of the crop is very labor intensive. On a typical tobacco plantation there was a white owner or an overseer (on the larger corporate plantations) and a couple hundred black workers, a demographic fact that would have profound political implications in the wake of the Civil Rights Movement. The shade tobacco industry withered after the war, and by the late-1950s the crop was no longer grown in southwest Georgia.

The mine on the other hand is still quite active. When I was a child, Standard Oil owned the site. Today BASF owns the mine and the company is the largest employer and taxpayer in Decatur County. I was a young boy during the great depression, and from beginning to end the mine remained open, albeit with limited production. The workers were not laid off; instead they were asked to accept shortened work weeks. Families in Attapulgus

3

survived the Great Depression this way. Folks were able to supplant their incomes by working on the shade tobacco plantations come harvest time.

•◆•

My father was born in Wilkinson County, Georgia, and upon graduating from High School he went to work for the Johnson Brothers Mercantile Company in Irwinton. He worked in a country store patronized by the men and women who worked the kaolin mines in Gordon and McIntyre, two nearby towns. News spread that a Fuller's Earth mine was going to open in southwest Georgia and the Johnson Brothers decided to expand. My father came to Attapulgus to establish and operate the new store. He quickly realized that the store was going to be successful and that it would make for a good investment. He saved up as much money as he could and then he bought out the Johnson Brothers. Around this time he was courting my mother, who was from a large, local family. He knew that she wouldn't want to leave Attapulgus, so he purchased a small frame house near the store. Earning an income and in possession of a home, he considered himself in a position to propose, which he did. My mother accepted and they were married in 1928. My father was 24-years-old and my mother was a year younger.

I was conceived in October, 1929, the month the stock market crashed on Wall Street. I was born on June 28, 1930, amidst the country's epic slide into the Great Depression. The pregnancy was my mother's first, and it proved uneventful until the onset of delivery. My mother went into labor early on a Friday afternoon and my father drove her to the Riverside Hospital in Bainbridge, to be delivered by Dr. R. F. Wheat. Dr. Wheat was not an obstetrician, rather a family practitioner who was well regarded in our community. Labor persisted through that afternoon and evening, and into the early hours of the morning. There was an abnormal presentation. A cesarean section was an extremely uncommon procedure then, and I doubt anyone in the rural hospital was an expert with forceps, so the labor went on. The protracted experience weakened my mother. The hours ticked by and she grew very fatigued. Dr. Wheat whispered to my father that she might not survive the delivery. In the prayers that followed, my father promised God that he wouldn't attempt another pregnancy if he spared my mother from this delivery.

I was ultimately delivered late Saturday afternoon, healthy in every way. Unfortunately my mother experienced significant pelvic damage. An adequate episiotomy had not been performed and she sustained a pelvic laceration, which produced urinary difficulties. Those difficulties would persist for many years until they were finally corrected by surgery.

•◆•

My father's store in Attapulgus sold everything from tuxedos to wagon-wheels. It was an old-fashioned general store and it was an integral part of the local tobacco culture; the place served as a commissary for the farm workers. This was partly because of the depression, which kept wages low, even on the more prosperous tobacco plantations.

I went to work on a local tobacco plantation when I was five. We arrived at dawn, worked under the hot sun, left at dusk, ate dinner, bathed, and collapsed into bed. In the morning, when it was still dark, we started all over again. Times were hard, and I knew that life was not easy for anyone, my parents included. The full-time workers on these plantations were usually black, but come harvest time white children would augment the labor force. I was only five but I can still remember those long, hard days. I also remember the camaraderie. I felt proud to produce something during the depression, even if all I took home was a small pay envelope. It made a good student out of me though—I didn't want to grow up to be a tobacco farmer.

The most productive male workers were paid 90 cents a day. Women not involved in piece work in the barns were paid 65 cents a day. Children and teenagers could expect to take home 40 to 50 cents a day, depending on their task. For my first job at the age of five I was paid 35 cents a day.

Being so young, the overseer had me 'mind the gate,' an undemanding task. My job required that I remain at the gate and open it each time the wagon loaded with tobacco barges arrived from the fields. I would open the gate, make certain that no livestock escaped, and then close the gate as fast as I could. The wagons proceeded on to the barns, where the piece work was done. I took up camp at the gate at sunrise, and left with the other workers at sunset. There was a short break for lunch and sometimes I would join the other kids who worked in the barn, but I usually ate by myself. It only took me a few days to realize that my lunch stood out. The black children ate leftovers in a tin can, dressed in syrup, which often led to hookworm and anemia. My mother prepared sandwiches for me. She would put an apple or an orange in my bag, and sometimes a slice of cake. To do this for me, she got up before dawn. My father used to get on my mother about those lunches. I would listen to him tell her that it was ridiculous to inconvenience the family so, preparing me a lunch that usually cost as much or more than I made for the day's work. My mother knew that I was working at a loss in economic terms, but she insisted that I had to learn the value of a dollar, and that I had to learn the value of hard work. She won that argument, and, aided by the mood of the depression, they instilled that sense of hard work in me.

My job minding the gate was not the only job I had on the plantations. Another task I performed earned me the title of *stick boy*.

During the tobacco harvest the women were largely employed in piece work. They would string the tobacco leaves with needle and thread onto a tobacco slat that would then be hung up in the rafters of the barn, where the tobacco would be cured. Sticks were supplied to the stringers in bundles of fifty. With each lot, a punch would be made in the stringer's ticket, which hung by her stall. The women then sewed thirty-or-so leaves to each stick, back-to-back, belly-to-belly, one after the other. When they were done they would place them up on the rack. Workers called rackers would carry them down to someone who passed them up to men in the rafters, who then hung the sticks. Then the process would start all over again and the women would get their cards punched another time.

Everyone was anxious to make as much money as they could during those lean years, and good stringers could make four or five dollars a day. The women would wait outside the barn at dawn, and they went to work as soon as there was enough light so see. They worked through the day, standing on little grass mats, stringing as fast as they could, and they only stopped when the sun set and the darkness made further stringing impossible. I was the stick boy in more than one barn, handing out the bundles and punching the women's cards. I quickly learned that fifty-one sticks in a bundle could create quite a bit of trouble between you and a stringer. Every additional stick in a bundle was an extra hardship and I double-counted my bundles to make certain that no one was called upon to string one more stick than they should. The necessity of performing this piece work as much as possible was brought home to me one day when a young pregnant woman came to work. She was there at dawn, like everyone else, and she strung tobacco until mid-morning. She then rushed home to deliver her baby. But she returned to the barn in the steamy late afternoon, anxious to get back to her stringing. I was only twelve then, but I knew that I did not want her on her feet working. So, as soon as she assumed her position on the line, I dropped by and punched her ticket several times and said, "Go home!" She walked out of that barn with a smile on her face.

I took a second job when I turned six. There were two newspapers delivered in Attapulgus—*The Atlanta Constitution* and *The Atlanta Journal*. Previously, two different individuals had delivered the papers. Through a bit of luck I wound up winning both routes. I combined them and held something of a monopoly on the newspaper delivery business, which I maintained until my senior year of high school. My parents thought this experience—delivering papers, collecting subscriptions, keeping proper records, and remitting to Atlanta on a timely basis—a meaningful and valuable use of my time. Until I could drive a car myself, my dad drove me through my route. I would jump out and hand-deliver each newspaper. During the week, people picked up their own newspapers at the post office, so it was only on Sundays that he would drive me, which he would do after we attended church.

As a young businessman of six, I grew to need a checkbook, so my father carried me to the bank in Bainbridge, some twelve miles away. Bainbridge was a substantial town, with a population edging toward 10,000 back then. Because Bainbridge was (and continues to be) so much larger than Attapulgus we drove there to patronize a number of different businesses.

In Bainbridge, there is a nice-sized square downtown and one and two-story businesses ring the park. Like most traditional southern towns, cars pull into diagonal parking spaces on the downtown streets. There are grand old oaks in the park, and hidden beneath the hanging Spanish moss there is an elegant white gazebo. Around the park there are two historical markers. One will tell you that Hernando de Soto and his army marched through the neighborhood in March of 1540. The Flint River runs just to the west of downtown and de Soto and his men crossed the river there, downing a few of the tall oaks to construct piraguas, a primitive sort of flat-hulled boat. The second marker notes the town's presence on *El Camino Real*, the Spanish Royal Road that cuts across the American south, through the southwestern desert, all the way down to the Vice-regal Capital in Mexico City.

In the Bainbridge bank, a slim white and gray marble building, I signed a card permitting me to write checks that would draw on my father's account. On the one hand I was the envy of my peers. None of them could write checks whenever they wanted to. My father, however, made clear to me that this was a privilege never to be abused. Most of my friends' parents gave them spending money every week. This spending money never amounted to much, but they could use those dimes and quarters as they wished. My pleas for spending money always fell on deaf ears. My parents told me to ask if I needed something, or to write a check. The money always had to be for a good purpose. Like this they made sure that I knew we didn't have money to waste on frivolous expenditures. I should say that we were not destitute, and we were better off than most families in Attapulgus.

Nevertheless, we were in the midst of the Great Depression, and though my parents might have described our family as living comfortably, this certainly was a relative term.

Comic Books were new and they were popular among my friends. I was eight when Superman first appeared in *Action Comics #1*. Batman arrived a year later in *Detective Comics #27*, and a later entry in this series was the first comic book that I ever purchased. Comic Books cost a dime, and my dad allowed me to buy them from time to time, but always only one. My friends often bought three or four comic books at a time, since we had to travel to nearby towns to purchase them. I was frustrated, and I asked him once, "Dad, you know we're not over there all the time, why can't I buy more than one?"

He looked at me and said, "No, no, no. You boys need to each buy one and then trade 'em around."

"I don't understand this at all," I said. "I know you got more money than so-and-so's daddy, and he buys five comic books at a time."

"Well Charles," he said, "we don't waste any money, and one day you'll want to go to college, and one day you'll want a car, and one day you'll want to make sure you've got the right kind of clothes, and you'll have all that, because you haven't bought five comic books at a time. So-and-so may not ever go to college, and he's not ever gonna have your advantages, but you'll have them, because we don't waste money."

• ◆ •

My mother and father had very different personalities, and in many ways, they were opposites. Perhaps opposites attract. At any rate, it was a happy marriage, and they were inseparable for sixty years. My father was a reserved man, a man of few words, but one who always saw the best in other people. My mother was vivacious and extremely energetic. She was quite outspoken, but very cautious in all of her relationships. They were active parents who took the responsibility of raising me quite seriously. My mother resigned from her bridge club when I was an infant so that I would not grow up with playing cards in the house. Similarly, I never once saw a bottle of alcohol in the house until I left for college.

Back from college one weekend, I remember asking my mother if I might have a couple of friends from Thomasville over for dinner. She said, "Of course," and we sat down to plan a menu. I was amazed when she mentioned that it would be nice to serve cocktails before dinner.

"Cocktails!" I exclaimed. "We've never had cocktails."

"No," she said, "your father and I didn't want to have drinks in front of you until you were grown, but it'll be perfectly alright for you to serve cocktails to your guests now that you're an adult."

From then on, there was always a very nice selection of liquors in a cabinet in the living room. My parents frowned upon beer and we only drank wine on special occasions. I never once saw my parents make a drink for themselves, but when I came home, if I asked if they would like to have a drink with me, the answer was invariably yes. Mother never took more than one drink, but dad always shared a second with me. Every now and then my parents would surprise me like that, but those stories are for later.

I grew up before the sexual revolution, before the pill, and before television was common. Experimental television broadcasts had begun the year before my birth, but sets were rare, and in 1942, production was suspended, as the war economy revved up. Dancing was frowned upon by many of the local churches. An unwanted pregnancy out of wedlock was *the* most feared complication of the boy-girl relationship. Getting pregnant was an absolute *no-no* for the girls, and participation in such a fiasco was equally feared among the boys. Given such restrictions on sexual activity, it was only natural that smooching and heavy petting were terribly enjoyable activities. I like to say I grew up in the age of heavy petting.

So what else was a child left to do for fun? Without television, movies were popular. At that time there was no movie theatre in Attapulgus, so when I wanted to take a date to the movies we would drive up to Bainbridge where there was a theatre on the town square. On many dates, after the movie, we would drive off and park somewhere, allowing for a session of light petting. We usually wrapped the night up with a late-night snack at one of the popular drive-ins.

My mother was rather critical of small indiscretions. She was particularly concerned about my relationships, and she constantly warned me that I could ruin my life in a single night! I came of dating age during World War II and almost all of the young men older than I were in the service. Those who were not were 4F status, which carried its own baggage. As a result of these demographics, I, and the other boys my age, tended to grow up quickly. We were invited to dances and parties by older girls and young women because we were the only game in town. My mother was not pleased at all with this development. She was concerned that I might have a sexual relationship with one of these girls, which could result in a pregnancy and a marriage of expediency. Bless her heart, she held on to two very questionable opinions: She believed that I should never date a girl whom I didn't wish to marry, and she tended to relate sexual promiscuity to social status. Thus, I was a bit surprised to find that the girls I met from fine families had just as much (and sometimes more) interest in sex as girls from the other side of the tracks.

Mother always waited up for me to return home from a date. She would sit in the living room until I returned. She expected me to sit down and have a conversation with her, recounting my evening. Her other big no-no was smoking cigarettes. Maybe it was because she grew up in the shade tobacco culture, or perhaps she somehow sensed the adverse health effects of cigarette smoking—whatever the cause, she condemned cigarettes so harshly that I never smoked.

My father was much more relaxed and laid back when I was out on a date. As the hours ticked by and my mother would ask him what time it was, he would always state the time in my favor. He did what he could to calm her anxiety. If I had been particularly late in coming in he might kid me the next morning and say, "You should try to come in a bit earlier. I can only go so far; your mother's not so easy to fool."

He also cautioned me against parking on lonely roads and lover's lanes where we might be attacked. He had an interesting position on this possibility.

"I know you would protect your date at all costs, and it would be *such* a pity to lose your life in those circumstances," he joked. "So, if you really feel you must park, be certain you find a safe place."

My parents may have been opposites, but there were many things they agreed on, education was at the top of that list. They emphasized a strong work ethic, consideration and respect for other people, black or white, honesty and integrity, and performance consistent with my abilities. Psychiatrists would have described me as "performance oriented." Looking back, I had a rather ideal situation from whence to launch a career. My father made it very clear to me that he did not have a business or property for me to return home to—my future would be up to me, and it would be no one's responsibility but my own to work hard enough to assure success. At the same time, my parents encouraged me to enter the field of my choice. They assured me that I was capable of doing anything I wished to do. The rub was, of course, that since they believed I *could* achieve whatever I wanted to, they *expected* me to achieve whatever I set out to do. Not everyone went to college in those days, especially those from a small town like Attapulgus, but my parents were quick to let me know that funds had been set aside for that purpose.

My parents committed themselves to my education. They did this because they believed that this was their duty, but also because they hoped that I might be successful. I like to think that they succeeded. I would be remiss though if I discounted the role the community played. Attapulgus, far from the handicap I once believed it to be, was instrumental in making me into the man I would become.

The Tobacco Culture

WHILE I WAS STILL LEARNING to walk and talk the depression was deepening. The bank in Bainbridge where my father kept his modest accounts failed—a major setback for a young couple with a small child. His store was profitable enough and they managed.

My first ten years on earth were marked by the Great Depression, and the next five years were spent living through World War II. Despite this, when I think back to my childhood, most of my memories are happy ones. By many standards my family was poor, but I couldn't perceive this because no one else in Attapulgus had a great deal of money.

Franklin Delano Roosevelt's election in 1932 helped our family out, if just a little bit. My father was a Democrat, and back then, when the presidency switched between parties, so did postmasterships. The Republican postmaster in Attapulgus was relieved of his duties and the local party leaders informed my father that he had been appointed postmaster. He made an addition to his store, and moved the post office there. The compensation was rather modest, but every little bit helped.

So while my childhood was marked both by economic hardship and war, these were not things that I really perceived. Of course there was one other dark mark on the world in which I grew up. The tobacco culture was paternalistic and though it did not exist in order to promote segregation, it did nothing to alleviate it. I was aware of some of this, even at a young age, but Attapulgus was a small rural town in southwest Georgia and the Civil Rights Movement was still a decade or so away. And, during the depression, and later during the war, everyone was just trying to get by. That's not to say that we were like Atlanta in the 1960s, "Too Busy to Hate," but in times of economic hardship people need not turn on each other; sometimes they do the opposite.

13

I saw the paternalism of the tobacco culture as benign and well intended. In addition to the daily wage, each plantation was responsible for the welfare of its workers. When plantation workers fell ill, the local doctors cared for them, and the plantation owners picked up the bills. Of course, if the patients were black, the service was delivered out the back door of the doctor's office, but those were the times.

At the end of the week, when the paychecks were handed out, part of the weekly wages were delivered as trade credits at local businesses, including my father's general store. This was to make sure that the wives and children were supported. By doing this the companies were obviously interjecting their judgments into a family situation. A worker should be entitled to his wages and to spend them any way he wanted to. However, they were not trying to tell them how to spend their wages; they just wanted to make sure that the women and children were taken care of. Was it right for the companies to do this? Perhaps. Perhaps not. Is it right for the federal government to take money out of your paycheck to finance your retirement for you? While some today say that we should be allowed to invest for our retirement on our own, most still support Social Security.

The workers were also given small plots of land behind their homes to farm or do with as they pleased. Some of the most amazing times of my childhood were spent over by the workers' houses. We called the neighborhood The Quarters. There might be five or six tenant houses, lined up in a neat little row on one of Attapulgus' narrow, newly paved streets. On those hot summer nights, the workers and their families would sing, play the fiddle, and barbeque under a blanket of stars. Everyone was welcome to come down and enjoy themselves. Just the same, I had a basketball half-court on the lot next to my dad's store and the black kids would come by to shoot hoops with me in the summer, when there was no work for them to do.

American Sumatra Tobacco Company operated most of the plantations in our area. This company owned several dozen plantations and each had its own superintendent, but they operated jointly. The company carefully selected the superintendent families, and almost invariably they were the pillars of our community. The plantation would be supervised by the manager, his wife and his family, and they would live a comfortable lifestyle. It wasn't that they were paid great wages, rather they had the free time to hunt and fish and ride horses. Labor was also very cheap, as I mentioned earlier, so with their wages these families were able to hire help around the house, a gardener, a cook, and perhaps a maid. As a child, I looked up to these people. They supported the churches, and the local schools, and they would ride their Tennessee walking horses about the fields. Those were popular horses at the time and the families who could afford them took great pride in them.

We used to have horse shows, which were very big events in the community. A lot of these shows were in Quincy, just across the border in Florida, and everyone would show off their horses at these shows. I remember General Patton came down from Fort Benning for one season. He headed the Fort's equestrian team and he came down to perform with jumpers and some excellent riders. This was before the war. Patton was still a Lieutenant Colonel at the time.

Some of the plantations were privately owned, and these were quite profitable. They were not as well maintained as those operated by the AST Company, and they did not always offer their workers the support and security offered by the AST Company.

Along with the general store, my father maintained the family farm, which he had purchased from my grandfather. He had become the Postmaster in 1932, and over the years he acquired a number of rental properties. Together these activities provided a comfortable standard of living, but it was still necessary to work hard and watch expenses. My mother worked part-time in the Post Office for a number of years, and she also assisted in the store at certain times. I worked as a clerk in the store after school and on Saturdays. The store was closed on Sundays.

By the time I was ten, I knew every adult in the community, white or black, and most of the children. As you could have guessed, blacks and whites were segregated during my childhood, but in practice all of our lives were intertwined in meaningful ways.

When I was very young, we had a live-in maid, a young black woman named Emma, who decades later would care for my mother during her terminal illness. Emma read me my first stories. She also took me to the movies, where I sat upstairs in the balcony with her. She was sweet and she was kind and I couldn't imagine having grown up without her. We also had a series of cooks, who were wonderful, and doted on me, preparing my favorite dishes.

My father taught me at a young age to be very respectful of all black adults, and to be friendly and honest with the black children my age. Growing up where and when I did, I can proudly say that I never once in my entire life got into an unpleasant racial situation. At the time I didn't think of the system as unfair or harmful to anyone. It was paternalistic to be sure, but not for unkind reasons, at least in our little community. Everyone was simply trying to get by during the depression. Attapulgus' black community respected my father because of his honesty and the fair way in which he treated everyone equally. He would never have thought of

15

joining the Ku Klux Klan, and he always did whatever he could for those whose circumstances were not comparable to our own.

Slowly though, I became aware that whites voted in the main, and blacks but rarely. There were two black men who voted regularly in Attapulgus, and they often participated in the political discussions that I witnessed. They were leaders in the community and they were respected by all. Turner Williams was one of these men. He lived on a small farm, which he had purchased from my grandfather. He was the father of Hosea Williams, a boyhood friend of mine who became a close associate of Dr. Martin Luther King, Jr., and an important Civil Rights leader in his own right. Hosea and I were to both end up in Atlanta, and when we were in the same crowd and he was making an address, he would usually call me out, refer to our boyhood, and state that no one had been nicer to him when he was growing up than my mother and father, for they had treated him just as well as they had treated me.

Back when we were boys, his nickname had been Hosey (pronounced hoe-see). Well, many years later he happened to be at Emory Hospital the same day that my mother had come up to Atlanta to watch over my father, who was in for heart surgery. He saw her coming down the hallway and, to the open-jawed shock of his whole entourage, he took his hat off and he called out, "Miss Vivian, Miss Vivian, you know me, I'm Hosey."

She came up to him, told him how nice it was too see him, and they chatted for a while in the hallway.

Hosea's mother had died when he was a little boy, and an aunt had raised him. Years later, he called me up, when I was working at Emory, and he told me that she had been acting a little strange. He asked me if he could bring her up to Atlanta so that I could check her out and see if it looked like she had Alzheimer's. I happened to be headed down to Attapulgus the next weekend, so we decided that he would bring her by the house down there. Unfortunately, when I checked Hosea's aunt out, it was quite apparent to me that she did have Alzheimer's.

It was only later, after we had both grown up and moved from Attapulgus that Hosea made me aware of his displeasure with the unfair situation that we had accepted as the normal state of affairs. He was a few years older than I was, and he served in World War II in an all-black unit, under General Patton's command. He was wounded during a Nazi bombing and returned to Georgia on crutches to spend Christmas with his father. The bus on which he was riding stopped in Americus, Georgia, and he stepped inside the little station to get a drink of water. The "colored only" fountain was out of order, so he went over to get a drink of water from the "white only fountain." Some redneck saw this and pushed him to the floor of the bus station. Lying there on the floor, he began to realize that if a soldier in the uniform of his country, honored with the Purple Heart, wounded and on crutches, at Christmastime, couldn't be allowed get a drink of water from the only working fountain, then something was terribly wrong, and he was going to devote his life to seeing that things were changed.

Hosea made his impact, and, white and black, we all profited from the Civil Rights Movement led by Dr. King and Hosea Williams, who served as a trusted lieutenant. Today most people take the accomplishments of the Civil Rights Movement for granted, but it's worth the time to stop and think about what the last three decades might have been like had the movement never occurred. Dr. King, Hosea Williams, and everyone else who participated in the movement may well have saved the United States as we know it.

Hosea was very cognizant of my position at Emory, and I of his position as a civil rights leader in Atlanta. Often we were able to help each other. On one such occasion, he was attempting to organize the food service workers at the Emory University Hospital. He had arranged for a group of picketers to take up positions on Clifton Road, near the front entrance of the hospital. Unfortunately, it was a very hot day. The Emory Clinic had an awning at its front entrance which provided some comfort to the picketers.

I turned on my television, and saw the name "The Emory Clinic" prominently displayed in the background of the news coverage of the protest. I rushed over to the clinic and explained to Hosea that he was picketing the wrong organization, that The Emory Clinic was a separate legal entity from Emory University, and that our service workers had no complaints. He apologized, explaining that he thought they were one and the same, as Emory's name appeared on both; but then he graciously asked all of his picketers to relocate to the hospital side of the street, though this meant that they would have to stand in the bright sun. While this might seem trivial, this misunderstanding could have easily escalated out of control had we not known each other.

Atlanta, especially in the 1970s, moved forward on the foundation of a delicate racial détente. Grievances existed, and people were wronged, but Atlanta saw little of the violence that racked other southern cities and towns.

Often, it was favors back-and-forth that ruled the day. When Hosea served as a member of the DeKalb County Board of Commissioners, I called on him on a number of occasions to assist me in obtaining variances to the building code. When we made additions to the hospital, and some other buildings, the projects were often in excess of five stories, which meant that we were required to obtain height variances. Invariably, Hosea would ask me—always in a very friendly way—if I planned to offer jobs to some of the 'brothers and sisters' in the building. And I always assured him that not only would they be involved in constructing the building, but that there would be employment opportunities when the project was completed. He would then laugh and say, "Well, don't worry about the variance. I'll show up and bring a friend or two, and we'll take care of that for you."

I would receive a letter from Hosea—usually a couple of weeks after the variance had been granted—which included the names and addresses of some of his 'brothers and sisters' whom he hoped I could employ. I would turn this list over to an administrative assistant, and if possible we would see that these requests were honored. Sometimes change came in dramatic ways—like our decision to lend a hand to the Morehouse School of Medicine at Grady Memorial Hospital—but often it was these sort of small favors, a job here, a job there, that were essential to Atlanta's steady march to modernity.

Mr. Henry Philyaw was another elderly leader in Attapulgus' black community. My father told me that Mr. Philyaw was a fine person, and he insisted that I treat him with special respect. I remember a phone call in the middle of the night, and my father coming into my bedroom to ask me to ride with him out to the Philyaw farm. He had just been told that one of Mr. Philyaw's sons had died in Newark, New Jersey, and that the only way they knew how to reach Mr. Philyaw was through him. So we rode out to the farm in the dark, rural night, under the moon and the stars.

Mr. Philyaw answered the door, startled awake at that late hour. My dad told him that he had bad news and that perhaps they should sit down. He came out on the porch and he sat down in the swing. My dad sat beside him, explained what he knew about the death of his son, and comforted him as best he could. We remained out on Mr. Philyaw's porch through the night, until the orange light of dawn peeked over his rolling fields. It was daylight when my dad decided that Mr. Philyaw would be all right, and only then did we take our leave.

There were so many experiences like these throughout my childhood, but my point here is not to list one after the other, as if they are a sheet of evidence. As I have stated before, things were the way they were. I was a boy and I attempted to understand the world around me. I was fortunate enough to have parents who taught me to respect all people, black and white, and also a boyhood friend like Hosea Williams, who years later could both show me and tell me the faults of the world in which we grew up.

There is one more story that I wish to share with you. In Attapulgus there was a kindly old black woman, Ms. Rosa Dixon, who was known by me, as well as my dad, as Aunt Rosa. The first time I waited on Aunt Rosa in our store, she had a precise list in her mind of the things she wanted. Looking back, I realize that she was ordering in priority fashion from the most basic grocery items on to something special and maybe a "sweet" or two.

Well, that first day she ordered flour. When I put the flour on the counter she took some money from a tied-up handkerchief and handed me a bill. I thought that was all she wanted, so I made change and gave the coins back to her. She then ordered meal, again handing me money that she took out of her handkerchief. I made the change and returned the coins to her. We repeated this process over and over again for a few minutes. She held out the money and paid me item by item until the money was exhausted, or her list complete. After she left the store that first day, with some annoyance I described what had happened to my father and said, "Why in the world would she pay for each item separately instead of just paying me after I totaled up the items she had purchased?"

"Charles," my dad said, "Aunt Rosa can't count, but she trusts you. She holds out her little money, knowing you will take only the right amount, and then she keeps ordering things she'd like to have until all her money is gone, and then she stops."

I was ashamed of my annoyance, and after that I not only let her shop the way she liked, but I sought her out among the other customers whenever she walked into the store.

•◆•

While the racially-tinged system of paternalism was the defining characteristic of the tobacco culture, there were also class divisions. As I've said, my family was not at all wealthy, but better off than many. Few families enjoyed a more comfortable lifestyle. My uncle was a general manager with the AST Company. He operated plantations a few miles from our house, in Amsterdam. Mr. Sam Candler Dobbs was the largest shareholder in the AST Company at the time, and he visited my uncle's plantation many times when I was a child.

Mr. Dobbs was the nephew of Asa Candler, who founded Coca-Cola, Georgia's most famous corporation. Mr. Dobbs' first job, he told me, was to travel around Georgia, introducing people to Coca-Cola. On the first day on the job he visited a small pharmacy, to hand out samples. Out of the first ten people, nine of them ran out the door and spit out the new drink. He shared with me that he was quite surprised after that episode that Coca-Cola became so popular.

Mr. Dobbs would come down to Amsterdam to fish and hunt, and to walk the grounds of the property. My parents and I would be invited to come by to visit him. The first time I met Mr. Dobbs I was five years old. My parents dressed me up in a little blue velvet Fauntleroy suit. There I was, a farm-boy who worked the gate at a tobacco plantation, chatting with a millionaire.

Later on, when my cousin from Amsterdam and I were attending the University of Georgia, we paid Mr. Dobbs a visit at his home in Lakemont, Georgia, up near the tri-state border with North and South Carolina. Mr. Dobbs was then in his 80s, and his wife had passed away. At the time of our visit, Mr. Dobbs was a lonely old man, but he seemed to really enjoy visiting with my cousin and me.

Some time earlier, during a hunting visit to Amsterdam, Mr. Dobbs had broken his leg, and his caretakers had taken him back to Atlanta to Piedmont Hospital. There he saw Dr. Lawson Thornton, a prominent orthopedic surgeon of the day. While hospitalized, a private duty nurse named Mrs. Wren took care of him; he became so enamored with her that he lured her away from the hospital to continue looking after him. His daughter took a dim view of this relationship, however benign it must have been. Faced with this criticism, Mr. Dobbs had left his home on Tuxedo Road, to live on his property in Lakemont. For convenience, and perhaps to make Mrs. Wren feel more comfortable, he built a small cottage at water's edge, all on one level, equipped with all the conveniences his advanced age required. Mrs. Wren remained with him until his death, and Mr. Dobbs left her the Lakemont Cottage in his will.

Mr. Dobbs' grandson, Sam Howard, eventually wound up at Emory to pursue his undergraduate degree. Mr. Dobbs had been grooming the boy to take over the AST Company, but that was not to be. He had a girlfriend in Atlanta and he told his grandfather that he wanted to marry her. Mr. Dobbs threatened that he would cut him out his will if he married before graduating. Well, he couldn't wait; he got married before he graduated, and he wound up being disinherited.

Years passed and one day I received a call from Sam. He had been diagnosed with oral cancer and he wanted to get whatever treatment he could. By this time I had risen up the ranks at Emory and I arranged everything I could for him. Unfortunately, he had resisted treatment for some time—he had only come to me at his children's repeated urgings—and he soon succumbed to the cancer.

Ironically, many, many years later, the poor farm boy from southwest

Georgia who had first met Mr. S. Candler Dobbs as a five year old, dressed in a blue Fauntleroy suit, like a pauper in his Sunday best before the king, would be the only person in the entire Emory University Administration who actually knew the man who had given the University Dobbs Hall and the Dobbs Professorships.

Three Churches

THERE WERE THREE CHURCHES IN Attapulgus—the Methodist, the Baptist, and the Presbyterian. Each church was unique, bringing something different to the community. I usually attended services at the Methodist Church, but from time to time I took in services at the other two churches. I was fortunate to participate in the activities of all three.

The Attapulgus Methodist Church was founded in 1830, and a new and quite impressive building was constructed in 1928. I grew up a stone's throw from the church, a classical white brick building with a set of gray steps and four columns in the front. Green shrubs encircle the building, and three proud live oaks stand nearby draped in Spanish moss. The church stands in the middle of a grass field, which is surrounded by narrow lanes, a few low-slung homes, and a small cemetery.

My parents were both Methodists. I was baptized in the Methodist Church and became a church member when I was twelve. I attended Sunday school and Sunday morning services there nearly every weekend of my adolescent life. My attendance at Sunday evening services tapered off in my teenage years, and mid-week prayer meetings were always somewhat optional. Several of our regular school teachers taught in the Sunday school. These ladies also taught Vacation Bible School. In the winter they put on the church's Christmas pageants.

The Methodist Church's membership in Attapulgus included most of the AST superintendents and many of the independent plantation owners, their families, and the top officials at the clay company. The congregation was rather conservative; our minister frowned upon beer, wine, and dancing, but rarely mentioned the evils of tobacco for obvious reasons. There was a great sense of decorum to the services and the men and the older boys almost always wore coats and ties, even when the minister invited everyone to take off their coats during summer services. My father considered this inappropriate, and he and I never accepted the minister's invitation to make ourselves a bit more comfortable.

My father served on the Church's Board of Stewards for over twenty years. During the depression, maintaining the church budget was quite difficult. As a little boy I noticed that my father didn't usually drop money into the collection plate on Sunday. I asked him about this and he explained that each December, the Board of Stewards met to divide up whatever shortfall had occurred in the annual budget. Since this was always a very significant amount, he was hesitant to make contributions throughout the year, which might make it difficult for him to meet his annual commitment. I remember one cold December evening: my mother sat in the living room by the fire, waiting for my father to come home from the annual board meeting. As soon as he opened the front door, she twisted her neck and asked, "How bad was it this year?" He didn't say anything; he just shook his head. Through the generosity of this group of men, the church managed to operate normally during those difficult years.

The Baptist church was a large and active organization, less formal than the Methodist Church, and it seemed to me, more focused on the youth. I enjoyed the fellowship and the relaxed atmosphere that defined the Baptist church. I attended services there from time to time, with my parent's approval. The Baptist Church and its small dirt parking lot sat on a plot of land that my grandfather gave to the church, and as a result everyone greeted me warmly whenever I dropped in for services.

I do remember mother warning me that the Baptists were known to invite a number of people down to the altar to express a variety of feelings. She gave me permission to attend services, but warned that I was to remain in my pew regardless of who was called down to the altar. Well, one evening, following a blustery evangelical sermon, everyone who wanted to go to heaven was invited to come down to the altar. The choir sang a lovely hymn and row after row, every man, woman, and child got up and marched to the altar. The choir kept at it until the last row of pews had emptied out and I was the lone person in the entire church left sitting in his seat. Later, someone asked me why I hadn't joined the group at the altar.

I smiled and said, "My mother told me to 'stay in my seat regardless,' and at the moment, I'm much more concerned about my mother's wrath than I am the Devil."

The third church in town was a little Presbyterian church with a handful of members, which held services once a month. Otherwise, the Presbyterians attended the Methodist church. The Methodist church didn't hold services on the Sunday of Presbyterian services, so there was very little change in services except for the building in which services were held.

In time, the little Presbyterian Church faded out of existence, and the Baptist Church acquired their property, in order to expand their cemetery. The old Presbyterian cemetery has been well maintained though, supported by a modest endowment. Friends and relatives of the old members often come to town to pay their respects.

The Baptist Church remains a vibrant organization, however, the failure of the shade tobacco industry, and an exodus of mine officials following the shuttering of Attapulgus High School have had profound effects on the Methodist Church. Today, the Methodist Church is lucky to round up more than a dozen people for Sunday morning services. Unfortunately, the demographics of Attapulgus are such that there are more people buried in the cemeteries than there are people presently living in the town. For years, as attendance dwindled, my mother and her friends remained committed to the Methodist Church. When they grew so old that they couldn't manage the steps at the front of the building, my mother sent the minister to me, instructing him to ask me for money to install an elevator, which I gladly gave him.

A Special Friend

JAMES MCGRIFF IS A MAN I have known my entire life. The story of his life, how it is intertwined with my own, and that of my entire family, is one that deserves its own chapter. The story of James and my family is one that explains much about the south. It is a story about how the south has changed so much during my lifetime. It is also a story about how some things remain the same. It illustrates an aspect of traditional southern life that is probably quite alien to northerners; a story that needs to be told.

James' father was the foreman on one of my uncle's plantations. This was the beginning of the long relationship between our two families.

James was born around the same time I was, and we knew each other as children. Eventually, I left Attapulgus to continue my studies, while James became a foreman at the Clay Company. My parents were fortunate to know James. As the years passed and my parents grew older, and my lengthy absences continued, he assumed the role of caretaker for them and their home. When the time came to make the decisions about an assisted living facility or a nursing home, I was fortunate to be in a position to arrange care for them, so that they could remain in their home. I hired three women, each of whom would work an eight hour shift. James headed up this team, making sure that my parents were cared for properly. He supervised the attending nurses, kept track of my parents' medicines, and when necessary, he drove them to their doctor in Tallahassee. A visiting nurse augmented these caregivers every day of the week.

I also prepared a house for James adjacent to my family's home. We extended the iron fence bounding my parent's house to ring James' new house. We needed to make it very clear to everyone else in the community that the house was a part of our family compound. We made this effort because James was the first black person to live in that part of Attapulgus.

At the time, the housing was quite segregated in town, and he had clearly moved to the white portion of town. As I said, I owed him a great deal for the lengths to which he went to take care of my parents. When he moved into the house, I agreed to have him and his wife stay there as long as they lived. The exception to this agreement was that if I needed the house for a caregiver to look after me and my wife or family, I would be relieved of the agreement, so long as I furnished him with a comparable house, someplace else in town.

Back in the mid 1990s, the Chairman of the Decatur County Board of Commissioners called me on the phone. There had been a death on the board, and they needed to appoint someone to serve out the rest of this man's term. They felt that times were changing, that it was time that someone from Attapulgus' black community served on the board. I agreed. They asked me if I thought James would like to serve. I told them that I thought he would like that idea. I called James and told him that they would like him to be the County Commissioner from our district. He was a bit surprised by this, but I reassured him the offer was genuine.

"James," I said, "it's an indication of the changing times. My family has looked out for us for a long time. The politics have changed. Now *you'll* be in a position to look after us."

"Well," he said, "I'll do the best that I can." He served out the term and then ran for reelection.

There is a festival in Attapulgus called the Dogwood Festival. There is always a Grand Marshall who leads a small parade through town. The organizing committee had asked me a couple of times if I would serve as the Grand Marshall. At the time, they had held the festival over the first weekend in April. For me, this presented a conflict with the Masters Tournament in Augusta, and needless to say, the Masters always won. Well, the year that James was set to run, they called me again. They asked me if I would be able to make it down to Attapulgus if they moved the Festival up a week. I told them that that would work fine.

I invited James to ride with me in the car as I led the parade. It turned out that this was the first time that a black man and a white man had ridden the parade route together in the lead car. We had my son and my step-son drive us in a convertible, and James and I sat up on the back seat.

I said to James, "Waive and throw candy out of this bag to all of the kids."

Well, he threw out a lot of candy that afternoon. Afterwards I joked to him that he was probably the most popular man in town after our little stunt. Sure enough he won the election that fall.

He ran again, but by the end of his second term, James had lost much of his interest in politics. The requests he received for road repairs and other improvements to county services became somewhat of an annoyance for him. He lost the next election to a retired white math professor who campaigned vigorously against the establishment to which James now belonged.

James, and his wife, Christine are a fine couple. He is a deacon in his church. James is a very thoughtful man. You might even say that he is sentimental.

James' mother, a widow, lived into her 90s—and she spent her final years in a nursing home. James made a point to visit his mother every day in the nursing home. He made certain to personally feed her one meal each day until she passed away.

He was a good father. Four of his five children went on to college. One of his sons served as an officer in the Navy. That young man was a whiz with computers and he helped run the Information Technology operations at Bethesda Naval Hospital. Upon completing his service commitment, he took a similar position at Emory Healthcare.

Having said all this, I think there is one episode that, on its own, perfectly sums up who James McGriff is, who I am, and what we mean to each other. As I said at the beginning of this chapter, James supervised the care of my parents as they grew older. When my mother ultimately passed away in the Tallahassee Hospital, he said to me, "Why don't I tell your father? I see him a lot more than you do nowadays, and it would be easier for both of you."

James is a deeply caring man whose friendship I treasure. Although we went into the room to talk to my dad together, James was the one who told him that my mother would not be coming home from the hospital.

Community

STRONG FAMILIES WERE THE BACKBONE of our small community and they were the rule, rather than the exception. Most children lived with two parents. A family headed by a single mother was highly unusual. A family headed by a single father was usually a temporary thing, the result of a death due to disease or an accident. Support for the family was omnipresent, and the community helped take care of and support all of the town's children. An adult wouldn't hesitate to come to the aid of an unrelated child, nor would he or she hesitate to correct and even discipline such a child. Questionable activities of any sort were promptly reported to parents by any adult observer. That's not to say we never got away with anything. There was my first kiss with the girl from around the corner, and as I mentioned earlier, the late-night petting sessions. But, most of the time we were under the watchful, though certainly sincere eyes of the whole community.

Most social activity centered around the local school. Parents participated actively in Parent Teacher Association meetings, attended school plays and other events, and of course they were there for all of our home basketball games.

There were only ten to twelve students per class at Attapulgus High School in the 1940s. As such, there simply weren't enough people to field competitive football or baseball teams, so we concentrated on basketball. In the fall, and the winter, and on through the spring we lived and breathed basketball. We were in the gymnasium, a building called *The Shell*, running lay-up lines and practicing shooting drills all year long. This concentration on one sport invariably produced a winning team. On a regular basis, little Attapulgus' team easily defeated the teams from southwest Georgia's larger towns. Since the school was so small, the coaches invited all of the students to join the team. Even the smallest and most physically inept were welcome to participate. Everyone had a chance to play and the composition of teams often varied from day to day.

The schools of the era were completely segregated of course, and the community's two schools made little contact with each other. We did make our gymnasium available to the colored school though, and I often attended the colored league tournaments that were held there from time to time. Although it would be a few more years before the NBA opened its courts to black athletes, after watching these games I could have told you that segregation on the professional level wouldn't last much longer.

I played on the Attapulgus basketball team all four years of high school, and I served as Co-Captain of the team my senior year. I was only an average player, neither tall nor especially strong. I did have the advantage of a regulation half-court for my use, and I was able to practice free throws and jump shots for hours on end. I developed a nice touch from outside, and playing point guard, I would bring the ball up court, dribbling my way to my favorite spot. If the opposing player was foolish enough to leave me space, I could toss up these shots with a good degree of accuracy. If one or two defenders did come out to challenge me, I was usually able to feed the ball to my teammates down low, who could quickly rack up points.

The principal, or a male teacher, would coach the team, but they never did too much. Everyone played all year, every year, so they spent most of their time with the uninitiated. Competence was learned and maintained through daily practices, which ran year round. The community turned out for the team, cheering us through one successful season after another. We usually lost only one or two games, and a betting man would give good odds that we would make it through the first few rounds of the state tournament.

• ◆ •

The grammar school and the high school occupied a handsome brick building, and the primary grades were instructed in the wooden addition to the school. There was no kindergarten class so the school had 11 grades in total. The teachers were excellent and highly motivated. When the county finally closed the school every single teacher held a masters degree or better.

From early on we were all made to understand the importance of education. I'll always thank my teachers for instilling in me a rewarding sense of pleasure that came with the acquisition of knowledge.

All of our parents emphasized the importance of satisfactory performance in school, though I do believe my parents were a bit more adamant in this regard than others. Inappropriate behavior would promptly lead to a visit to the principal's office, a small dreaded room where corporal punishment was known to be dealt out on occasion. Any student having such a problem in school would arrive home by bus to find his parents aware of the situation, even though his family had no telephone! To this day some of my friends have never figured out how the news spread so quickly. Luckily I never suffered this fate. My mother let me know that when I was very young, my father had not hesitated to punish me when I deserved it.

A favorite story was told that one evening I managed to receive three separate switchings. Eventually my father got his point across, because that evening was said to be the turning point in my behavior. I never challenged my father so aggressively again. In fact, I don't have a single memory of my father so much as raising his voice to me. My mother, on the other hand, did not hesitate to scold me until I went away to college.

My parents, like everyone else's, gave the teachers their unwavering support. When the principal meted out punishment at school, you could expect further punishment once you got home. It certainly never occurred to any parent to sue the teacher or the school over a behavior problem concerning their child. With such unwavering support, the teachers instructed us in a rather ideal environment. Learning came easy and school was always interesting, even exciting.

My parents placed such an emphasis on education that nothing was allowed to interfere with my attendance at school. My friends might be excused by their parents to attend the circus or go on an educational trip. It was not so for me. Nothing was as important as school; consequently I moved from the first grade through graduation with perfect attendance, not missing a single day of school in those eleven years.

As I progressed through school, my teachers quietly and unobtrusively let me know that I was a rather gifted student. My grades consistently placed me at the top of my class, and my teachers assigned me extra homework on a regular basis. In high school, if one of our teachers was unexpectedly absent, I would be called upon to substitute for the day. Even now, looking back on those days when I taught my own classes, I cannot remember any resentment or hostility on my peers' faces. I was kidded now and then, of course, about being a 'brain,' but I was careful never to forget that I was just a fellow student.

I was quite aware of my teachers' high expectations, and sometimes I secretly bemoaned the fact that I couldn't slip into the inconspicuous position of an average student. My parents arranged for an aunt of mine to teach me Latin and French with a couple of other students, and that was added to my course-load, which was always the maximum the high school would allow. While students today fill their afternoons and evenings with endless extracurricular activities, building up resumes for college, this sort of thing was quite rare in a small town like Attapulgus in the middle of the century.

One activity that I did participate in was band. I also took private violin lessons with a local music teacher. Though I was still young, I will never forget the day the Japanese bombed Pearl Harbor. I was practicing with the church pianist for a violin performance at the Sunday night service when the news came to us by radio. That evening I played "Amazing Grace", which was a favorite of my grandmother.

I was a serious student of the violin for ten years, but I played in the band for fun, and fellowship. Of course the violin lessons benefited me in my band assignment as solo trumpet. When I arrived at college, I tried out for the band, and quickly won a position. Unfortunately I found the drills for halftime performances at football games to be time-consuming and tedious for a pre-med student. The band director graciously offered me a music scholarship, but I felt that I needed to drop band from my activities and concentrate on my academic work. In retrospect, if I had not had an academic scholarship, I would likely have been happy to play in the band—football drills and all!

•◆•

During my junior year of High School, Georgia held its first Boys State. A mock state government would be set up in Atlanta, and students would be elected to various positions: Governor, Lt. Governor, Attorney General, etc. Those elected would spend the day working with their real-world counterparts at the capitol.

The American Legion had conceived of Boys State a decade earlier, amidst depression-fueled fears that American democracy was faltering. American civic leaders looked at Nazi Germany and Fascist Italy and saw the governments indoctrinating their youth with propaganda glorifying the state. The American Legion decided to go directly to the American youth, though with a markedly different approach. Instead of spewing propaganda, the Legion conceived of Boys State as a way to *show* American youth just how democracy worked. The assumption underlying this approach was that once we saw democracy in action we would naturally see the wisdom of the system.

Decatur County asked each of its schools to nominate an outstanding student to be considered for the honor of representing the county at Boys State. From this group, the committee selected me to represent Decatur County. I enjoyed attending this initial Boys State, which was held at the Georgia Military Academy in the Atlanta suburb of College Park. I was a lively participant in the political activities, and was selected by my peers for several leadership positions. When I returned home, the Bainbridge Rotary Club invited me to speak at their next meeting—my first address to a civic organization!

In 1945, I attended the State HI-Y (High School YMCA) and Tri-HI-Y meetings with several students from the Bainbridge High School. This was the first time I ever drove up to Atlanta on my own. My dad loaned me his car and gave me fifty dollars. I thought he had gone crazy. Fifty dollars was a lot of money at the time. We stayed at the Georgian Terrace, the hotel where the premier reception for *Gone With The Wind* had been held seven years earlier. We had dinner on Friday night, and then we caught a movie. I remember the movie well. It was *The Outlaw,* and Jane Russell had the starring role. The movie was somewhat notorious, and I can still remember Jane Russell and her heavy breathing, thrashing around in the hay, as the lights dimmed. We had breakfast the next morning, ate lunch and dinner, spent that night at the hotel, had breakfast Sunday morning, and then drove home. The money I spent on the movie and the meals added up to a grand total of $17.50. Fifty dollars had been way over the line. Dad was making sure that I had what I needed, but he was also confident that I wouldn't spend *anymore* than I needed to spend. If he had only given me twenty-five dollars, well, he probably would not have gotten any change back.

The following year HI-Y and Tri-HI-Y convened a similar program, and I planned on attending. The year was 1946 and the Assembly would be overshadowed by one of the most tragic events in Atlanta's short history. Hundreds of students had come to Atlanta for the December conference, joining thousands of other tourists who were anticipating festivities marking the fifth anniversary of Pearl Harbor. I had been set to join some of my classmates from Bainbridge in Atlanta, who were staying at the Winecoff Hotel, but to my dismay, my basketball coach refused to let me go, as I would have missed a Friday evening game against Climax, Georgia, a traditional rival. He suggested that I drive up to Atlanta early Saturday morning. He didn't know it then, but by refusing to excuse me, he very likely saved my life.

The call came into the Atlanta Fire Department at 3:42 AM. The Winecoff hotel, a fifteen-story brick building, was engulfed in flames. A fire had broken out on the fourth floor and the flames quickly shot up the elevator shafts. The 'fireproof' building, like the 'unsinkable' Titanic, which lacked lifeboats, was absent of sprinklers and fire escapes. Eight students from Bainbridge, as well as their teacher, died in the fire. They were all on the tenth floor and the fire company's ladders could not reach them. Many of these students were girls, including two friends who leapt from the building, hand in hand, tragically missing the outstretched nets.

Ambulances from all over the metropolitan area rushed to the scene. Taxicabs were converted into makeshift hearses to cart away the singed dead. Some on the upper floors managed to escape the flames, knotting bed-sheets together in order to rappel down to the extended fire-ladders.

A Georgia Tech student stood on Peachtree Street, with a camera in his hand and five flashbulbs in his pocket. He snapped some shots of the plunging victims, and then, with his last bulb, he took a photo of a woman leaning against the side of the building. The Associated Press bought the photograph for three hundred dollars, distributing it to hundreds of newspapers, which all printed it on their front page. For the photograph, he became the first amateur to ever win the Pulitzer Prize.

There were 280 guests that night. There could have been 281 had I not had a basketball game. One hundred nineteen of them died in what still remains America's worst hotel fire.

In a city where the skyline seems to change every day, old buildings crashing down, orange cranes swinging against the horizon, and concrete spires growing up like trees, the Winecoff has stood at the corner of Peachtree and Ellis Street for over a half-century. A group of investors tried to rehabilitate the hotel in the 1950s and later, another optimistic group converted the building into a home for the elderly. As the century came to a close the building stood empty, the ground floor boarded up, wind gusting through the blasted out windows on the upper floors. Interestingly, the brick tower refuses to come down, and today the construction crews have returned, dispatched by a developer who is attempting to convert the sad old building in to a boutique hotel.

• ◆ •

Most of my high school years were spent during World War II. A great spirit of patriotism and civic cooperation united the community and the nation. War movies, newsreels, magazines, and newspaper articles all made the older boys eager to serve in one of the Armed Forces. I won't rehash what so many others have already said in words more eloquent than I could ever hope to write, but I grew up in a world where good and evil were clear and if good did not stand up and defeat evil then civilization would be lost.

Many people—teachers, parents, and peers—suggested that I consider seeking admission to West Point or Annapolis upon graduation. I found the idea quite appealing. Just after my Rotary Club address, our Congressman, Mr. E. E. Cox, of Camilla, Georgia, invited me to visit him at his home, as Congress was out of session. Upon that visit, he graciously offered me an appointment to either of the Service academies. We discussed the matter and we both concluded that Annapolis would be a better fit for me. I returned home, delighted by the prospect of serving in the Navy. With the appointment already assured by my congressman, I had only to qualify for the Naval Academy. Because of my academic performance, I was allowed to pre-qualify by certificate, and was spared from the entrance examination. I was in perfect health and my admission seemed assured.

My father expressed significant reservations about my entering the Naval Academy at Annapolis just after World War II had ended. He hoped for me to choose a career that involved service to others and he imagined me trapped in some bureaucratic office in a peacetime navy. Despite these reservations he graced my application, honoring his pledge to allow me to follow my wishes.

I was shocked when a letter arrived from the academy a few weeks later, pointing out the unfortunate fact that I would not be old enough to enter Annapolis with the class of 1951! Regulations stated that a cadet must turn seventeen six months prior to entering the Academy. I would turn seventeen exactly three days before my anticipated admission. I was heartbroken and distressed. My future had seemed so clear and now everything was up in the air. Congressman Cox's offer had made acceptance at the academy a seemingly foregone conclusion and I had not bothered with college applications. A few weeks later I received another letter from the Navy. This letter was from Admiral Chester Nimitz, the Chief of Naval Operations. He apologized for the snafu, and said that Congressman Cox had already been contacted, and he had assured the academy that he would provide me with another appointment next year. Admiral Nimitz closed the letter advising me to begin my college education as I saw fit, reiterating that I would be welcomed with the class of 1952. I was disappointed to be sure, but it seemed that my father's wishes would be honored, at least for the time being.

As I already mentioned, both of my parents were clear that I should choose the career I desired. That is not to say that they didn't have opinions. In particular, my father had reservations about the possibility of my pursuing a career in law.

"Charles," he asked, "if you're perhaps smarter than some of the other boys, do you really believe it would be a proper use of your talents to outsmart other people, or to use them defending criminals?"

He was pleased with my eventual decision to become a physician, but he did not understand the system of postgraduate medical training or the nature of academic medicine. When I completed my internship in surgery at the Johns Hopkins Hospital and decided to take the first two years of my residency at The Peter Bent Brigham Hospital in Boston, he naively asked if I had failed, or had found the Hopkins program difficult and was having to repeat the work in Boston. I jokingly assured him that it wasn't possible to fail out of Johns Hopkins and then repeat your work at Harvard. Years later, as my training in general surgery and cardiothoracic surgery continued, he took me aside.

"Charles," he said with a concerned look on his face, "you're our only son, so whatever you want to do is alright with your mother and me, but you've been in school and training for so long that I don't know what to tell people who ask me what you're doing."

I muttered something about my records and performance at the leading medical institutions in the country, and stated that I might someday wish to be a Professor of Surgery.

"My God!" he exclaimed. "A school teacher after all I've spent on you!"

In time he came to understand the various facets of academic medicine, and he was very proud that I was involved in teaching and research, in addition to patient care. That was a long time coming though, and in 1947, in late June, what concerned me was my delayed entrance to the Naval Academy and the troubling fact that though I had graduated from high school, I had no arrangements for college. A few months earlier, The University of Georgia had offered me a Regent's Scholarship based on my academic record. Hoping that the offer was still on the table I called the University. Thankfully the offer was still valid and I accepted the scholarship eagerly anticipating fall in Athens.

Section Two: Athens, Marriage, and Major Decisions

A Personal Word

I entered the University of Georgia in the fall of 1947. To me, UGA was a very large school with 20 times as many students enrolled there as there were people living in my hometown. It was definitely a big adjustment for me. My teachers and parents had always encouraged me, my grades in high school had been excellent, and I had been assured for years that I was gifted. Could it be possible that this wasn't really the case? I declared pre-med since that seemed to be the best course of study for a good student wishing to keep all options open. When I had decided to pursue a career in medicine I had set three goals: 1) to make it into medical school by twenty; 2) to finish training for my specialty by thirty; and 3) to be the head of my department by forty. Through hard work and a fortunate coincidence I achieved the first goal by the end of my junior year, setting myself up to work toward the second and eventually the third. I became a husband with a new set of responsibilities but before I would leave medical school, there were some tough choices to be made.

Athens

Before I left for Athens, my dad called me into the living room one afternoon. He said to me that he didn't think that my asking him for money all the time would be the best situation for him or for me.

"Why don't I just let you have several of the rental houses?"

As I mentioned earlier, over the years, my father had bought up a handful of small homes in town, usually as a favor to a tenant or owner. In this way he had been able to gradually increase his cash flow to a more comfortable level. And now, he proposed to pass a few of them on to me.

"You can keep them up, and paint them in the summertime, whatever you want to do. That will provide you with enough money for you to be independent in college."

Obviously, I accepted his offer on the spot. I thought that this was a pretty nice arrangement indeed. Those same houses, many years later, would become a bit of a thorn in my side. They were little frame houses and by the late 1980s it was no longer financially possible to keep them in good condition, renting for what they did. I had to find a way out, as the situation had the potential to become embarrassing. By then I was a prominent doctor in Atlanta and someone might have stumbled upon them and called me a slumlord. As you may remember, Lady Bird Johnson fell into this same trap with some Alabama tenant houses when her husband was the President. Thankfully, I found a solution in allowing the renters to homestead the properties.

I entered the University of Georgia (UGA) in the fall of 1947, anticipating spending a year there, before leaving for the Naval Academy in Annapolis. I declared pre-med, since that seemed to me the best course of study for a good student wishing to keep all options open.

To me, UGA was a very large school, although there were less than

10,000 students enrolled there at the time. I had graduated from a very small school, with only twelve students in my graduating class. There were 20 times as many students enrolled at UGA as there were people living in Attapulgus, so Athens was definitely a big adjustment for me.

In 1947, entrance examinations were required, and they determined where you would be placed in certain subjects. Still rather frightened about the unknown, I was reassured by a call from my high school principal—I had scored so well on the entrance exams that a college official had called to congratulate him. This official was interested in learning more about me personally.

I started off in the usual freshmen pre-med courses. Inorganic chemistry was quite interesting, though I approached the class as if I were walking through a minefield. My professor invited me to drop by his office after two or three weeks. He tried to reassure me, joking that I must be the most frightened student he had ever had. He found this amusing because I was doing just fine.

Academically, I had never taken a chemistry course, and I had very minimal laboratory experience in physics. It was a frightening period for me. I really didn't know just exactly *what* I was. True, my teachers had always been encouraging, my grades had been excellent, and my parents had assured me for years that I was gifted. Could it be possible that this wasn't really the case? Had I merely excelled in a small, atypical environment? The proverbial big fish from the little pond suddenly lost, dropped in the ocean, I was concerned that I might not perform satisfactorily at the collegiate level given the limitations of the small high school which I had attended.

I made the only B+ in my collegiate career at the end of my first quarter. I developed an increasing confidence when I made five A+'s in my second quarter. I was subsequently called in to meet with my professor in inorganic chemistry. She informed me that all the schools in the university system for the state of Georgia were given standardized final examinations in this course, and congratulated me for having set the state curve in inorganic chemistry that year. I was quite pleasantly surprised by this turn of events, and I remember her statement of amusement that she didn't think I had any comprehension of how outstanding a student I was. She was certainly correct in that assessment!

I was seventeen years old, not exceptionally tall, and if I wasn't young and physically undistinguished enough, the average male student that year was twenty-seven-years-old. Facilitated by the GI Bill, thousands of World War II veterans had flooded UGA's campus. These were grown men, grown men who had gone into battle against Evil and came back alive. I had the utmost respect for these fellow students of mine, but I cannot say they made this young country boy feel any more comfortable on the large, unfamiliar campus.

The Attapulgus high school had offered an excellent algebra course, and I was somewhat amused by the first examination I took in my freshman algebra course. The professor returned our papers with the apology that he must have made the examination far too difficult since almost everyone in the class had failed. He was therefore going to add ten points to everyone's grade on this examination. I received my paper with a bit of trepidation, but there it was, in big red ink, a 110! Throughout that course, and two additional math courses that year, my average never fell below 100 because of that ten point cushion. The chairman of the math department invited me to dinner, and several key professors in the department spoke with me about majoring in math, suggesting that I pursue a Ph.D. I thanked them profusely, of course, but thought to myself that this was all a big mistake. All I had done was solve a few simple problems. I will readily admit, I am no mathematician!

My aunt had been an excellent French tutor and I scored quite well on the French entrance exams, winning myself a place in an advanced conversational French course. I could certainly read and write in French, but I did not feel comfortable speaking the language in informal conversation. I took my *drop and take* card to the Dean of the College of Arts & Sciences and I expressed to him my concern. He asked where I had taken French, and when I explained my situation, he laughed and said, "By all means, drop the French. You're not adequately prepared for this course. I suggest that you start over in Spanish or German."

Well, his tone and demeanor irritated me just a bit too much. I reached over the desk and took the *drop and take* card out of his hand, thanked him for his advice, and told him that I had decided that I would remain in French. I subsequently made the highest grade in the class, and was invited to join the French Club.

As I said previously, at the end of the first quarter, I received what I felt was a terrible blow. I had received two A+s, an A, and a B+. A B+ in English Lit! It was the first grade that I had ever received that was not an A or an A+. I felt somewhat ashamed. I was also a bit confused, because there had only been three examinations in this English course, and I had a 96 average on those tests. I went to my professor, who assured me that I had gotten the highest grade in the class, but informed me that as a matter of policy he just didn't give As to freshmen. I went to the head of the Department and offered to take the course again, under a professor with a different philosophy. He laughed and said, "don't be ridiculous, you have a long way to go. A B+ is a fine grade, and you have many courses yet to take. Suppose you took the course over and made an *A*, and then made a *B+* in another quarter or two."

I made my peace with that *B+*, eventually realizing its relative insignificance, but when I graduated four years later, it was still the only *B+* I had made in high school or college. Nevertheless, I maintained one of the highest academic averages in the college and graduated Magna Cum Laude. That lone *B+* given by that professor—unjustifiably, I still believe—simply because I was a freshman, kept me from graduating Summa Cum Laude. Alas and alack, how serious things seemed to this young country boy!

Looking back, I set too high a bar for myself, and thus I caused myself quite a bit of unneeded anxiety. By expecting perfection, in the event that I received an A- and not an A+, instead of celebrating an excellent grade, I wallowed in disappointment. I *did* have to keep myself in the top ten percent of my class in order to maintain my scholarship, but in truth, a handful of less-than-absolutely-perfect grades were not going to put me at risk of falling out of that rarified range.

•◆•

During my freshman year, I was required to take ROTC drills every Tuesday at eight in the morning. The war had been over for three years and the Russian threat had not yet fully emerged. I began to question life in the military and my father's apprehensions became my own. The following spring my appointment to Annapolis came up again. It was 1948 and I had serious doubts about my carefully laid plans. My pre-med grades had been excellent, and my faculty advisor was strongly encouraging me to qualify for medical school. On the other hand, my professor of Military Science & Tactics thought that I would be a fool to pass on an appointment to Annapolis. My parents were divided. My father, as I expected, strongly favored a medical career. My mother leaned toward Annapolis, even if I didn't plan on sustaining a career in the Navy. Ultimately, I decided to remain in Athens.

Congressman Cox didn't have any problem with this. He had already endeared himself most deeply to my family and friends, and now he could pass the appointment on to an alternate and reap additional political benefit.

My change in plans was not without its own disadvantages though. I had not rushed a fraternity, expecting to leave Athens in a year. By now my study habits were defined, and I had the new goal of obtaining admission to a top-notch medical school. I decided to remain focused on my academic work, and limit my social activities somewhat, knowing that I would still have years ahead in which to expand my horizons beyond the classroom. I anticipated graduating from college with an excellent academic average, and attending medical school at Harvard, Johns Hopkins, or some other prestigious institution.

I was not a recluse at UGA though. My first year there I only missed Sunday church once. With Annapolis out of the picture I did develop more of a social life.

I only had one roommate during my stay in Athens—James Martin of Albany, Georgia. The university paired us in our freshman year. I found him to be a great roommate and we stuck together the rest of the way. James majored in radio-journalism, quite a different course of study than my own, and we obviously pursued different careers, but we have remained friends throughout the years.

Dempsey Guillebeau was my closest friend. We lived across the hall from each other in the dormitory and we became fast friends. Dempsey was brilliant and easily the most intelligent student I had ever met. He was pre-med and a year ahead of me, but often we wound up in the same classes, and whenever we did, you could be sure that we would finish first and second grade-wise. The only question was who would be *one* and who would be *two*. We would study for tests together and other students would pay us for the privilege of sitting in on those sessions.

•◆•

That first spring, three friends and I drove down to Augusta to attend the Masters Golf Tournament. It was quite a small, comfortable operation at that time. We drove down Magnolia Lane. A member of the Club was selling tickets just in front of the Club House. A Saturday ticket was $5 dollars—still a lot of money at that time. Movies were nine cents and a gallon of gas cost about seventeen cents; $5 dollars seemed like quite a bit to my friends and me. I asked the gentleman selling the tickets if we could pull out of line, so that we could discuss the matter. We did so, and had a significant debate about whether to buy tickets, and whether we in fact had $20 dollars among us. Fortunately, we had $20 dollars with a little to spare. We decided to pay the outrageous charge, and attend the tournament, since we were in Augusta for that purpose!

We had a wonderful time, and had the unique pleasure of watching Bobby Jones play that afternoon in a twosome with Bobby Locke of South Africa. Ultimately, Claude Harmon, father of Butch Harmon (the famous golf instructor who was one of Tiger Woods' earliest coaches), won the tournament; he was the last Club professional to win the Masters, or any other Major.

Afterward, we realized that we didn't have enough gas to return to Athens. Gas cards and other credit cards were not yet available, so instead we tried two or three service stations, inquiring in advance if they would accept a check. These attempts were refused, so I offered to handle the situation. I pulled into the finest station I could find, jumped out of the car, and asked the attendant to fill her up. He did so, and when this was done I gave him a choice: *You can either take my check, which is perfectly good for this purchase, or you can siphon the gas out of the car.* He was a friendly sort, and seeing the humor in the situation, he agreed to take our check for the gas, and agreed to let me add an amount which would permit the four of us to have a nice dinner in Augusta.

Augusta National and the Masters hold a very special place in the hearts and minds of Georgians, so I hope you will forgive me if I step out of time for a bit. While we all take some pride in the elegant way the tournament is presented on CBS, and to the public in attendance, in the early days, the Masters was not the financial success that it is today. And so, churches and civic groups were obliged to sell a certain number of tickets. I am lucky to have had season tickets since 1962, and although I have attended more than fifty Masters tournaments, I still enjoy going down one day each tournament, and inviting guests from around the country to join me for this event. Although I have been on the request list for additional tickets for over forty years, my allotment of tickets has never been increased. Through the years I had friends and patients who were members of Augusta National, and I have been invited to play the course many times. The best I ever shot was a 76, but this feat was achieved from the members' tees, which are not comparable to what you face during the Tournament.

Following the death of Bobby Jones, a fund was established to permit Emory University and St. Andrews University to send four or five exchange students across the Atlantic, to the two campuses. Over time the program's funds have grown, so much so that at present it affords each student a stipend equal to or greater than a Rhodes Scholarship. In addition, a small van is furnished to the students from Scotland; the students are encouraged to tour the United States whenever they have a bit of free time. These students are given the opportunity to attend the Masters Tournament. While in Augusta, on the Saturday morning of each tournament, they are invited to attend an affair behind Butler Cabin. Each of the young men and women are given an opportunity to tell their hosts from the University (a role I was afforded on more than one occasion) about their activities here in the States, and to discuss their plans upon return to Scotland. I can remember being put on the spot by one attractive Scottish lassie who asked me, "And what was your connection with Bobby Jones, Dr. Hatcher?"

I quickly replied that I didn't really have a connection with Bobby Jones, but then I added that I, of course, knew Bobby Jones, and that I had in fact performed surgery on his wife, Mary. Getting into the situation a bit more, I added that I had performed emergency cardiac surgery on Frances Jones, the wife of Bobby, III. Before the morning was over, I realized that I had as much a "relationship" with Bobby Jones and his family as anyone at Emory University.

One Masters winner was Tommy Aaron, of Gainesville, Georgia. Tommy had led many tournaments until the final day, when he frequently blew his lead. The year that he won the Masters Tournament, his mother had been referred to me for removal of a tumor of the lung. He was very concerned about his mother's outlook, and he was tremendously relieved when we were able to discharge her in a week. She was able to go up to Augusta and walk the course with him, all four rounds. I've always felt that the satisfactory management of his mother's condition gave him just the extra push he needed to finally win the tournament.

Interestingly enough, I had invited a new Chairman of the Department of Surgery at Emory University School of Medicine to be my Masters guest that year. We were standing on the 18th Green when Tommy won the Tournament, and he spoke to us as he made his way to the Scorer's tent. I then asked my guest if he would like to have a drink.

"Where in the world can you get a drink here?" he asked.

I pointed to the Jones Cottage on the 10th Fairway, and said that I had been invited to drop by whenever I wished during a tournament, a courtesy extended to me by Mary Jones. We entered the cottage and my guest, who loved country and bluegrass music, was delighted to find that Tennessee Ernie Ford, a friend of Bobby Jones, III, was also in the cottage; they struck up a warm and very pleasant conversation.

• ◆ •

My second year at UGA was uneventful. It wasn't until my junior year that my future began to take shape.

I had a friend in Chi Omega, and she introduced me to a girl named Celeste Barnett, who had just transferred from Agnes Scott, the all-women's university in Atlanta. Celeste was sweet, she was pretty, and she was intelligent. Our mutual friend asked if I might show Celeste around and take her to a party or two. I agreed, and we quickly took to each other.

Celeste was from Washington, Georgia, a town rich in history and customs. People from Washington can be a bit different, so whatever I might have noticed in Celeste as a little odd I surely wrote it off as cultural quirks.

Washington is the small town where the final meeting of the Confederate cabinet took place. The infamous General Robert Toombs was also born in the town. With the collapse of the Confederacy imminent, Tombs slipped out of the country, barely managing to evade the Union troops sent to arrest him. He took refuge in Cuba then made his way to London and Paris before finally returning to the states some years later. He refused a Congressional Pardon, which would have required him to swear an Oath of Loyalty, and though he never regained his American citizenship he once again became active in politics, playing an important role during Georgia's 1877 Constitutional Convention.

The second important development of my junior year occurred during an April visit to Augusta, Georgia. My good friend Dempsey Guillebeau had invited me attend the Masters Tournament. He would be graduating in a few weeks and he had already been accepted to the University of Georgia School of Medicine, which was in Augusta. We took in the tournament, watching Sam Snead play his way to his first win at Augusta.

That weekend Dempsey insisted that I at least ride over to the Medical School campus and let him show me around. Well, he was a very close friend, and it seemed like the least I could do to take a look at the medical school.

As we drove by the Administration Building, Ms. Janet Newton, the Director of Admissions, happened to be walking down the steps. Dempsey asked me to stop the car. He got out, greeted Ms. Newton, and then introduced me. He told her that I was completing my junior year, and that I had the highest average at the College in Athens, and that he thought the University of Georgia School of Medicine should accept me as a junior—otherwise, in all likelihood I would be going up north to continue my medical education. She asked me if I had the academic record that Dempsey claimed, and I told her that I did have an A+ average.

"Well, young man," she said, "let me go back in and get you the application forms. I believe the Admissions Committee will accept you as a junior. The College of Arts & Sciences will let your courses in the freshman year of medical school count as your electives. You can return to Athens next summer and graduate, and then come back in the fall as a sophomore in medical school."

I had never given this a thought, but the idea was intriguing. To finish college at nineteen, and medical school at twenty-three sounded good to me, especially since the returning veterans had greatly increased the number of medical school applicants, making competition for class positions especially fierce.

We took in some more of the tournament and then we returned to Athens. I completed the application forms Sunday evening, stamped them, and dropped them in the mail. On Tuesday, an admissions officer at the medical school called me, inviting me to come down to Augusta for an interview. I drove down for the interview on Wednesday, noting a dry hacking cough, only concerned that the cough didn't cast a negative pall on the interview.

I thought the interview went well, and I had a good time meeting a number of professors. By the following morning, it was obvious that I had measles, and I admitted myself to the campus infirmary. The next day, Friday, I received an acceptance letter from the School of Medicine, read to me by the campus physician in my room at the infirmary, which had been darkened because of the photophobia of measles. It was an astonishing turn of events and I was quite flattered. In one week I had moved from application to acceptance, and I would be attending medical school with my two best friends. That other friend was LaMar Scott McGinnis. I shared an apartment with him in Augusta, as Dempsey was about to wed Peggy, his high school sweetheart.

I could hardly wait to relay the news to my parents. I justified this most recent change in plans by telling them that I would do my Internship and Residency at Hopkins or Harvard that all medical schools were Grade A, and that where I took my specialty training would be what counted anyway. So I was nineteen years old, headed off to Medical School in the fall.

When I decided to pursue a career in medicine I set three goals: 1) to make it into medical school by twenty; 2) to finish training for my specialty by thirty, and 3) to be the head of my department, wherever I wound up working, by forty. I didn't know if it would all work out just yet, but through hard work and a fortunate coincidence I had achieved the first goal, setting myself up to work toward the second and eventually the third.

A Country Practitioner?

ALTHOUGH CELESTE HAD ANOTHER YEAR to go at Athens, we continued to date, and we visited each other often. I was in Augusta, a college senior and a medical school freshman, one of the few people at the University of Georgia to occupy such a position. I felt a great sense of relief, which was soon replaced by enthusiasm and anticipation. Classes began in the fall, and immediately I ran into some difficulties, though none that would compare to what would happen the following April.

That fall was not all doom and gloom. Dempsey and Peggy got married over the summer and LaMar ("Mac") McGinnis and I got an apartment together. LaMar was an excellent roommate and went on to enjoy a distinguished career as an oncological surgeon, and as a clinical professor of surgery at Emory University School of Medicine. He eventually served as the President of the American Cancer Society and President of the American College of Surgeons.

In the spring of 1950 we made several get acquainted trips down to Augusta, visiting friends and fraternities and getting familiar with the city. There was no doubt that the three of us would pledge the same fraternity. There were four medical school fraternities and we became quite familiar with each. During rush week the following fall we were pleased to receive a strong rush and bid from each of the four fraternities. Each one had its own strengths and weaknesses, but in the end we made the decision to pledge Phi Rho Sigma, because of the members we had known in Athens and because of the preferences of members of our own class whom we considered special friends. This proved to be an excellent choice and resulted in four years of fellowship and close friendship.

Mac and I rented space in a private home for the first year of school. The son of this family, the Benson's, had just joined the navy and his room, bath and private entrance were available, along with parking spaces for our cars. The Benson couple was very friendly and they made us feel most at home. The house was located near the Phi Rho Sigma house and convenient to the medical school campus. Mac and I spent a pleasant year there before we moved into the fraternity house our sophomore year.

That first fall Mac and I spent a lot of our time over at Dempsey's house. Peggy went out of her way to take care of us. We would come over to study and she would brew coffee and bake cookies and such.

Among our freshman classes there were two that stood out initially: gross anatomy every morning, consisting of human dissection, and histology in the afternoon. Gross anatomy was a very structured class with sections of the body dissected one by one. Upon completion of each particular portion of the body, our professor would administer a personal examination to each of us.

My histology course was a different matter and my professor in that course caused much of my stress that fall. Histology is the study of thin slices of tissue. Anatomy on a microscopic level is an easy way to think of what histology entails. The man who taught the course was a crotchety old cuss, and carried out an extremely unpopular testing policy. That fall we had anatomy in the morning. We would break for lunch, and review, thinking our histology professor might give us an exam that afternoon. Well, we got underway that first week. There was no exam on Tuesday, no exam on Wednesday, and no exam on Thursday and so on. For a few days there was that fleeting sense of relief that accompanies a lack of examinations. After two weeks though, that sense of relief had turned into a sense of dread among many of us in the class. With each passing day the material for that first exam kept piling up. The whole month of September went by and still, no exam. The whole month of October went by and still, no exam. Soon it was November and homecoming at the University of Georgia edged closer on the calendar. Now, a lot of us in the class went back to Athens to attend the football game and take in homecoming. On Sunday night, my friends and I drove back to Augusta. On Monday afternoon we walked into the histology classroom, and there our professor was, strolling up and down the aisles of desks, passing out the first exam of the year!

I don't think there was a person in that room who didn't feel like we needed to get drunk after we finished the exam. Either way you needed to hit the bars if you had done so poorly that you needed to drown your frustrations, or if you were just so glad the exam was finally over with that you wanted to celebrate. The whole class went out and partied that night. We walked into the room Tuesday afternoon and damned if Dr. Bowles wasn't passing out the year's second exam!

That year we also had a course in Osteology, the study of bones. We had the responsibility of memorizing the descriptions for every single bone listed in *Gray's Anatomy*. This knowledge was not merely needed to pass our examinations; our professor often called upon us during his lectures, always without warning. Dr. G. Lombard Kelly taught these classes on Saturday mornings. At the time, he was the Dean of the School of Medicine. I thought the course had very little practical value, but it was a "rite of passage," and the school had required it of freshmen for years. It also afforded Dean Kelly an opportunity to demonstrate his unique knowledge of a subject soon to disappear from the curriculum of most medical schools.

• ◆ •

I drove a little two-door Pontiac that first year, and a few weeks before classes were to end, in April, I was driving up to Washington to pick up Celeste for a fraternity party. It was raining and I skidded off a little wooden bridge, plunging fifty-five feet into the Little River, a tributary of the Savannah River. I wasn't far from the Savannah River Site, where they were working on the hydrogen bomb and the water was about twenty feet deep here. The car landed on its top, with the driver's side angled into the water. I was dazed but I quickly realized that the car was taking on water. Soon I knew that I was taking what would be my last breath. I was either going to get out or I was going to die. Luckily, the windshield had shattered in the crash, and I crawled out through an opening on the passenger side, sustaining quite a few lacerations in the process. Although it was raining, two fishermen were out on the river in their boat checking their lines. They had seen me skid off the bridge and they navigated over and pulled me to shore.

Quite a number of guests from the medical fraternity party met me at the hospital. I had compression fractures of my T12 and L1 vertebrae. I wore a body cast for about four months. We then took the cast off, and replaced it with a body brace, which I wore for another couple of months. When I got back to school I worked through the inconvenience, draping big and tall clothing over the cast and later the brace. In the end, the accident did wonders for my academic career. Any sort of socializing was out of the question, especially that spring. I would go to class and then I would return home and study. My grades were so good that semester that some of my classmates grew troubled.

One of them, our Class President, took me aside, and said, "Now look,

Charlie, because you're in that cast all you can do is study, but we've all got regular lives to live, so you've gotta ease up, your killing the curve man!"

In August, in my body brace, I made the trip back to Athens and graduated with my old classmates. Even though I'd been away for the year, I still managed to be elected to Phi Beta Kappa. Celeste graduated with most of the class in May, and had been elected to Phi Beta Kappa as well. To celebrate graduation, she and a girlfriend took a trip to Europe. The next fall, when she returned, she began work on her masters, with the plan to teach the following year.

•◆•

I started my sophomore year in medical school a college graduate like everyone else in the class, at last. 'Killing the curve,' was not the only development related to the car crash.

Dad called me a few days after the wreck. He asked me if I needed a new car. The Pontiac had been totaled and so I did. He asked me what kind of car I would like. Seeing as I had just driven one car off a bridge, I told him that anything would do just fine. He saw things a bit differently.

"Oh, no, no, no," he said, "I want you to have a nicer car than the one you wrecked. I wouldn't want anyone to think that I was displeased, or that I had lost confidence in you."

Well, that was how I got my first *Oldsmobile 98*. The *98* was Oldsmobile's top-of-the-line model, featuring a large V-8 engine. I don't think many dads would have reacted that way, not that I was complaining.

The second thing that came out of the crash was a bit trickier. Although alcohol had not been involved whatsoever in my skidding off the bridge, I could tell that the seeds of a pressure to 'settle me down' had germinated in my parents' minds. *I needed to get married. I needed to be off the road, etc.* My mother and father never said any of this directly, but they began to find a lot about Celeste that they liked very much. It was obvious that they wanted me to end my days of bachelorhood and get married.

•◆•

We took a pathology course that year and on the first day of class the professor announced that we would take ten exams. A couple of weeks later we took the first exam and I thought there was nothing to it, but when I got it back, I had made a *B+*. Well, I said to myself, that's interesting, maybe I need to be a little more attentive next time. We took the second test a few weeks later and again, it came back *B+*. This time I said to myself, maybe I'm being too verbose. I thought it might be a good idea to just outline things on the third test—take a "less is more" approach. The test came back *B+*. I reversed tack on the fourth test, figuring that maybe they wanted more material. Same result. Ten exams, ten *B+*s. *Oh well*, I thought, remembering my early *B+* back in Athens.

In the spring we took a physiology course, and most years the school exempted two or three students from taking the requisite final. This was a great accolade and the professors enjoyed this little game. The thing was, they wouldn't tell you until the afternoon before the test, so that even someone who wound up exempted would still have to study. A professor would come out of the department offices and post a single sheet of paper on a bulletin board around five o'clock, on his way out of the building for the day. Dempsey and I figured that we would make the list, but we couldn't presume so. It would be poor form, and manners aside, if we hadn't bothered to study and we didn't make the list, then we could be in real trouble. We studied diligently, but deep down we both thought that we would be exempted. Sure enough around five-fifteen a professor came out and pinned up a little sheet of paper to the bulletin board with both of our names on it, and that of one of the other students. That night Dempsey and I went out and we had two big steaks and split a nice bottle of red wine, and thought about all of our poor friends who were stuck in the library.

Come May I got my grades for the year, and to my great surprise, I received an *A* in pathology. Well, now I was really confused. I didn't understand what I'd left out on those ten exams, and now I was trying to make sense of how ten *B+*s could add up to an *A*. I found my professor in his office and I asked him about the grade.

"Oh," he said, smirking, "that was just the grade we put on your paper. We just wanted to keep you working, make you sweat. You've been making straight *A*s all year."

I would be lying if I told you that I wasn't ready to clock that man. What right did he have to make me miserable all year, just to put me in my place? I was confident in my abilities, I don't deny that, but I wasn't at all cocky and I didn't think I deserved his playing games with my grades. I was never arrogant or rude about my performance, and to this day, the whole thing still rubs me the wrong way. I was very diligent about my work and I took great pride in my grades and to find out that he had just been playing a game really bothered me.

I think that incident, and my histology professor's "unique" testing policy, along with a raft of other little things, all helped to put the idea in my head that some of the school faculty resented excellence for excellence's sake. It's not that they didn't like students sticking their head up a little bit, rather they just wanted everybody to do their work and quietly graduate. The school was interested in training doctors to go back to the small towns of Georgia and practice family medicine there. That's really what their mission was back then. That's not to say it was a bad mission, not at all. The state needed doctors just for that purpose. That wasn't my mission though. I can't blame the school for my displeasure. It was I who chose to attend Georgia despite my aspirations to head north to Hopkins or Harvard.

Nevertheless, there were some professors who encouraged me to strive, and I would be remiss if I didn't recognize them. Dr. Robert B Greenblatt, an endocrinology professor, was first among these men. For nearly thirty years Dr. Greenblatt chaired the Endocrinology Department, which he himself had founded in 1946 (the first in the nation). Whenever Dr. Greenblatt became starved for particular patients he would actually *bring* patients to Augusta. He would mail people throughout the state money (out of his own pocket), in order to pay for their bus fares to Augusta. Working doggedly like that, he made sure that his students received the best education they could. Professionally, he built up a legacy of groundbreaking research in the field of female infertility. I took his course and we developed a friendship. Senior year, I nominated him to be the honorary member of our class. This honor was given to Dr. Sydenstricker though, as he was near the end of his career (he was also of course an excellent professor). Dr. Greenblatt knew that I had nominated him, and it helped forge a special bond between us.

A few years later, after I had graduated from medical school, he came up North to deliver a lecture at Harvard. He visited me at The Peter Bent Brigham Hospital, where I was a resident and we went out for lunch. That was not the last time our paths would cross.

Many years later we would come together again in Atlanta. Dr. Greenblatt's son had married Bob Hope's daughter, and we were all invited to WSB's 25th anniversary party, where Bob Hope would be the MC. WSB was Atlanta's first television station, having begun broadcasting in 1948 as a member of the NBC affiliate network, and they planned a gala to mark twenty-five years on the air. Dr. Greenblatt called me to ask if I could find a proper date for his daughter, a student at Gaucher College in Towson, Maryland, and preferably a nice Jewish boy. I flipped through the Emory Medical School yearbook and picked the best looking boy I could find. Alas, he had just become engaged the weekend before and he thought it would be unwise for him to go out on a date. My fallback was a very handsome resident on my cardiothoracic surgery service, a young man named Dale Waters. Dale was up for it, and I told him to make sure that she had a lovely evening, that she thoroughly enjoyed herself. Perhaps I should have been more careful with my words.

We joined the Greenblatt's at the hotel and we piled into a limousine to head over to the party. Later that evening, when we got back to the hotel, Dr. Greenblatt's daughter smiled sort of sheepishly and said that she was not coming inside; Dale had offered to show her some of Atlanta and that she was eager to get underway. They stayed out much too late, and arrived back at the hotel about the time that Dr. Greenblatt and his wife were sitting down to breakfast. Dr. Greenblatt was most annoyed with me, and the next day I spoke with Dale about his behavior.

In the hospital, I took him aside and asked, "What in the world possessed you to do that?"

"Well," he said, "you urged me to be sure that she had a good time, and Dr. Hatcher, she sure had a good time last night."

I just shook my head and laughed, for there was not much else I could do. In time, Dr. Greenblatt of course forgave me.

Getting back to Augusta, the school's clinical faculty was made up largely of teachers and clinicians. Research was encouraged but not overemphasized. Perhaps top among the clinical teachers was Dr. Virgil P. Sydenstricker, Professor and Chairman of the Department of Medicine. Every student was in awe of Dr. Sydenstricker, who seemed to have infinite knowledge and excelled at solving the most difficult diagnostic problems. Unfortunately, by the time our class came along, Dr. Sydenstricker had been largely confined to a wheelchair. He still possessed his unique intellect and in fact, he could derive so much information from a simple stool exam that it was a student joke that the government had engaged him to sit beside the Savannah River and take the census for Augusta and Richmond County.

During his years as Professor and Chairman of the Department of Medicine, Dr. Sydenstricker had trained quite a number of outstanding internists. Among these had been Dr. J. Willis Hurst, Candler Professor and Chairman of the Department of Medicine at the Emory University School of Medicine, and a wonderful colleague throughout my years at Emory.

I finished my sophomore year and then my junior year and soon enough it was time to choose a specialty. Celeste spent my junior year practice teaching, working as a classroom assistant. Since graduating she had traveled abroad, worked on her masters, and begun teaching; all very socially acceptable things to do back then, all things which indicated that she was biding her time until marriage. This was not lost on me as I began to seriously think about my career in medicine.

Over Christmas break, I proposed to Celeste. A few weeks earlier, my parents had asked me what I was giving Celeste for Christmas. I told them that I hadn't thought about it yet.

"Why don't you give her an engagement ring," my mother suggested.

I told her that I couldn't afford to purchase an engagement ring. She replied that my father would be happy to help me out with the cost of a ring.

·◆·

I got a summer job at the Archbold Memorial Hospital in Thomasville. The hospital in Thomasville is now and was then the leading medical center in southwest Georgia. How this little town ended up with such a fine hospital is an interesting story.

Following the Civil War, a number of northerners bought up the great plantations in the area. Directors from Standard Oil, U.S. Steel, and the other large conglomerates of the day were among the wealthy industrialists who maintained sprawling plantations in the region. Mark Hanna was foremost among these men. A Clevelander, he had made his fortune in the transportation business. He enjoyed politics and assisted William McKinley with his Ohio gubernatorial election campaign. When McKinley ran for President in 1896, Hanna oversaw the fundraising effort as the Chairman of the GOP. Hanna was a hardnosed businessman with vast financial resources and a network of wealthy contacts, which he put to work in what was at the time the most expensive Presidential campaign in American History. McKinley won of course, and Hanna went on to serve in the Senate.

Hanna built a winter home in Thomasville, a plantation named *Pebble Hill*. He had a son named Melvin, and he built a second plantation named *Melhanna* in honor of his son's name. Some people say that Hanna and McKinley plotted the latter's successful Presidential campaign at one of these plantations. A lot of other men and their families followed Hanna down to Thomasville. Eventually, these wealthy men realized that Thomasville was lacking in two things: a good club and a good hospital. They established the Glen Arven Club, and then in 1925, John Archbold, a Standard Oil heir and the proprietor of *Chinaquapin*, donated $1 Million dollars to build a state-of-the-art hospital. This hospital still bears his name today.

I spent half of the summer with a surgeon, Dr. Charlie Watt, Sr. and the other half with an internist, Dr. Ernest Wahl. Both doctors were considered leaders at the hospital and they had both trained at Johns Hopkins.

I split my time with the two doctors and I quickly realized that the better student you are the easier it is to be an internist, probably more so than in most medical tracks. To be a successful surgeon requires more than intellect, it requires excellent eye-hand coordination and, perhaps most importantly, a good bit of nerve. Based upon my grades a career as an internist certainly seemed like the path of choice. At the end of the summer I thought things over, and I decided that I had had a lot more fun in surgery. Years later I looked back and realized that it hadn't hurt matters at all, that while Dr. Wahl had only his one nurse and a receptionist, the operating room was filled with attractive young nurses.

· ◆ ·

Celeste and I were married in August, 1953, the summer before my senior year of medical school, at the Methodist Church near her home in Washington, Georgia. We had the reception at her home, a beautiful antebellum building now on the National Register of Historic Places. Celeste was a lover of colonial history and we honeymooned at the Poinsett Hotel in Greenville, South Carolina. The Poinsett was an elegant brick hotel, standing on South Main Street, in Downtown Greenville. The hotel was built in 1925 by W.L. Stoddard, a New York City-bred architect who designed a number of hotels throughout the country.

From there we drove up to Colonial Williamsburg, where we stayed at the Williamsburg Inn, a stately white-columned hotel built by John D. Rockefeller in 1937. Celeste loved the hotel, and we had the chance to meet royalty. Japanese Crown Prince Akihito, who was nineteen at the time, happened to be staying at the hotel while we were there. He was on his first overseas trip that summer.

After a brief stay in Myrtle Beach, South Carolina, we returned to Augusta. I bid Mac, my roommate, adieu and Celeste and I moved in together. We rented a small flat in the Monsano Apartments, where we would live while I finished up my last year of medical school. Our apartment was nice. We filled it with furniture borrowed from both sets of parents, and we had good neighbors. Another student living in the building, who was a ham radio buff, helped me mount an antenna on the roof, which we hooked up to a small black-and-white television set. While I continued my studies, Celeste taught at a local high school.

Soon the year was underway. I was a young husband with a new set of responsibilities and the time was nearing when I would leave medical school behind. But first there were choices to be made. Over the summer I had enjoyed working with Dr. Watt and the notion to go into surgery became even clearer during the year. Dr. Robert Major was the acting Chairman of the Department of Surgery, the Chief Thoracic Surgeon, and a professor of mine during senior year. I worked closely with him and I found him to be an excellent professor. On occasion I served as a special nurse for some of his patients, overnight from eleven to seven. I was grateful for this early thoracic surgery experience, and I do believe that it helped nudge me onto the path that I would follow for decades to come.

Training with Dr. Major at the time was Dr. Robert Ellison, whom I came to respect a great deal. In time Dr. Ellison would become Chief of Thoracic Surgery at the Medical College of Georgia and a nationally recognized figure in the field. He was endeared by scores of residents on his service. Dr. Ellison, a very small man, was affectionately known as *The Little General*. His wife Lois was also a Fellow and she became an outstanding physician and medical administrator. Together, the Ellisons had five sons, all distinguished young men.

There are a handful of other professors whom I remember quite fondly. There was Dr. Harry B. O'Rear who developed an exceptional pediatrics department. He was well liked and in time he would go on to become Dean of the Medical School, and President of the Medical College. A disproportionate number of my classmates, influenced by Dr. O'Rear, would enter Pediatrics.

In Pathology, Dr. Pund was an excellent Chairman, who would also serve as President of the Medical College. In Anesthesia we had an outstanding residency, headed by Dr. Perry Volpitto. His Anesthesia program was the leading program in the region at the time. The dynamic duo of Dr. Hervey Cleckley and Dr. Corbett Thigpin entertained us and taught us in psychiatry. They subsequently published a book, which was later made into a movie, *The Three Faces of Eve*. I had the opportunity of having Eve as a patient when I was on psychiatry. She was the first triple split-personality on record—there was Eve Black, Eve White, and a combined personality which ultimately emerged with their help. In the fine film adaptation, Joanne Woodward played Eve, and she won an Academy Award for this role.

My first encounter with an open chest in thoracic surgery occurred on a rotation at the Augusta VA hospital. I was fortunate to witness an open thoracotomy for a pulmonary resection; the surgery was being performed by Dr. Nelson Kraft, a Senior Resident who would go on to have a very distinguished and successful career in thoracic surgery in Tallahassee, Florida. I can still remember walking into that operating room—the lights were dimmed, soft music was playing in the background, the operating field was absolutely spotless, and the chest was open, the lungs shining under the bright lights. The field was beautifully draped and a portion of the lung packed away with soft moist sponges. There were minimal traces of blood at the operative site, and the dissection of the pulmonary vessels and bronchus had been quite precise. Suddenly, I realized that this was the way I had always imagined surgery should be performed, and it contributed significantly to my ultimate decision to be a cardiothoracic surgeon.

The first time you're in the OR and you see the heart beating, it's just the most miraculous thing. The thing that impresses you more is when you use chemicals or some other technique to stop it beating, but then two hours later you start it back up again. First it will quiver, and then it gets back into a regular beat.

Laparotomies with yards of intestines and fat were not particularly appealing, nor was orthopedic surgery with hammers and an assortment of rather crude instruments. That left cardiothoracic surgery and perhaps neurosurgery. I was drawn to cardiothoracic surgery because the success rate in this discipline was superior to the success rate of neurosurgery at the time; I was not sure that I possessed the personality to be content achieving success one or two times out of ten. I much preferred to succeed with nine patients out of the ten than to help an occasional patient.

I hoped to obtain my surgical training at Harvard or Hopkins and in my senior year I set my sights on winning a position at one of these two fine institutions. I decided that I would apply to the internship program at Johns Hopkins and the internship program at Peter Bent Brigham Hospital, which was affiliated with Harvard Medical School. My professors in Augusta thought that I was foolish not to apply to some safety programs, that perhaps I didn't see the rocks out in the stream in front of me. I understood the logic of their suggestions, but I was confident, and in truth it was a pain to fill out all of those applications.

In order to eventually enter the Halsted Surgery Program at Johns Hopkins, you had to do your internship there, which elevated Hopkins to a practical first choice. They evaluated you while you worked through your internship, and then, at the end of the year, they allowed two or three interns to enter the Halsted Residency Program. This whittling down almost put the skids on my forward motion a few years later, but when I received my acceptance that was the last thing on my mind.

Before I could be accepted into the internship at Hopkins, I first had to travel to Baltimore for personal interviews. It was 1954 and air travel was not quite that common yet, so instead, I rode by rail. In Atlanta, I boarded the Silver Comet, a train that Strom Thurmond had made famous six years earlier, when he and his associates walked off the floor of the 1948 Democratic Convention in Philadelphia. They rode the Comet in the opposite direction all the way down to Birmingham, Alabama, where they held their own competing convention.

Dr. James Cantrell showed me around the Hopkins campus. He took me to meet Dr. Alfred Blalock, who was in charge of the Halsted Program, and we sat down for the interview. Dr. Major had given me a letter of introduction, which I presented to Dr. Blalock. In the letter Dr. Major had noted that I was at the top of my class, and that my position in any group would be whatever I wanted it to be. I thought this was very kind of him and I'm sure it helped my eventual admission along. Overall I thought the interview went well and I left Baltimore feeling confident.

The final spring in medical school was uneventful. Guillebeau and I, as well as LaMar McGinnis had been elected to Alpha Omega Alpha. When final details of graduation were released, Guillebeau and I and another excellent student, A. D. Wright, were selected to graduate Cum Laude. And LaMar was elected the permanent president of our class.

Some weeks before graduation I received official notice of my acceptance for Internship in Surgery at Johns Hopkins. In June Celeste and I drove to Baltimore. We stayed a night in Washington, D.C. at the Shoreham, a grand old hotel on the edge of Rock Creek Park. The young husband and wife thought it would be nice to have one last enjoyable weekend, spent in the lap of luxury, before reporting to duty. When I got to Baltimore the next afternoon I found out that I had only one hour to spare before my first meeting. I didn't leave the hospital that evening until well after midnight. When I finally returned home I regretfully informed Celeste that not only was I due in surgery at seven a.m., but that I would be in the operating room assisting Dr. Earl Walker, the Chief of Neurosurgery. The baptism of fire had begun.

Section Three: From Baltimore to Boston; to The Dunes and Back

A Personal Word

I was fortunate to begin my training at such a pivotal moment in history. If I had been born just a few years earlier I might never have had the opportunity to make a career out of operating on the heart and the aorta, avoiding the pair like every other physician had for the last 2,500 years.

The Baptism of Fire

I RETURNED TO THE HOSPITAL the following morning, unexcited but ready to assist Dr. Walker. I was not at all interested in neurosurgery, but that was the division I had been assigned to and you had to do what you had to do. So, for a month I worked in the neurosurgery department, dealing with what can only be described as a bizarre lot of patients. You see, the night before, the intern who had previously been assigned to neurosurgery had shown me around the wards. He introduced me to everyone on the service. I didn't know it at the time, but one of the surgeons was studying possible surgical ablation of a focus that was related to athetoid movements (think of someone who has cerebral palsy). Well, as I said, I didn't know it at the time, and as I walked through the ward, spying patient after patient exhibiting uncontrollable movements, I thought, *good god, this is the strangest group of patients I've ever seen in my life.* Of course, I eventually found out that they had all come in from a nearby mental institution for the doctor's study.

When I left the hospital that first night around midnight, I had assumed responsibility for all of the patients whom I had seen.

I said, "Well, I'll be responsible for them, but damnit if I can find them without a map." They were all over the hospital but I did have the locations of their beds written down, so one by one, before I met with Dr. Walker the following morning in the operating room, I sleuthed my way around the hospital. I checked on all of them before I went in to surgery because I might be tied up in the operating room for hours, and as I said, these patients were now my responsibility.

The first month was like this, day after day: checking on the patients at the crack of dawn, followed by surgery at seven or so, and then filling out orders and checking on my patients again. There was usually a meeting in the early evening, where tea and coffee would be served, and then there were the evening's teaching rounds. All of the house staff would gather and the Chief Residents would give a lecture on some point relating to an interesting patient in the hospital. When that was done, usually around nine, I would head back to the floors to check on my patients and work up my new patients, before finally leaving for my apartment sometime around midnight. Everyone was very nice to me, but the work was quite demanding and there were several quirks to the place.

Dr. Frank O'Tenasek was the leading active surgeon in the neurosurgery department, and in order to simplify his life, he just called all of the interns *Joe*. I felt like this was a sort of slap in the face. Maybe it was a bit presumptuous of me, but I figured if I were going to be looking after his patients for a month, he could at least bother to learn my name. Well, he just didn't fool with it, so instead it was, "Joe, what are you planning to do this weekend; Joe, where are you from?"

Back when I had come up to interview at Hopkins I had met a senior student who was going to be an intern in the fall and I had asked him how much scut work the interns were responsible for. He drew himself up and said, "We do not refer to routine laboratory work as *scut work* at Johns Hopkins."

Well, I looked at him skeptically and asked him how long he had been like this. He asked me what I meant.

I smiled and said, "They might still be able to help you."

He didn't appreciate that comment, and a few months later, when I returned in the fall, our paths were to cross again. He was on the laboratory service, which meant that he ran the blood bank. I was working the emergency room and I received a patient with trauma one afternoon. I sent up a request for blood to be typed and cross-matched. Then we waited, expecting a call to let us know that the blood was matched and ready. The minutes ticked by and the call didn't come. Finally I called upstairs. He listened to my query and then he said, "We have not acted on the request because the form was improperly filled out."

"What do you mean," I asked.

"You didn't specify the number of pints that you wanted."

"Well," I said, anger slipping into my voice, "I at least wanted one, didn't I?"

The chief resident happened to overhear this and he asked me what the problem was. I told him, and I said that I hadn't specified a number of pints because my patient was actively bleeding and I didn't know just yet how much blood I was going to need. He grabbed the receiver and tore into the fellow.

I enjoyed the second month of my internship much more than the first, as I had moved on to general surgery. The two chief residents in the department that year were Dr. Frank Spencer and Dr. James Maloney.

Frank was a workaholic and I worked hard for him that month. I can remember being on the floor the last night of my month-long assignment to his service. He came by and we spoke for a while before saying our goodbyes. He started down the hall, but just before he got to the doors, he stopped, turned around and came back and said to me, "Charlie, you just perform every month as well as you have this month and one day you'll be the Halsted Resident."

Well, that sounded great, because the Halsted Residency was the reason I had come up to Hopkins to do my internship in the first place.

Anyway, I did this and I did that, and I rotated through the different services. It was enjoyable and it was exciting, but there's no denying that it was tedious. For months on end I was at the hospital before dawn and I rarely ever got home before midnight. It wasn't all a matter of hard work though. I also realized that perceptions would play an important role in the advancement of my medical career.

You can picture me like a duck, gliding across the surface of the pond calmly, but underneath that water, my feet were kicking like hell. To this end, I kept an anatomy book in my locker in the OR dressing room. Whenever I was going in for surgery, I would always make a point of showing up about fifteen minutes early, so that I could flip through the book and review the anatomy for whatever surgery we were doing that day. That way if the attending doctor asked what we were looking for, or what little thing he might be pointing out, I always had the answer on the tip of my tongue. I also made an effort to keep up my physical appearance. We all worked slavish hours and fairly or unfairly, one of the doctors in charge of your future might look at you and judge you poorly if you looked like a slovenly mess with your eyes bloodshot and your whites messy and wrinkled. Of course the most important thing is to be a good surgeon, but it also helps to look like a good surgeon. Recognizing this I was always clean-shaven and I made sure to keep a freshly pressed, clean white suit in my locker, which I would change into before conferences with the senior staff.

The position I wanted more than any other was that of the Halsted Resident. As Chairman of the Department of Surgery and Surgeon In-Chief, Dr. Alfred Blalock was in charge of the Halsted Residency Program, and I knew that he cared about appearances. He collected all of his residents' uniforms at the end of the year and gave them all new ones, so that you wouldn't have any that were frayed and ragged. Now, anyone who would go to the trouble of collecting the old house staff uniforms at the end of the year was obviously a man who was interested in having his house staff look sharp. I knew that it would make a good impression on him if he saw me cleanly shaven and draped in a fresh white suit at every conference that I attended. The effort was not for naught—the nurses that year also voted me the neatest intern!

In the same way, it was important to develop friendships with as many people as I could in the hospital, because as good a doctor as I hoped to be, a lot of people could help me or hurt me depending on whether they liked me or not. The head nurse in the cardiac surgery ICU was one of those people. If Dr. Blalock came in to check on one of his patients and he said, for example, "I think this patient is behind at least one unit of blood," the situation could play out two decidedly different ways. If this nurse did not like you she might say, 'I think so too, and I mentioned that to Dr. Hatcher, but he didn't agree', or 'I haven't been able to reach Dr. Hatcher', or so on and so on. Well, you might never know that had happened, and it could really hurt you. On the other hand, if she liked you, she wouldn't say anything, but as soon as Dr. Blalock left she would grab the phone and call you up and say, 'Dr. Blalock thinks the patient is a pint of blood behind.' Upon hearing this you would rush down to the patient and arrange the additional blood to be administered. That way when Dr. Blalock called you to ask what you thought of this patient you could tell him, "I think he's at least one pint of blood behind and I've ordered it for him."

"Good boy," he would then say, "That's what I thought."

Dr. Alfred Blalock was a graceful man in his late fifties with an athletic build when I first came to know him. As a boy, he had access to a tennis court at the family home. He was apparently quite a good athlete, and played on the tennis teams at the University of Georgia during his undergraduate years. Outside of the operating room Dr. Blalock was a perfect gentleman; in the operating room he was somewhat of a whiner, pleading for help by his assistants. Trained in the years before blood transfusion had been developed, Dr. Blalock was never at home with a major hemorrhage. On a few occasions that I recall of major hemorrhage, Dr. Blalock would wrap his hands in a towel and take a seat on a stool placed against the wall of the operating theater. He would matter-of-factly ask me to get control of the situation. I would shift to the opposite side of the table and undertake the repair of the vessel or vessels involved, or otherwise seek to control the hemorrhage. Every few minutes he would ask if I had things under control, and if I said "not yet," he would say "well hurry, we can't be here all day" or something to that affect. The thought passed through my mind that he expected me to correct any error that he had made, and to do so in short order! Of course he would always be most gracious when the surgery was completed, and frequently praise his assistants personally to the family of the patient involved.

Dr. Alfred Blalock

I say it was tedious, but there were moments that affected me deeply, that shaped my entire career. During my internship I joined Dr. Blalock while he performed a closed mitral commissurotomy. Dr. Blalock had placed a purse string suture at the base of the left atrial appendage, and after amputation of the tip of the appendage, had slipped the index finger of his right hand into the left atrium to evaluate the status of the mitral valve. He confirmed the presence of mitral stenosis with fusion of the anterior commissure, but before attempting the commissurotomy, he withdrew his finger and applied an atraumatic vascular clamp to the atrial appendage. He then invited me to come around to his side of the table and carefully instructed me in the insertion of my own index finger. I have never forgotten the feeling of having such intimate contact with a beating heart.

Dr. Blalock carried me carefully through identification of the mitral valve apparatus, and then guided me through the withdrawal of my finger and the application of the vascular clamp. We then swapped places at the operating table, and Dr. Blalock completed the surgical procedure without difficulty. From that moment, I knew that cardiac surgery would be a major component of my surgical career. Interestingly enough, I came to appreciate that these basic techniques in closed cardiac surgery, i.e., mitral valvuloplasty, etc. were quite stressful on the senior surgeon giving the instruction. The heart rate of the senior surgeon is significantly increased during this period of instruction of a resident when the finger movements within the heart cannot be seen, and in the excitement of this operative experience, the resident may acknowledge faulty landmarks, and his finger may be quite out of proper position.

Dr. Dwight Harken

70

The experience with mitral stenosis was repeated in Boston with Dr. Dwight Harken, who termed the procedure mitral valvuloplasty rather than accept the term mitral commissurotomy, which had been advanced by a surgical rival, Dr. Charles Bailey of Philadelphia.

Dr. Harken was typical of so many of the first generation heart surgeons, some of whom tended to take themselves a bit more seriously than they needed to. For example, when Dr. Harken helped organize the Mended Hearts Club in Boston, he arranged for their annual meetings to be held on his birthday. Patients to be operated upon were routinely referred to Dr. Harken's business manager who informed them that the cost of the surgery would be one tenth of the previous year's income, and that this income needed to be verified with a copy of their tax return. I thought the selection of this "tithe" was somewhat amusing. Nevertheless, I appreciated the unique stresses endured by these cardiac surgery pioneers.

• ◆ •

That fall was not only difficult for me; it was also rough for Celeste. I was at the hospital nearly eighteen hours a day, and the few hours that I was home I usually spent in bed, trying to rest up for the next day. In addition, I was always on call when I was home, so it was hard to find any time to relax. She found Hopkins to be very demanding and not very supportive. She was only able to handle the situation for about a month or so at a time. After that she would head back to Washington, Georgia to spend a few weeks with her family.

I earned twenty-five dollars a month as an intern, and we occupied a small apartment. This apartment was very close to the hospital—in fact, Hopkins required that my residence be close enough to the hospital for my telephone line to be hooked up to the hospital's switchboard. We tried to enjoy ourselves that fall, but it was not to be. One night, I signed out of the hospital for the evening. Celeste and I went out to Housner's Restaurant for dinner. I received no less than four phone-calls from the hospital before I just gave up and drove on back to work.

Celeste left for home a couple of weeks later. She returned to Baltimore a few times that fall, but she just couldn't handle the harsh situation.

My residency really depended on those first six months and, as the winter approached, I felt more confident in my chances of earning a surgical residency position in the Halsted program. I had put in long hours, and I was eager to see the results of my hard work. The rewards came but they did not present themselves easily; rather they came in the form of tough decisions.

In December of 1954, Dr. Blalock began his interviews with the year's interns. Out of the eighteen of us, only two or three would be allowed to enter the residency program directly. Dr. Spencer was presiding over the rounds the night before this process began and he took me aside. He told me that the interviews would begin the following morning, and he asked me if I would stick around after the meeting. After the rest of the staff had left the room he congratulated me on being one of the top ranked interns in the group. He then told me that Dr. Blalock would speak to me in the morning, at seven-thirty, to discuss my future plans.

The next morning I met Dr. Blalock in his office. He declared his desire for me to go into the Public Health Service at the NIH (National Institutes of Health) in Bethesda, Maryland. He had a former resident there, Dr. Andrew Morrow, who was in charge of Cardiac Surgery at the National Heart Institute. Dr. Blalock thought this would be a good research opportunity for me, but more so, he wanted to make sure I had my military commitment out of the way before I got into the residency program. Having passed on going to Annapolis seven years earlier, I had yet to complete any military service. I was eager to serve my country, but at the same time, I hoped to do so in a way that would not interrupt my medical training. So on this point I agreed with Dr. Blalock. Moreover, the United States Government had introduced a Doctors Draft in 1950, so there was always the possibility that I might be called into service on terms not my own, which Dr. Blalock obviously feared as well.

I was glad to hear that he thought enough of me to consider my future plans in respect to a possible residency position at Hopkins. At the same time I did not want to do lab work; I was eager to perform surgical work. Furthermore, if I were to serve, I wanted to put on a uniform. So the position at NIH, which Dr. Blalock had proposed, had two strikes against it. I thanked him for his advice, but told him that I didn't wish to go to the NIH.

"Well," he asked, "what do you plan to do then? You know I told you that you can't begin the residency until you've made your military commitment, and I've arranged this for you so that this would be your military commitment."

I told him that I thought I would like to go up to Boston for a couple of years, to The Peter Bent Brigham Hospital, where I could work under Dr. Francis Moore. Dr. Moore was well-known in the surgical community at the time, and today he is remembered as one of the greatest surgical scientists of the entire 20th Century. I had met Dr. Moore that fall at a conference of the American College of Surgeons in Atlantic City. We took a walk along the boardwalk and we discussed my career. We hit things off, and a few weeks later he wrote me a letter offering me a residency position at Brigham if I wanted one.

Peter Bent Brigham Hospital as it was in the mid-1950s
(artist unknown)

I must admit that there was something aside from the opportunity to work with Dr. Moore that appealed to me about going up to The Peter Bent Brigham Hospital. The hospital was affiliated with Harvard Medical School, and the residency program was extremely competitive. Whereas at Hopkins entrance to surgical internship was just a matter of sitting down for a series of interviews, the Brigham required that you take an entrance exam. This exam had both an oral and a written portion. I had taken the exam in my senior year of medical school, as a part of the internship application process. One-hundred sixty-six people took the examination that year, all striving for one of two available places on the Brigham House Staff. I wanted to get this exam out of the way, so I decided to fly up to

Boston. I had about ninety dollars in my bank account and I spent seventy of them on my plane ticket. I got up to Boston and, lacking in funds, I managed to get myself a bed at one of the local hospitals, as I knew a house officer there. The situation was not ideal, but if you wanted to get into the program, you had to do what you had to do. Looking back, flying up to Boston, spending almost all of the money I had in the bank to do so, sleeping in hospital house staff quarters, all for a two or three in 166 crapshoot, was a bold and admittedly dumb move.

Anyway, I went to take the test, and man did I stick out like the lone southerner that I was. Everyone in Boston was wearing dark gray flannel suits, white oxford button downs, red silk ties, and plain-toed cordovan shoes. We hadn't gotten to that dark gray in the south yet, and I sat down for the test wearing my light gray suit.

Some of the doctors joked with me, saying, "Well Charles, one thing about you, we'll always remember that fellow in the light gray suit."

I scored well on the exam and they did remember me, because when I came back looking for a residency position two years later, my application sailed through. With the position in hand, I told Dr. Blalock that I would like to go up to Boston to the Brigham to work under Dr. Moore. He asked me if I thought I could get an appointment up there, and I told him that I thought I could. He then asked me if the position would be on the house staff or in the laboratory, and I told him that I thought I could manage either one or both.

Dr. Blalock stared at me for a while, smoking on his cigarette in a long holder. After what felt like an eternity he leaned forward in his chair and said, "That appeals to me."

I let out a sigh of relief.

"Too many people go on to NIH for their research work," he continued. "I'd like for you to work with Francis in his metabolic lab and when you come back you'll be a little different."

Unbeknownst to me at the time, Dr. Blalock had another reason for supporting my decision. He and Dr. Moore had crossed professional paths in the past, and they had clashed a few years earlier at a meeting of The American Surgical Association. The meeting had been held in Baltimore that year and Dr. Blalock invited Dr. René Leriche, a French surgeon to attend. During the War, the Hopkins staff had, for the most part, worked with General MacArthur in the South Pacific, whereas the people from Boston were stationed predominantly in Europe, headquartered in London. Dr. Elliot Cutler and many of the surgeons from Boston were intimately familiar with Dr. Leriche. They had gone into France with the Allied Forces and helped liberate the hospitals, and they knew about Leriche's collaboration with the Nazis. There was no question that Dr. Leriche was a collaborator. However, his younger assistant would explain, after Leriche's death, that they just couldn't imagine that anyone could beat the Germans, having seen their country overrun by the Nazis in ten days. Dr. Leriche was not fond of the Nazis, but he thought that it was necessary to do business with them or to get out of surgery and close his clinic. He made the decision to continue practicing medicine. At any rate, Dr. Moore and his people from Boston objected to Leriche being a guest. Dr. Moore asked who had invited him.

Dr. Blalock took this as a personal affront and he stood up and said, "I invited him, and Francis, Professor Leriche was making contributions to surgery when you were still wet behind the ears."

This episode created a good bit of awkwardness between the two of them. A few years passed before I came along. By then, both Dr. Blalock and Dr. Moore saw me as an opportunity to repair their damaged relationship. I would pass friendly messages between them whenever I drove back and forth, and years later, when I served as the Chief Resident at Hopkins, I had the opportunity of inviting a guest professor of my choosing. I invited Dr. Moore, who stayed in Baltimore for three days. Dr. Blalock joined us at a number of events. He enjoyed the trip and the night I took him back to the airport he told me that I had made the right decision in finishing my residency at Hopkins. This was mostly because Hopkins was a much larger hospital than the Brigham at that time.

With Dr. Blalock's blessing of my decision, and a vague assurance that I would be able to return to Hopkins in the future, I finished out the second half of my internship. Things let up just a bit in the spring, and I even had the chance to attend a party or two with the residents. I drove to Boston at the end of the summer, excited to begin my residency with Dr. Moore, acutely aware of the fact that I had yet to complete my military service.

"Has Adolph shined his shoes yet?"

I HAD GONE AGAINST THE conventional wisdom. Dr. Spencer said to me, "Dr. Blalock is going to offer you a place in the program in the morning. You're one of the top-ranked interns, so he's going to talk to you at seven-thirty. Do whatever he says. Don't question it, just do whatever he says."

But I didn't want to go to NIH at the time.

"Charlie," he warned me, "Don't say a damn thing. If you object to that then he's got a lot of pressure on him. He's just trying to figure out where all these boys are going to go and if you don't want to follow instructions and you don't do what he says he'll just wash his hands of you right quick and that'll be that."

I realized I was taking a gamble. If it came to my never returning to Hopkins, I was prepared to live with that. I would be at the Brigham and I reasoned that I could just stay there, work as hard as I could, and get my training in Boston. I probably would not have gone on to be a heart surgeon, just a general surgeon, as their cardiac surgery program was not nearly as developed as Hopkins', but I believed that it was worth the risk.

None of this was really on my mind though. I wanted more than anything else to be in Boston, and I was very excited to be there.

Dr. Francis D. Moore

Throughout his life, Dr. Moore suffered from asthma. As a result of this condition, he was deferred from military service. When Dr. Elliott Cutler, his predecessor as surgeon in chief at the Brigham, developed cancer of the prostate and could not return to Boston from World War II, Dr. Moore assumed the position of Moseley Professor of Surgery, the oldest endowed chair at Harvard Medical School, at the young age of thirty-six. He had been featured on the cover of *Time* magazine, billed as the most brilliant surgeon of his generation.

In addition to *Time* magazine, I read an article which stoked my excitement. The piece had been in *Collier's Weekly*, which was a very popular magazine until the mid-1950s. The article was entitled *Adolph Watzka: The World's Foremost Orderly*. Watzka was a little man from Czechoslovakia who had immigrated to the states years earlier, and answering a help wanted ad, he got a job working at the Brigham Hospital. He applied himself to watching what was going on in the operation rooms. He quickly made a name for himself by developing mechanical attachments for the operating room table that better positioned people for surgery.

Aside from Dr. Moore and Watzka there was one other doctor whose eminence drew me to the Brigham, and that man was Dr. Harvey Cushing. Dr. Cushing had come to Harvard from Johns Hopkins. He was a brilliant pioneer in the field of neurosurgery; widely regarded as one of the greatest surgeons of the 20th century. He epitomized the elegant neurosurgeon. He was quite handsome, wore tailored scrub suits, and had his own personal driver. Adolph caught his eye and soon enough he became Dr. Cushing's personal orderly. He designed instruments for Dr. Cushing, arranged patients on the equipment before surgery and so on and so forth. Dr. Cushing passed away in 1939, but Adolph continued to work in the hospital, serving under Dr. Cutler, who died in 1947, and then, by the time I arrived, under Dr. Moore.

Soon after I got to Boston I met Adolph. He was very dedicated, and he had Dr. Moore's ear when it came to number of important matters. Adolph would roam around the ward, watching everybody operate, and if he thought you were a good surgeon, he would begin to polish your operating shoes each night. The next morning they would be back in the rack, clean and gleaming. It was so well known that this was his way of evaluating people that Dr. Moore would ask about someone who was questionable for a promotion, "Has Adolph shined his shoes yet?" If Adolph had shined his shoes, he likely got promoted. If he hadn't then the guy most likely did not win the promotion. Some guys would go through the program and never get their shoes shined. I got my shoes shined early on, in part I think because he related me to Dr. Cushing, on account of our both coming up from Hopkins.

One morning, a few months in, Adolph and I were chatting while I stood at the sink, scrubbing my hands before a case. Well, Adolph had a heart attack and he fell right into my arms. Unfortunately, we could not resuscitate him. The first inkling of an urge to come up to Brigham had been my reading about Adolph in *Collier's* and there I sat, on the floor, with Adolph's lifeless head in my lap.

On the day of his funeral the operating room went dark. Adolph Watzka, without the benefit of a day of formal training, had won such respect and admiration within the hospital that when his coffin was carried out, all of the pallbearers were full professors at Harvard Medical School.

Dr. Elliott Cutler was another doctor at Brigham who was gone by the time I arrived. He had led the Harvard Medical unit in London during World War II. He had a lot of bright young surgeons working for him, and one of these men was Dr. Dwight Harken. Dr. Harken was a cardiothoracic surgeon who was very interested in war wounds of the heart and possible surgical repairs. He got into this work while serving in the European theater, and this led him to the idea that you could mechanically break up adhesions in the mitral valve. This technique is called valvuloplasty. By the time I got to Brigham he was past his three-thousandth attempt at the procedure. This surgery was performed almost every day in the hospital, and early on I assisted in a number of mitral valvuloplasties.

•◆•

I came up to The Peter Bent Brigham Hospital at a very exciting time. Dr. Joseph Murray who would ultimately be awarded a Nobel Prize for his groundbreaking research on transplantation, had performed the world's first successful kidney transplant a few months before my arrival. He had operated on the nineteen-year-old Herrick identical twin boys from Oklahoma City, removing a kidney from one and implanting it in the other. I had the honor of assisting Dr. Murray on the second transplant, this time with a pair of forty-year-old twins, the Heilman brothers from Washington, D.C.

I spent much of my time at the Brigham Hospital discussing cases and making differential diagnoses. I did a good bit of laboratory work that fall—exactly what I had hoped to avoid at NIH—though the work in Boston was far more practical to a working surgeon. The hours as a junior resident were long of course, though not nearly as demanding as they were the year before during my internship. Thus I had some free time so I spent it exploring Boston.

I had moved to Boston with Celeste, and on the way we visited a cousin in Southampton, on Long Island. We spent a day or two with her and had a very nice visit. We went to her beach club and I remember seeing Gary Cooper there.

In Boston, I had the good fortune of borrowing an elegant Beacon Hill townhouse from one of the neurosurgeons, who had left town for his beach house for the summer. He lent me the house for a month, affording me some time to find more permanent arrangements while I got acquainted at the hospital. The house was on Mt. Vernon Street, a block up from Louisburg Square, which is of course quite a famous little private park. At one end there is a statue of Christopher Columbus and at the other a statue of Aristides. Local legend has it that Reverend William Blaxton's spring was in the square. The street's many famous residents over the past three hundred years include John Hancock, Robert Frost, Silvia Plath, and today Senator John Kerry.

The month went by quickly and I soon needed to find a new place to live. Celeste had just departed on a trip around the world with her mother. Her aunt was living in India at the time, so she and her mother decided to visit. They slowly made their way through Europe and then down to India.

They stayed with Celeste's aunt there for several weeks before making their way back to the states through the Pacific.

A professor of dermatology at Harvard, Dr. Lane, had recently died, and Mrs. Lane wanted to take an extended trip to Europe. Since he was a doctor she thought it would be nice to let somebody from the Brigham "house-sit". Dr. Lane had interned at Johns Hopkins and she remembered how hard the internship had been, leading her to choose me from among the other names on the list of applicants. She had a lovely townhouse at 287 Commonwealth Avenue, in the heart of the Back Bay. Comm Ave, as it is often referred to by Bostonians, is an elegant street with a wide median of lush trees running down the center of the traffic lanes. I was a block over from the shops on Newbury Street, and five blocks from the Public Gardens, both lovely places to take an evening stroll.

In the winter, I moved to a third house, and this is where Celeste joined me when she returned from India. Brigham maintained a rotation for surgical fractures, and they sent a doctor to the lodge in Sun Valley, Idaho, for three months during the winter. The doctor cycling out that winter had a home in Wellesly Hills, a close-in suburb of Boston, and he allowed me to house-sit for him. The way things came together, Celeste was due to return to Boston the day that I was supposed to check the place out. I obviously wanted to meet her at the airport, so I asked a nurse colleague to check the house out for me. It was snowing that day, and in trying to unlock the door, she must have fumbled the key, because she lost it in the snow. She couldn't find the key and she called the fire department, who had to break their way into my newest borrowed home.

There was very little permanency to the way I was living back then. I was jumping between houses, often just sleeping over at the hospital, and Celeste, after she got settled in, was in and out of town for weeks at a time, visiting her family in Washington, and traveling. My first six months went by very quickly, shuffling between houses, assisting on a handful of interesting cases.

About six months had passed, and it was around Christmas that I received two very important letters. Dr. Blalock had written me a Christmas message, wishing me well. In the letter he revealed that he had been thinking about our last conversation and that he felt that he had not been as definite as he had meant to be.

"What I meant to say," he wrote, "was that I will have a position for you here whenever you wish to return."

Well, that was something else.

I also got a letter from Dr. Moore. He wrote that he was very pleased with my progress, and that I would be the first junior resident appointed to a senior residency position. So it was a good Christmas. At the same time the future was beginning to take shape and choices would have to be made. I seemed to be quickly coming up on a fork in the road. On the one hand I had Dr. Blalock's clear assurance that there would be a residency position for me open at the Halstead program in Baltimore. On the other hand I had Dr. Moore's praise, and not so subtle insinuation that the ladder to the top of the residency program at Brigham would be mine to climb.

The snow melted and spring bloomed in Boston. The days and months continued to fly by and the fork in the road was now plainly in sight. But before I finally made my decision, I received a third letter, informing me that both choices had just been yanked off the table.

Uncle Sam Comes Calling

IT WAS A GOOD CHRISTMAS. The two letters confirmed what I hoped—that I had probably nailed it down at Hopkins and that I was managing the competition quite handily in Boston. I still had not made a decision about where to go next, but I was set to begin the second year of my residency at The Peter Bent Brigham Hospital. Unfortunately the United States government had different ideas.

The news that I was being drafted was very disturbing. Interrupting my surgical training was going to present me with a number of real problems. First, I was being drafted in the 18 – 25 regular draft by the Draft Board in Bainbridge, Georgia. I made a point of never finding out who of my neighbors were on the Draft Board. Subsequently, I was visited by the FBI one evening at the Brigham to inquire if I were a conscientious objector. I said, "of course not". They then informed me that I was going to be drafted as a private in the Army unless I volunteered for the Medical Corps. I assured them that I would indeed "volunteer" at the proper time. In this manner the Army limited the number of physicians brought in through the Doctor Draft.

As soon as I found this out I contacted one of my Georgia Senators, Richard B. Russell, Jr. Senator Russell was the Chairman of the Senate Armed Services Committee, arguably the second most important position related to the military at the time, second to the president of course. He had been there for many years, and he said to me, "I'll ask if you can be deferred until you finish your training."

I said to him, "There's no question about my willingness to serve—I just would rather finish the residency than go right now when I'm not yet a surgeon but a little more than a general medical officer. I think I'd be a lot more valuable to the service after I finish training."

Well the Army Command wrote him back and said that they needed general medical officers and that they could not allow a deferment. A notice from the military arrived in June, though not the one that I expected. The military had now decided that it was unnecessary to accept me through the draft because they now had more general medical officers than they needed. My services were no longer required. I sent Sen. Russell that note with a little sarcastic addendum: 'You and I were told that I could not possibly be deferred because I was desperately needed as a general medical officer and now I've received this. I've let my apartment go. I've let my residency appointment go, at the worst possible time, and it's now going to cost me two years to get out and get back in somewhere, all because they are doing what we asked them to do before.'

The Senator called me and said, "You just go ahead and proceed to Fort Sam Houston in Texas as if you were in the Army, and your orders will be cut by the time you get there."

A couple of days later, I got an annoyed phone call from a Colonel with the 1st Army in New York, and he said, "I think you should know that the Army doesn't appreciate the manner in which you have used political influence."

I was rightfully frustrated and I said back to him, "Now look, I didn't want to use political influence but you people have just given me no consideration whatsoever. I asked to be deferred, was told I couldn't be deferred, so I burn all of my bridges behind me, and now I am deferred and I don't want to be deferred because I've given up my apartment and my position and all of that."

"Well," he said, "we're sorry that's happened..."

He mumbled on and then hung up the phone.

After this, I called up the senator in his office and told him that I was a little bit uneasy going into the Army, with the Army annoyed with me.

"Well," he said, "it's alright to use political influence as long as it's *real political influence*, so don't you worry about this."

He told me that there was a military rule that forbade your being sent out of the continental United States without forty-eight hours notice in peacetime. So if I got any foolish orders, say sending me to Greenland, I'd still have time to go to the telephone, and he'd be able to abort the orders. He told me not to worry about any tension, assuring me that I would be fine.

In the meantime, Dr. Moore—who was also surgical consultant to the Surgeon General of the Army—had requested that I be assigned to the Walter Reed Army Medical Center, specifically the WRAIR (Walter Reed Army Institute of Research). The WRAMC (Walter Reed Army Medical

Center) in Washington, D. C. was the Army's preeminent medical facility, and this is very much where I would have hoped to be stationed.

I left Boston and drove down to Fort Sam Houston for six weeks of basic training. Toward the end of this training they interviewed everyone, asking us, among other questions, where we would like to serve. I said that I would like to be stationed at Walter Reed.

The interviewer laughed and said, "Are you crazy? You're not going to Walter Reed. That's for regular Army Officers. It's our most distinguished post."

"Well," I said, "you asked me where I would like to go and I told you where I wanted to go. If that's not possible then don't worry about it."

About a week later, when my orders came in, directing me to head up to Walter Reed, I dropped by his office and said, "Well, sometimes it pays just to ask for what you really want."

He couldn't believe it and rightfully so—I was one of only a very few two-year guys assigned to Walter Reed. The hospital is typically reserved for people who are career officers in the Army, who are nearing the end of their service, the kind of place to which you receive your final promotion. I was just very, very fortunate to have Dr. Moore pulling for me.

I had a great time at Walter Reed. Dr. Moore would come down every couple of months, as he liked to visit their laboratories, where some of the newest research in his field was being done. Each time he would request that I be detached that day to accompany him, and we would go around the laboratories together and he would always introduce me, "You know my boy Charlie?" If they didn't, they quickly learned who I was. I was treated very well because he was so attentive to me when he was at Walter Reed; it was a good two years. Of course I was intimately involved in some fascinating research. The initial chaos that the Army had sown seemed to be settling into a very fine situation after all.

•◆•

The year was 1956. The Korean War had come to an uneasy ceasefire three years earlier and the strange new reality of the Cold War was beginning to ferment in the American consciousness. The notion of a proxy war between the United States and the USSR was now real, and the nuclear arms race had begun. I was relieved to be at Walter Reed, for I believed it was my duty to serve my country. I had felt squeamish about the prospect of going to NIH and now I had exactly what I wanted—a position in the Army and the uniform to go with it.

The Navy had presented an interesting possibility to serve, but I believed that the Army represented a better situation for doctors. The Army has Medical Centers spread across the country, whereas the Navy just has Bethesda in Maryland. The Army had Walter Reed, Brooke Army Medical Center in San Antonio, Fitzsimmons Army Hospital in Denver, Letterman in San Francisco, and Tripler in Honolulu. With five medical centers, your chances of seeing interesting patients were much greater than in the Navy.

I was assigned to the Army Institute of Research upon my arrival at Walter Reed. In the Army this department is often abbreviated to WRAIR. I moved around, carrying out a number of different experiments, working with assorted departments, but for most of my time at WRAIR I shared an office with some doctors in the Department of Experimental Surgery.

For my first major project, I helped the Army establish a blood-gas laboratory at Walter Reed Hospital. With this laboratory one could analyze drawn blood to determine the oxygen and carbon dioxide content, as well as the pH of a sample. Dr. Moore was a pioneer in the field and I drew upon my work with him in order to set up the lab.

I was also instrumental in getting Walter Reed's open heart surgery program up and running. I was a cardiac surgeon (in training), but Dr. Roger Sherman, with whom I worked closely, was not. He had, however, worked with the people who had developed the heart-lung machine in Cincinnati. He worked very hard to make sure that the department got itself a reliable heart-lung machine. My tack was that the Army used consultants from Georgetown and George Washington, which were both nearby in Washington, D.C; I proposed that we arrange for additional cardiac surgery consultants from Johns Hopkins and offered to speak to Dr. Blalock in this regard.

I made some phone calls and Dr. Blalock arranged for Dr. Frank Spencer and Dr. David Sabiston to become consultants to Walter Reed. I felt that Walter Reed Hospital should have access to the best available people in a particular field, and I was pleased to assist in these arrangements.

Just before my arrival at Walter Reed, General Linton Heaton, the commandant of the hospital and the chief of surgery, had operated on President Dwight Eisenhower. Subsequently, General Heaton was awarded with a third star, the first medical officer to be accorded that rank. He left his post at Walter Reed thereafter to become the Surgeon General of the Army. He returned to Walter Reed weekly to conduct surgical rounds. Whenever possible, I tried to attend those rounds. Instinctively, I referred to him as Dr. Heaton on several of these occasions. After joining a few of these rounds, a senior officer in the medical service corps called me into his office. He told in no uncertain terms that I was to refer to the man as General Heaton, not Dr. Heaton. I replied that everyone knew he was General Heaton, as he had the stars to prove that, but that he was making the effort to return to Walter Reed for these weekly rounds to show that he was still a doctor.

"Well you may think that Captain Hatcher, but that's not your decision. I shall expect you to call General Heaton, General Heaton, not Dr. Heaton in the future."

Years later, after his retirement, General Heaton was a guest at the Cloister in Sea Island, Georgia, and invited me to play a round of golf with him. He attempted to suggest that I call him "Lin" during the round, and of course I demurred. He then mentioned that he recalled me because I was the only young surgeon at Walter Reed who had called him "Dr. Heaton." I told him that I had been soundly criticized and admonished for calling him "doctor", but that I was very happy to know that he understood the gesture I was making.

At Walter Reed, I assisted on various experiments to see what happened to soldiers who had post-traumatic sequelae from war wounds. One of the positive developments of war is that conflict is usually accompanied by medical advances. Many gains in the field of modern surgery were made at the edges of the battlefields of the past century's greatest conflicts. Whenever there is a deluge of traumatized victims, there is almost always an improvement in care accompanied by the development of new techniques. Amputations, prostheses, and many other medical advances are the direct result of war.

Wounded soldiers in World War II, who made it off the battlefield and made contact with a medic suffered a fatality rate somewhere between five and ten percent, toward the high end of that range. Korea saw the deployment of MASH hospitals. Wounded soldiers were flown in by helicopter, right off the battlefield. The reduction in the period of time between the initial wound and when that soldier made his first contact with a doctor was significantly reduced. As a result, the mortality rate dropped below five percent. Vietnam saw further improvements in care and evacuation procedures, and the mortality rate was even lower. And now, in the Iraq and Afghanistan theatres, the mortality rate is lower still. Whereas in Korea doctors were working out of actual tents, the field hospitals the Army deploys today are literally mobile pre-fab hospitals. As advanced as those field hospitals are, soldiers spend far less time in them than they used to. Fifty years ago it took almost an entire month for a wounded soldier to get back to the States; today it takes about three days to get them to the Army's large facility in Germany. From there it is simply the matter of a single flight across the Atlantic.

During the early days of the Korean War, the Army decided to centralize the earlier scattershot studies of battlefield trauma. The doctor in charge of this effort was Dr. John Howard, who later became Chairman of Surgery at Emory University. He and his team published over two-hundred papers on various metabolic studies in wounded men. The work continued on well after the war reached a stalemate in 1953.

One of the many things that Howard and his team observed was that if you lost a certain amount of blood, the kidneys could fail. This condition is called post-traumatic renal insufficiency. The Army was very interested in the condition and I worked on an experiment to see how much epinephrine or norephinephrine had to be released to cause the artery to the kidneys to spasm. This would result in changes to the kidney that could be either reversible or irreversible, depending on how long the cessation in blood flow lasted.

Of course there were other experiments going on at Walter Reed; these investigators often called upon me to perform the surgeries that they needed done. I remember one experiment I that assisted on in particular—the researchers were performing adrenalectomies on various animals. Simply stated, an adrenalectomy is a procedure to remove the adrenal gland. I ran out to these follows' laboratory once a week and I worked on a couple of dogs for them.

These efforts were all prequels to the most important project I became involved with, Biomedical Project 4.1. Project 4.1 had the highest priority of anything that was being done at Walter Reed at the time. This was before the space race had begun—that would be a year later with the launching of Sputnik—instead the nuclear arms race between the United States and the U.S.S.R. was beginning to escalate, and all sorts of complimentary projects to the actual weapons development program were being carried out in research laboratories across the country.

Everything was shrouded in secrecy and my team and I were vaguely led through the routine of what we were to do: we were going to go out to the desert, we would have a field hospital, we would have certain circumstances that would mimic civilian and military life, and we would be using pigs as test subjects. Animal casualties were expected and the military felt that the general public would not be sympathetic to the deaths of hundreds of dogs.

We were to participate in Operation Plumbbob, the largest and most controversial series of nuclear tests ever conducted in the continental United States.

Room One-Twenty-Three and the Chester Whites

My medical unit set out for Las Vegas in the spring of 1957, under the command of Colonel Bill Moncrief. Our team was made up of people from a number of units from more than one service. I was serving in the Army of course, and there were also personnel from the Navy and the Air Force. The assignment was considered a hazardous one, and our wives were not allowed to join us out in the desert. Las Vegas at the time was a very different town than it is today. Before we go any further, I think it's necessary to set the stage:

In 1931, the state of Nevada legalized gambling. A handful of legitimate casinos quickly sprang up on Freemont Street (there had been other, less than legitimate operations already in business). The Hoover Dam was completed a few years later, and as the cheap electricity began to flow, the nascent hotels reclad their exteriors in garish walls of neon lights. Though the Hoover Dam construction project had brought thousands of workers to Las Vegas, the city's population had still yet to reach 10,000 by the close of the decade. Two important events occurred in 1941, which together changed the face of Las Vegas forever. First, the Army began construction on what would eventually become Nellis Air Force Base, and second, Thomas Hull opened a new resort, El Rancho Vegas. This resort was the first in the city built outside of the downtown area; instead it was on the road which is known today round the world as *The Strip*.

After the War, the city grew rapidly and a number of resorts opened on The Strip, the most famous among them The Sands, The Sahara, The Tropicana, The Dunes, The Desert Inn, and Bugsy Sigel's Flamingo Hotel. In 1951, the Atomic Energy Commission opened the Nevada Test Site with a big bang, an atomic one actually. Over the next ten years the AEC would detonate over one hundred atomic bombs in atmospheric explosions, before moving the tests underground with the passage of the Partial Test Ban Treaty in 1963.

I arrived in Las Vegas in the spring of 1957. There were a dozen large resorts on The Strip and perhaps 50,000 people living in the city. The Strip was not yet paved all the way to the Dunes. It stopped right at the Flamingo, which was across the street and we would walk across a construction site where the concrete turned to dirt. The place was more like a big town than a small city, and by virtue of your being in the hotels for weeks and weeks, you got to know all of the employees and they treated you differently than the tourists. Everything was cheap or even better free—the buffets cost a silver dollar and drinks in the casino were comped so long as you sat at the tables. The towel boys at the Dunes' pool knew us and they always fixed us up with good lounge chairs. Most of them did not even expect tips for this. If you could be of service to the employees, then they particularly went out of their way for you. I can remember this very pretty girl from one of the shows who had been in a little automobile accident. She got a cut on her face and the emergency room doctor on duty had stitched her up with large silk sutures, which could leave a prominent scar. She came by and showed the laceration to my friend Roger and me, and immediately we said, "No, no, no, we can't leave you like that. That's not right."

So we took her back to the hospital and told the doctor that we didn't have any credentials in the state, but that we were perhaps further along than he was. Roger had completed his training and by that time I already had two years of experience under my own belt. The young doctor told us that he would be very happy for us to redo the stitches. So we took those stitches out and then closed the wound with a subcuticular stitch, which hides the stitching between the dermis and the epidermis. Well, I'm telling you that spread like wildfire. All the showgirls up and down the Strip heard about what we had done for this girl. We were golden—we were the two dudes who had taken this girl's stitches out and gotten her fixed up right.

Back then the resorts gave all of the showgirls chits so that they would not have to spend their own money in the building. The chits could be used to purchase drinks and such at the bars and lounges. The resort asked them to sit in the lounge between performances and sip on drinks, so that men would come up and ask to join them and spend money at the bar. Some of these girls would also sit at the tables and gamble away casino money in order to attract some unlucky suckers. The girls would be given three chits a night. Well the good looking girls *never* bought but one drink. The girls all knew me because of the stitches episode; after that, they didn't want me to have to spend any money, so they gave me their extra chits. I didn't want to lose any of my money in Las Vegas, and those chits certainly helped me in my efforts.

•◆•

All in all about 18,000 Department of Defense personnel came out to the desert to take part in Operation Plumbbob. There were dozens of different experiments being carried out and aside from scientists and doctors, there were thousands of enlisted men who participated in troop maneuvers during the twenty-four "shots." A shot, each of which was named—Boltzman, Franklin, and so on—was how the military referred to the individual atomic detonations.

The enlisted men lived in army barracks out in the two desert camps. I shared an apartment in town with several doctors, including Tommy Armour, a major in the Air Force. When we weren't out at the test site, the men in my unit spent most of our time at the Dunes, on account of a little stunt that I pulled.

The Dunes had its own myth—*The Miracle in the Desert.* The Dunes was no miracle though, and in its early years it changed hands a number of times before coming under the control of Major Auterburn Riddle. Major Riddle made headlines in January of 1957 by booking *Minsky's Follies* for the resort's stage show. *Minsky's* made the papers because it was the first stage show on the Strip to feature bare-chested showgirls.

Anyway, just before I left for Las Vegas, it had come to my attention that Major Riddle and I shared a mutual friend. My friend gave me a letter of introduction and I drove over to the Dunes with it in hand. A giant fiberglass statue, The Sultan of The Dunes, stood above the hotel's entrance clad in a turban and a cape. I entered the hotel, passing under the stucco-walled porte cochere, under the gaze of the fiberglass sultan. I presented my card at the front desk and I asked the receptionist if he would give it to Mr. Riddle, and tell him that Dr. Charles Hatcher of Georgia would very much like to pay his respects.

A few minutes later the receptionist returned. He told me that Major Riddle would see me. I sat down in his office and we talked and he asked me what he could do for me. He obviously thought I had a little chutzpah to come in and see him on pretty slight pretenses. I was young and filled with confidence, and I think he liked that. So, seeing an opening, I said to him, "I can tell you right now, we want one hotel that we could sort of think of as our Officers' Club. We're going to have 500 scientists and a few thousand enlisted men, and there are going to be more enlisted men in town for each shot so that they can witness the mushroom cloud and feel the earth shake and not panic. There will be Congressmen and officials from Washington coming out for these shots, and we'd like to be able to pick them up at McCarran Field, come by and meet and have a drink."

I had obviously piqued his interest and he waited for me to go on.

So I said, "I am confident that whichever hotel is the place where everybody knows to meet as the unofficial club will double its lounge's profits overnight!"

He smiled, "I'll be happy to accommodate you."

He stood up and offered to show me around the hotel. He took me out on the casino floor, introducing me to the pit bosses, and out to the pool and through the nightclubs, introducing me to the people in charge of all of the different hotel activities. Finally we came back to the front desk and he said to the receptionist, "I'd like the key to room one-twenty-three."

He turned to me and said, "C'mon, I'll show you to your room."

The room was very nice, overlooking the pool in the central courtyard. We walked back to the front desk and my curiosity getting the better of me, I asked, "Sir, it's a nice room, but I can't help but wonder why you wanted me to have room one-twenty-three?"

"My boy," he said, putting his hand on my shoulder, "I don't care how drunk a woman is, you tell her you're in room one-two-three and she'll never forget that."

I spent the summer in and out of room 123. I had my apartment of course, and my friends and I shared the room amongst ourselves whenever we needed an extra bed, or wanted to stay on the Strip for the night. The room had two beds and we kept a cot in there, but every now and then, that would still not be enough.

One night we had a friend join us, but there wasn't any room for him, so we suggested that he sleep on one of the chaise-lounges by the pool. When the pool-boy came by in the morning he recognized him as one of our friends, so he just left him alone. He didn't want to disturb him, deciding that this fellow probably just needed to sleep it off. We didn't come down till about noon, and hell, when he woke up he was just cooked. He had been lying in his bathing suit completely exposed and we had to treat him with crumbled up saltine crackers and milk and all sorts of things so he wouldn't have to go to the hospital.

Of course there was actual work to be done in Las Vegas and we did spend a good bit of our time out at the test site, which is about sixty-five miles northwest of the city. Every night we would drive down the Strip to the Atomic Energy Commission building, and if a shot were on, a pennant would be up on the roof, fluttering in the desert wind. If there was no pennant then you knew that the winds were not blowing in the right direction and you would stay in town. Utah and Idaho were very sparsely populated and a decision was made that shots would only be detonated when the prevailing winds were blowing to the northeast, to prevent the fallout from traveling west to California. The people living in the remote towns of Utah and Idaho were to be unwitting "participants" in the experiments.

The military detonated twenty-four shots that summer (as well as five zero-yield safety shots), starting with Boltzman on May 28th, and ending with Morgan on October 2nd. There were dozens of experiments carried out that summer. Of course they were testing the bombs themselves, but the Department of Defense also carried out complimentary medical, scientific and psychological experiments. As absurd as it may seem today, in the late 1950s, the arms race heating up, World War III against the Soviets seemingly inevitable, the government was very interested to see how soldiers would handle, physically and psychologically, a battlefield scared by tactical nuclear strikes. These doomsday scenarios never came to pass, of course, but back then their threat seemed very real.

Project 4.1 was a series of biomedical experiments to study the 'Effects of Nuclear Detonations on a Large Biological Specimen (swine)', in official military parlance. We had five goals: 1) To determine the effectiveness of field medical procedures in a mass casualty situation; 2) To investigate the effects of combined injuries from supralethal to nonlethal ranges; 3) To derive the LD-50-30 (midlethal doses in 30 days) for a large biological specimen; 4) To obtain information on blast injuries in a large biological specimen; and 5) To obtain information on thermal injuries in a large biological specimen.

In order to carry out these experiments we maintained a herd of 150-pound Chester White pigs. We chose the pigs because they were similar in size to humans and they responded similarly to ionizing radiation. No detail was too small in our attempts to simulate human likeness, and we went so far as to dress the pigs up in military uniforms. The pigs were strapped into chairs and desks and cars, and dosimeters (used to measure radiation exposure) were placed inside the pigs, in various organs. In one experiment, the physicists arranged rows of plate glass between the animals and the blast, so that we could predict how many of each particular kind of injury would occur. Interestingly, we found out that you could take the small intestine in a pig and cut it in two and drop both ends back in and the pig would be alright. A wound of the stomach however was uniformly fatal. All in all, I found the methodology to be a bit questionable—extrapolating human fatality rates from a hundred or so pigs, who were strapped into seats, while an air raid siren blasted in the room. I think they were asking far too much of us, with such a set of experimental materials and unpredictable variables, but the Defense Department really thought that we could come up with precise fatality predictions. How will the glass shatter? Will the glass fragment in just that many places? Will the blast velocity carry the glass on an absolutely true trajectory? Will the animals remain in the position in which they were placed? I don't think we could truly account for any of these questions.

The dosimeter implantations were far more significant work, in my opinion. We were trying to determine what a fatal dose of radiation would be, absent external effects. We would have a certain blast of so many kilotons and people within a certain range would receive x amount of radiation. We implanted these dosimeters in various organs and came up with LD-50 figures. LD-50 means that if you have had this amount of radiation, fifty percent of people will live and fifty percent of them will die. With that standard you can begin to treat people. The thought was, in a mass casualty situation, medical supplies and personnel would be limited and the Army would not want to waste time tending to a soldier who had already received a fatal dose of radiation. On the battlefield there is little sense in mending someone's broken leg if it has been preordained that he is going to die of radiation poisoning within the week. You would give the guy some morphine and perhaps a cigarette, but that was about all you could do for him. We have never seen this come to pass, but we needed to know what the LD-50 was for each organ in order to prepare for the possibility.

We trotted the pigs out for three of the shots: Franklin, Wilson, and Priscilla. Priscilla was the largest of the three, with a yield of roughly 37 kilotons. To give this figure some meaning, the bomb dropped on Hiroshima produced a yield of 12 – 15 kilotons, and the bomb dropped on Nagasaki a yield of 20 – 22 kilotons.

The winds kept acting up and the Priscilla shot was delayed a number of times, but finally, we saw the flag fluttering on the 23rd of June and we headed out to the test site. The army had built a huge base out in the desert, two bases actually—Camp Desert Rock and Camp Mercury. There were barracks for the enlisted men who were stationed out there for weeks to months at a time and hundreds of tents for the more transient visitors like my unit. There was an officer's club, a noncommissioned officer's club and a beer hall. Thousands of people were stationed on the base that summer and there were some wild parties out there. With thousands of soldiers living on the camp at any given time, the military had to erect a small town. Secretaries and clerks and waitresses all needed to be hired. The assignment was considered a hazardous one, and the pay was commensurate. I met the man responsible for hiring the young women who filled these positions. I said to him, "It seems to me that all these girls are party girls."

"Well that's not happenchance," he said, smiling. "I check that out before giving them the jobs."

The Priscilla shot went off in the morning, just as the sun peeked over the mountains. As a member of the Nuclear Research Team, I was called upon to go to ground zero on a number of atomic explosions, including this shot. During the moments just before the explosion was to take place we stood waiting at the required distance from the tower where the device was to be detonated. In those brief moments, I always wondered ruefully if some physicist had misplaced a decimal point, and if we were all about to be vaporized!

You looked away from the intense light, and felt the powerful earth tremor beneath your feet, which usually knocked you back to the ground. We would then see the characteristic mushroom cloud rise up in the desert sky. The beauty of the explosion was so great that it was hard to believe that this was the deadliest weapon man had ever devised. Hard to believe until we inspected the aftermath.

At the predetermined moment, our team got into our jeeps and speed across the desert as rapidly as possible. In radiation safe clothing and gear, I had a driver, someone to utilize a Geiger counter, and one or two photographers to photograph details of the explosion and its effects that I thought were pertinent.

The morning of the Priscilla shot, some of the pigs were dressed in various different uniforms, to see which ones might best guard against radiation. Six hundred other pigs were dispersed around the site, from about a half mile from ground zero to nearly two miles out. These pigs were the ones we used to try and predict debris trajectories. Once the shot had been dropped and the mushroom cloud had puffed high into the sky and the fallout had settled, the safety inspectors allowed us to check on our pigs. The scene in the pen was not pretty—few of the pigs had survived, and those of them who had were in a sad state.

We recorded as many observations as possible until informed that we had reached the limit of tolerance of the radiation present. Then we hopped back into our jeep and sped out of harm's way as rapidly as possible. We were then checked at decontamination centers, removed our radiation safe clothing, and took a series of showers until cleared by radiation control personnel.

The destructive power of these devices was quite awesome, and I had the opportunity to evaluate explosions in excess of the bombs used in

Hiroshima and Nagasaki. We were taking the best precautions we knew at the time, and I do not remember being apprehensive about the role I played. Years later, I began to worry, particularly about birth defects in my children, or my own likelihood of certain malignancies. For each shot, about five thousand enlisted men would be positioned quite some distance from the explosion in order that they might experience the earth tremor, the blinding light, and the appearance of the mushroom cloud, making them less likely to panic in a mass casualty situation. Over the years, various individuals, farmers, some of these enlisted men, and others would challenge the government about these experiments through litigation. Since the actual exposure of these individuals had been quite minimal, I felt that I should make my position known to the Army. With a call, I did so. I reported to them the amount of radiation I had on my badges, and stated that I would never consider a suit against the government because of these experiences, but that I also did not wish to learn that people so minimally involved had been granted financial settlements.

All in all, I think we took the best precautions we knew to take at the time. The work was extremely important to our armed forces and our government, and I was happy and honored to participate in some small way in these attempts to learn more about atomic explosions.

On July 4th, I borrowed one of the pigs, incurring the wrath of an overzealous officer. I thought that it would be nice to give one of our pigs to some of the enlisted men, so that they might barbeque him for their Fourth of July celebration. Well, when this officer caught wind of what I had done, he came after me.

"You've appropriated government property," he shouted, humorously misplaced righteousness filling his lungs.

I just shook my head and said, "Make a case out of it."

Sense seems to have gotten the better of him, because I never was reprimanded for my illicit 'appropriation.'

•◆•

I came back to Washington, D.C. at the end of the summer, and I continued my work at Walter Reed. My military obligation was coming to an end and it was finally time for me to choose whether to continue on at Brigham or to return to Johns Hopkins. Dr. Moore had written me a letter, offering me the Chief Residency position at the Brigham Hospital and The Arthur Tracy Cabot Teaching Fellowship at Harvard. The offer was quite alluring, to say the least, but at the end of the day I knew that Halsted was where I wanted to be. There was less operating at Brigham than at Hopkins. There was also the question of how long it would take me to complete my residency. Before arriving at Walter Reed I had spent a year at the Brigham, and the Chief Resident at the time was already ten years out of medical school. Hopkins was not any less rigorous than Harvard; Dr. Blalock just knew when it was time to kick people out into the professional world—either at Hopkins or at another hospital that he found acceptable. So, for a second time, I bucked the conventional wisdom and chose uncertainty over certainty. When I say I bucked the conventional wisdom I mean that only a fool would turn down the Chief Residency at the Brigham Hospital, and in fact, no one ever had turned down such an offer.

The uncertainty at Hopkins was the following. The Halsted Program was structured like a pyramid and there were two seats at the top. The number of residents accepted in a given year might vary, but eventually there could only be two at the top of the pyramid—essentially the position I had been *offered* at Harvard. By this time Dr. Blalock had trained a number of doctors who were in charge of the cardiac surgery departments at their own hospitals, places like UCLA, St. Louis and Vanderbilt. He called this network his farm club. If he had too many people in a particular year ready to rise to the top he would call up one of these alumni and arrange a chief residency position for them there. The third or fourth choice at Hopkins was usually on par or superior to their own first choice candidates.

In my year, those two positions seemed to already have two names attached to them. Robinson Baker and George Finney were in my intern class and they both had solid familial connections to the Halsted Program and the Board of Hopkins itself. That is not to say that they were not more than qualified in their own right. The upshot of this was that an already difficult situation was now near impossible. People would shake their heads and tell me, "If you'd only been a different year..."

I always told them that I thought Dr. Blalock would work things out, which is exactly what he did, accepting three of us from my year, taking one resident the next. Because George had already made his military commitment by serving in the Navy, he was eligible to enter the residency before Dr. Baker and me, and in 1961-62 Dr. Baker and I were the Halsted Co-Residents. I could not have had a finer colleague with which to share this experience.

With the letter in hand, I drove over to Baltimore to see Dr. Blalock. A friend told me that I was foolish to bring the letter with me, that he would just congratulate me, thinking that I was trying to force something upon him.

I said, "Hell, he's a human being, you just got to talk to him. If he wants me to be his resident then I'm going to be his resident. If he doesn't, I think he's a gentleman enough to say, 'Look, Charles, I think this is a good opportunity, I see a lot of competition here and I'm not sure how this would come out.'"

Well I went down and visited him in his office. He read the letter. He asked me what I wanted him to do.

"I want you to tell me what to do."

"I want you to tell Francis that you're coming back to Hopkins and get that over and done with."

So that's what I did.

Section Four: Halsted Finally!

A Personal Word
I thoroughly enjoyed my time serving as chief resident. I was excited to have finally reached the position I had worked towards for so long, and yet, I was even more excited by the prospect of real employment.

The Pyramid

Surgical House Staff, Johns Hopkins Hospital 1961-62

I RETURNED TO BALTIMORE IN 1958, ready to enter the Halsted Residency Program. The Halsted program was the first of its kind in the United States. Dr. William Halsted came to Hopkins in 1889, the year the hospital opened to the public. He began training residents soon after, developing the surgery program in the European tradition. Dr. Dean Lewis continued this program, when Dr. Halsted passed away in 1922, and he was succeeded by Dr. Blalock in 1941. The program's concept was a pyramid of graduated responsibility. A trainee started at the bottom, with not a lot of responsibility, one among many interns. Then the trainee progressed up, graduated to an assistant resident and gained more responsibility, and so on and so on until those eighteen or so interns eventually whittled down to two survivors—the two chief residents. In this way, as you progressed up the pyramid your responsibilities and your surgical opportunities grew, as there were fewer and fewer people with whom to compete. There were also fewer and fewer people to rely upon for aid, which helped harden your nerves. A year later you left Hopkins or joined the Hopkins faculty.

In the past, every now and then there had been someone who did not want to leave. This fellow might be having such a great time that he desired to stay right where he was. It was grueling work to be sure, with horrific hours, but if you had come to Hopkins to participate in the Halsted program, then you most likely had a passion for surgery, and so it did occur that people enjoyed themselves so much in this environment that they did not want to leave. Dr. Halsted allowed people to stick around for years, but by the time I arrived at Hopkins, Dr. Blalock had instituted a strict one year limit for his chief residents.

Dr. Blalock was in charge of the Halsted program and we were all in awe of him. At the time, he was one of the most famous surgeons in the country, foremost for developing shunts in order to relieve cyanosis from Tetralogy of Fallot. In more lay terms, he had developed methods to attack and alleviate blue baby syndrome. The importance of this achievement cannot be overstated, and I'll emphasize it more later.

Everyone on the service had a great respect for Dr. Blalock, and we were all more than willing to live and die by his whim. The Halsted Residency was thus a dictatorship of the nth magnitude. As I said, the place operated like a pyramid, and whether you went up or down or sideways was purely a matter of what Dr. Blalock thought of your surgical skills.

Dr. Blalock was a Georgian from the little towns of Culloden and Jonesboro, which also appealed to me. In Boston, I was, as a deep southerner, rather in the minority. Hopkins on the other hand attracted a larger number of southern students. Hopkins is in Baltimore, Maryland, and you might remember from American history classes that Maryland was a 'border state' during the Civil War. The state never seceded, but the population and government were divided, and its citizens fought for both the Confederates and the Union. The level of excellence that Dr. Blalock demanded also helped to draw me back to Baltimore. He had assembled the best and brightest surgeons of the day at Hopkins, and these were the people from whom I wanted to learn. Many members of the first generation of American heart surgeons came out of the Halsted program. In fact, at one point in the late 1950s, half of the heart surgeries done in the United States were performed by members of this small group. Often, a doctor would finish his residency at Hopkins, and the next day go some place and be the professor and chairman of his department, which was of course unheard of. I would not be so lucky.

The blue baby operation was Dr Blalock's calling card. A "blue baby" is cyanotic. With crying or struggling, the cyanosis deepens from a lack of oxygen. Some children even pass out during these cyanotic episodes. Dr. Helen Taussig, a pediatric cardiologist at Hopkins, had seen a large number of children suffering from this condition. There was no treatment available, and there were literally hundreds of blue babies. Sadly these parents were told that nothing could be done and that their children would not likely survive.

Dr. Taussig approached Dr. Blalock with an idea for a new surgical procedure—the creation of a permanent ductus arteriosis. It was understood that normal babies circulated blood through the ductus (an artery between the pulmonary artery and the aorta) before birth. When they began breathing with their lungs at birth, the ductus gradually closed. She observed that the blue babies tended to do reasonably well until the ductus closed, as it normally does soon after birth. At that time, they would slip into a much more serious condition and often die. She asked Dr. Blalock if it would be possible to create an artificial ductus, building a new, permanent connection between the pulmonary artery and the aorta. The blood pressure in the aorta is approximately five times the pressure in the pulmonary artery and thus it would not take a very big connection to handle a great deal of blood, as you are moving from a high pressure system to a low pressure system. Dr. Blalock thought things over with Vivien Thomas, his laboratory assistant. Vivien Thomas was a black man, not a physician, but very skilled in surgery. They decided that they could take the subclavian artery, which normally goes down to the arm, and divide it, swing it down and implant it into the pulmonary artery. Serendipity was on their side, for it just happened to work out that the subclavian is about the perfect size. If they had used a bigger shunt it would have led to heart failure. If they had used a smaller shunt it would not have remained open.

Vivien Thomas

At first Dr. Blalock could not get an anesthesiologist to put the first little child to sleep, in order to carry out the surgery. They told him that he was crazy, that it was too dangerous to anesthetize an already weak infant. He eventually found a nurse anesthetist who would put the child to sleep, and from then on he was partial to nurse anesthetists, for the surgery was a great success. They performed their first successful subclavian pulmonary anastomosis (joining of the subclavian and pulmonary arteries) in 1944 and the news electrified the surgical world. It was the first time that anyone had been treated for an intracardiac birth defect. The procedure came to be called the Blalock-Taussig Shunt and Dr. Blalock himself performed hundreds of these operations, saving the lives of many children who would have otherwise died.

I came to Hopkins for my internship in the summer of 1954. The heart-lung Machine had been invented a year earlier, but it was not until a few years later that it came into widespread usage. This was an important development, which changed the nature of cardiac surgery. Cardiac surgery, as a field, had only very recently come in to its own. The story of surgery performed by one trained human being on another is a long one, stretching back to the beginning of recorded history. A famous physician named Sushruta who lived in India around the year 600 B.C. is credited with authoring what is perhaps the oldest surgery text in existence, the *Susrutha Samhitha*. The field continued to develop, but over 2,500 years would have to pass before a truly revolutionary breakthrough occurred. In the 1840s, the discovery of anesthetics such as ether and chloroform allowed surgeons to undertake hitherto impossible procedures. Progress continued at a steady clip, as technological advances were made. The whole time, from ancient India, to late 19th century America and Europe, there was perhaps one constant, and that was to stay away from the heart at all costs. The first procedure that would be considered cardiac surgery was performed at the very end of the century in Europe. The heart-lung machine, which debuted in the early 1950s, was just as revolutionary to surgery as anesthesia had been 100 years earlier. The oldest axiom of surgery was about to be tossed aside. I was fortunate to begin my training at such a pivotal moment in history. If I had been born just a few years earlier I might never have had the opportunity to make a career out of operating on the heart and the aorta, avoiding the pair like every other physician had for the last 2,500 years.

I had planned to be a unique surgeon, with two sets of skills. I would learn the blue baby operations with Dr. Blalock at Hopkins, and learn how to do closed mitrals on Dr. Harkins' service in Boston. Closed mitrals involved sticking your finger into the heart, to feel for the adhesions which were blocking the mitral valve. The heart-lung machine made this unnecessary, allowing you to perform an open mitral valve reconstruction. I had learned the skill in Boston in 1955-56, as the heart-lung machine was still a very new device; so I had this expertise, and I made use of it sporadically throughout my career.

Dr. John Gibbons, while a resident at the Massachusetts General Hospital, had assisted in the care of a young woman who died from a massive pulmonary embolus. At autopsy, he realized how easy it would have been to remove the embolus if only the circulation could be maintained artificially for a few minutes. Over the next several years he concentrated his research efforts on the development of a heart-lung machine, and ultimately successfully demonstrated its clinical use in cardiac surgery. For this remarkable contribution, Dr. John Gibbons should be remembered as the father of the heart-lung machine, and of the technique of cardiopulmonary bypass. Interestingly enough, I had the opportunity of removing a massive pulmonary embolus on cardiopulmonary bypass while a resident in cardiac surgery at the Johns Hopkins Hospital. At that time, it was the third case in the world in which this technique had been successfully employed.

Heart-lung machines opened up a whole new avenue of heart surgery. The machine circulates the blood for the heart, allowing the heart to cease beating, which makes a number of surgeries possible. With these rapidly unfolding developments, I decided when I returned to Baltimore that I would like to be a heart surgeon. I intended to go back to Georgia, so that I could be close to my parents, as an only child, and by entering the nascent field of cardiac surgery, I would be able to advance without stepping on established doctor's toes (at least that was my thought). I did not have to commit to this decision right away at Hopkins, for in your first year you performed all types of surgery.

•◆•

The first year was progressing nicely, though right around Labor Day I received a call from my old friends at the Department of Defense. First, a little history: From the mid-1950s, the Soviets had been calling for a ban on nuclear tests. President Eisenhower was open to this position but his cabinet was divided, and the Atomic Energy Commission recommended that the United States continue with its testing. In March of 1958, the Soviets announced that they would unilaterally cease all nuclear tests. World opinion quickly turned against the United States Government. A conference of the nuclear powers—the United States, the British, and the Soviets—was convened over the summer and an agreement was reached. In late August, President Eisenhower announced that the United States would halt all nuclear testing for a year, so long as the two other powers would agree to do the same. A meeting to hammer out the details of a permanent moratorium on nuclear tests would be held on October 31st.

In the interim, the Department of Defense scrambled to conduct as many tests as possible, detonating eight separate bombs on the 29th and the 30th of October alone.

There were still many experiments in the pipeline when Eisenhower made his announcement in August, and he was anxious to see them completed. The Army called and said that they were going to try to get the work done. They figured that in order to pull off the operation, which would amount to thirty-seven shots (the most of any test series to that date), that they would need experienced personnel who had already participated in nuclear experiments. They told me that I would have to come back out to the desert, as I was clearly qualified for the job.

I was distraught and said, "I just got back to the residency here and if I have to go out for three months it'll cost me this year and I'll have trouble getting back into a residency next year."

They seemed sympathetic to that and finally they said, "We'll continue talking to people who might qualify for the job, and if we can fill the team without you, we'll certainly realize the hardship that it would cause."

And so they called back a few days later and told me that they had found people who would not be quite so inconvenienced. You see, if I had already finished the program I would have gone, but at this point, after having completed two years worth of duty, it was time for me to focus on my career. And I do believe that they got on just fine without me.

•◆•

When I was stationed at Walter Reed, the hospital had a VIP floor, which was maintained for senior officers who had fought in World War II. Shortly after my return to Johns Hopkins I received a wedding invitation which started off: *General and Mrs. Curtis Emerson LeMay invite you....*

I was surprised, because we had not had General LeMay as a patient, and I had never had the occasion to meet him personally; I wondered why in the world had I gotten this invitation. I read on: to *Dr. James Lawton Lodge.* Good grief, I said to myself, LeMay's daughter is marrying Jim Lodge from Whigham, Georgia, right down the road from Attapulgus!

I determined immediately that I would drive over from Baltimore to attend the wedding. It was a glorious affair. General LeMay had just been made Chief of Staff of the Air Force, and the wedding reception was held at one of the larger officer's clubs in the Washington area. General LeMay stood on the terrace of the club to acknowledge the flyovers arranged in his honor. Every squadron in the United States Air Force flew over our heads that afternoon. I believe that almost every country that had diplomatic relations with the United States sent their military attaches in full military dress to attend the wedding and reception. Certainly I had never witnessed such a spectacular crowd.

When I arrived at the critical point of the receiving line, Mr. and Mrs. Lodge of Whigham, Jim's parents, were so glad to see me that they gushed their greeting and hugged me enthusiastically. I believe I was one of the few people they had known who had passed by in the previous two hours. In time, Dr. James Lodge would transfer from the United States Army to the United States Air Force. He was an excellent pediatrician, and a very good friend. General LeMay would briefly enter politics as the Vice Presidential candidate on Governor George Wallace of Alabama's ticket.

•◆•

Dr. Blalock had told me that he would like for me to come back to Hopkins. That conversation occurred while I was still at Walter Reed. Well, I went back and we didn't talk about my future again for some time. I certainly had enough work on my hands to keep my mind off such matters. I could have been happy never having seen Hopkins, but once I had I knew that I wanted to complete the residency program on top. Of course, this was not a unique mindset amongst my peers. So, while I worked to exhaustion, there were always reminders that there were people who were willing to work just as hard, if not harder.

I do think that some people took things a bit too far. In Boston, most of my peers had considered it 'poor form' to take your allotted vacation. They reasoned that you should always have some project that you were dying to do in the laboratory. So when Christmas came, instead of visiting family, you would be dying to hole yourself up in the lab. I never understood this. Maybe I lacked the motivation that drove my contemporaries. I don't think this is the case, but I'm not sure what other explanation there is to offer.

While we usually forsook our allotted vacations at the Brigham Hospital, at Hopkins we were not provided with vacations in the first place. I think I had one two-week vacation in my five years at Hopkins.

Sometimes you were forced to compete with your fellow residents. Cardiac surgery was usually your last rotation before sliding up to the chief resident spot. I had just finished a six-month thoracic surgery rotation, working at the Baltimore VA. I was back on the Hopkins ward, ready for the first day of my cardiac surgery rotation. Of course, I did not expect to do much that day. Fate, or more accurately, Dr. Blalock, had different plans. Dr. Blalock invited me to join him in the operating room; he had a blue baby operation scheduled. Dr. Blalock stood on one side of the table, and I stood on the assistant's side. For some reason, he decided that I was up to the task.

"Charles, would you come around here, and let me trade places with you," he said. "I'll help you with your first blue baby."

Well, Dr. Henry Bahnson, the number two guy in the department, was not at all pleased with this. After I finished up the surgery, he took Dr. Blalock aside and told him that he thought that he had acted unfairly, that it was wrong to allow me to operate on my first day as a cardiac resident, and that in doing so he had set a bad precedent. Dr. Blalock listened to him, but his rule was unquestioned, so that was the end of that as far as he was concerned.

Dr. Bahnson spoke to me later on, "I want you to know that I didn't think it was right for Dr. Blalock to let you do that case, seeing as you just came on the service."

"Now Henry," I said, "put yourself in my position. Do you think I was going to tell Dr. Blalock, 'No Dr. Blalock, I can't do this operation. You really shouldn't be letting me advance this much.' *You know* that's not an option Henry. If he says 'Do it,' you do it."

And you better do it as well as you possibly can.

No Crutches

AFTER FINISHING OUT MY SURGICAL assistant residency rotations, it would at long last be my turn to ascend to the ultimate position of chief resident. As chief, my surgical rotations were a lot of hard work but they were also a lot of fun.

The Chief Resident had his own operating room five days a week. After he finished operating he'd make his rounds, and then there would be formal teaching rounds at eight o'clock. After that he'd go back to the ward to see his new patients and check on his old ones. He'd finish around midnight, grab a bite to eat, go to bed, and then start all over again at six in the morning.

I challenged Dr. Blalock to let me, the new Chief Resident, have two operating rooms three days a week, so that I could stagger the cases. I thought I could do almost as much operating that way, while leaving Tuesdays and Thursdays open for teaching rounds and clinics. It was much, much more efficient. He offered to let me try it. We didn't lose anybody, except for patients with advanced cancer. The patients who were supposed to get well, got well. After a few months he suggested that I finish out the year with the new system. The wives and the house staff all loved the new system, as it allowed everyone to get out of the hospital more often. Hopkins kept this system, and in fact it is now common around the country.

It was finally time to have another talk with Dr. Blalock about my future and I was quite nervous. Dr. Blalock had not done anything to assist the chief resident ahead of me in finding a job. He had not offered him a position at Hopkins and he had not told him about any promising opportunities anywhere else. I thought, *Well, Dr. Blalock has gotten old and that's the way things are.*

Apparently that was not the way things were.

The day after I became Chief Resident, early July, 1961, Dr. Blalock paged me up to his office. He was cordial and relaxed, and quickly put me at ease.

He said, "Charles, it's time for us to plan for your future. I would like very much to have you remain on the faculty of the Department of Surgery and work with Henry Bahnson and Frank Spencer. The three of you can develop the Adult Cardiac Surgery Program and I'll get David Sabiston to do the children."

Of note, I had the opportunity to assist Dr. Henry Bahnson on some very interesting cases. A few years earlier Dr. Bahnson had performed the first successful resections of saccular aneurysms in the aorta. He and Dr. Spencer went on to develop a number of workable repair techniques.

I was quite surprised, to say the least. I was flattered by his invitation to remain at Hopkins as member of the faculty, but I had no intention of staying in Baltimore, so I demurred as tactfully as I could.

"I've never really thought about staying in Baltimore, because I'm an only child and one day I will be responsible for both of my parents."

Dr. Blalock understood my position, and said, "Well, if you're going to be in Georgia, I would like for you to be at Emory. Why don't you fly down to Atlanta as soon as you can arrange a day or two off, and see what you think."

I made arrangements to fly down to Atlanta in a couple of week's time. My career was the first thing on my mind those days, as I was no longer merely a young husband; I was a young father.

•◆•

The year before, Celeste and I had decided to have a child. Celeste had already stopped teaching by then. I was the chief resident in cardiac surgery, about to be promoted to the top of the pyramid, and I figured that with my career looming, it was time to have a child.

As soon as Celeste's pregnancy was confirmed, I referred her to the favorite and most active private obstetrician at Hopkins—not one of the regular full-time members of the Department of Gynecology and Obstetrics. I did not think the pregnancy would demand maximum professional experience, and I felt Celeste would appreciate the treatment and amenities of an obstetrician who worked with private patients all the time. This proved to be a happy relationship.

The delivery took place in 1960, during a meeting of the American

Surgical Association at the Homestead in Hot Springs, Virginia. Fortunately, the surgical schedule was extremely light that day, and I was able to spend time with Celeste, though in those days it was rare for a husband to join his wife in the delivery room.

Working with me on the cardiac surgical service was Dr. Richard Van Praag, a Fellow in Pediatric Cardiology and an expert in the embryology and the anatomy of the heart. He graciously and enthusiastically offered to examine the newborn to determine if there was any evidence of congenital heart disease. Though congenital heart disease only occurs at a rate of about one per thousand infants, if every child you've seen for months suffers from the affliction, you tend to feel that it is much more common. At any rate, he took the baby out of the isolette and did such an exacting physical examination that the nurse called me to protest his behavior. Fortunately, at that moment Dr. Van Praag pronounced the baby totally normal!

The baby was lovely little girl, and her mother and I quickly agreed to name her Marian, after her maternal grandfather, who was the oldest of her four grandparents. Her name was to be spelled Marian, as she was a girl; her grandfather's name had been spelled Marion. The family name was included as a middle name. We were pleased that her grandfather was aware Marian had been named for him, but perhaps were unduly concerned—Mr. Marion Barnett ultimately lived to be 100 years old!

Celeste was an attentive mother, perhaps a little obsessive, but this was her first child, so such behavior was hardly unexpected. Over the next year Celeste and Marian spent a great deal of time in Washington, Georgia, as I finished up my Residency at Hopkins.

Celeste never adjusted to the residency. There were a number of married residents at the time and they all struggled to make their marriages work. Most of their wives were able to adjust, and though Celeste could not, we would soon be leaving the stress of Baltimore behind.

Looking back I can now see the small hints of instability that she exhibited those years—her inability to order meals at restaurants, her pricing out antique furniture when I was earning $25 dollars a month— little, meaningless things that in the moment seemed like the manifestations of struggling to live with a largely absent husband in an extremely stressful environment. Celeste first became difficult a couple of years after we moved to Atlanta, but it was not until 1968 that she was first hospitalized. She struggled for many years, before taking a manic turn in 1976. The cliché goes that hindsight is 20/20, but in truth, when I look back to Baltimore, the picture is still a bit unclear.

Celeste was always somewhat appalled by surgeries I performed. When

I would attempt to tell her about some new operation or describe what I had done for a particular patient, she would not want to talk about it. Just thinking about these cases was too much for her. During my residency at Johns Hopkins, I limited her opportunities to interact with Dr. Blalock and others out of the fear that she might express her negative feelings about the training program. I felt that she should be given every opportunity to pursue her own interests while I pursued my training. I was quite happy when we were together, but I had to organize my life so that I could function effectively when she was not present. During my internship and residency I had a series of maids who cooked for me, kept the apartment clean and neat, and laundered my white uniforms. Having such revulsion at the thought of my surgery made it difficult for Celeste to share in my promotions or successes. When finally we moved to Atlanta, she was quite pleased to leave Baltimore behind.

In retrospect I have two thoughts on those years in Baltimore, and the rest of the history that followed in Atlanta. One is that I had been so dedicated to my work in Baltimore that I was not able to be the man she needed me to be. Perhaps if I had made more of an effort to spend less time at the Hospital and given her more support, then she would not have gone on to have a nervous breakdown in Atlanta.

On the other hand, she was eventually diagnosed with schizo-affective disorder. Throughout the late 1960s and early 1970s we consulted with the chiefs of four major psychiatry services. Each of these men performed extensive evaluations, and they all came to basically the same diagnosis. It seems to me, as a man and as a doctor, that her fate was largely predetermined. There was little I could have done to alter her situation.

•◆•

The University of Georgia and the Medical College of Georgia, it probably goes without saying, were both segregated institutions when I attended. The Peter Bent Brigham Hospital was the first integrated environment where I had ever worked. Hopkins was not, and the training program in surgery was divided into a white service and a colored service. The two chief residents spent their final year in charge of each service for six months. The chief resident assigned to the white service also served as the administrative resident, because the volume of clinical work was less on this service. The administrative duties included making out the rotation schedules, reviewing house staff materials, and evaluating the junior residents. On each service the chief resident was the surgeon in charge backed by a senior faculty member serving as his consultant. Dr. Henry Bahnson and Dr. Frank Spencer served as my consultants for adult patients and Dr. David Sabiston served as my consultant for pediatric patients. All patients were presented to the consultant every week during formal rounds, and all consultants were available at any time for urgent or emergency cases if needed. The racial implications were a product of the times. The segregated wards were abolished shortly after I finished training, and the number of chief residents increased over the next several years.

One day, while I was working on the white ward, a girl came in who had suffered a massive pulmonary embolism, a blood clot in the pulmonary artery. I think at the time there had been two successful pulmonary embolectomies performed on cardiopulmonary bypass in the world. I was making my rounds with Dr. Bahnson and he offered to scrub in and help me with the case.

"Well Henry," I said, "I don't mind, but you know how Dr. Blalock feels about this."

Dr. Blalock believed that as chief resident it was your duty to perform the cases assigned to you, and yours alone. Dr. Bahnson told me not to worry about that, as the case was so unusual. Having voiced my objection, I told him that it would be quite okay if he joined me across the table. Dr. Blalock strolled into the Operating Room a little while later, to see how things were going.

As soon as he caught sight of Henry across the table he turned red and said, "Dr. Hatcher, I would like to talk to you in my office as soon as you finish this case."

"Yes sir," I said.

So I went down to his office and he asked me if I had requested Dr. Bahnson's help.

"No sir," I said. "Henry volunteered his help and I was glad to have him. I didn't ask him though, and in fact I warned him a little bit against it."

"I don't want to tell you this again. I don't ever want to walk in that operating room and find anyone senior to you scrubbed again. If I lose confidence in your ability to do the operation, I'll scrub, but I'm the only person in the hospital who has that privilege. You can make an argument that Henry could probably have done that operation better today than you did, but you can do it better tomorrow because you did it today, and who's to say in ten years whether you or Henry are going to be better. You're not allowed to have a crutch at your level."

Despite some tense moments, I thoroughly enjoyed my time serving as chief resident. I was excited to have finally reached the position I had worked towards for so long, and yet, I was even more excited by the prospect of real employment. There are a couple of more stories that I want to share with you before I leave Hopkins behind and head back down to Georgia. I think each of these stories reveals a lot about my mindset back in those days.

Doctor?

ONE MORNING, A FEW MONTHS into my tenure as cardiac resident, I woke up feeling a little tight in my lower abdomen. I thought that it might be appendicitis, as I had heard patients describe similar feelings to me. I decided that I would have to wait for the pain to localize in the right lower quadrant. I had a full schedule of surgery so I scrubbed in and went to work. The pain became more severe and more localized, but I made it through the surgery.

At lunch time I went to the chief of anesthesia and said, "Don, I think I have appendicitis. I'm not going to eat or drink anything for lunch today so I'll be ready just in case. I wanted you to be aware, and I'm also going to go to Frank Spencer and ask him to be ready to operate if I need him to."

I returned to the operating room to go to work on my second patient. About half way through the second case, the pain finally grew too great to bear. I began to break into a sweat and my face became pale. The nurse asked me if I felt alright.

"No," I said, "as a matter of fact I've got acute appendicitis."

Dr. Spencer was ready within minutes, and having finished up the surgery, I left an assistant to close the chest for me. I walked next door, where Dr. Spencer and the anesthesiologist were waiting. Before the appendix is removed for appendicitis, it is necessary to perform a rectal exam to confirm the diagnosis. I was not keen to have this done, but I knew that it was required, so I said, "Let's just have one rectal exam. Everyone who needs to know can get the necessary information." Similarly, blood would need to be drawn for a white blood cell count, so I suggested the anesthesiologist insert a needle for his use and obtain the needed blood work at the same time.

Meanwhile a nurse had come by, telling me that a friend or family member needed to be notified before I went in to surgery. Celeste was in Washington, and as I said, her state of mind was less than optimal, so I didn't want to bother her. I told the nurse not to worry about it, that the procedure was a simple one and that I would be fine. She insisted and again, I politely told her not to worry about it, all the while slipping out of my operating room scrubs, getting ready to be operated on. She kept at it, finally telling me that she would make the notification call herself if I would quit being so stubborn and just give her someone to call. Seeing that she wasn't going to quit, I told her to call my maid at our apartment, and to have her bring over a change of clothes and the items I would need for a short hospital stay.

An appendectomy is a rather simple procedure. I also had planned everything out beforehand. Therefore it was rather soon after I had left my patient on the operating table that I found myself awake in the recovery room. As it happened, my second patient was recovering on a bed next to my own. He took a little while longer to wake up from his anesthesia, but when he finally did, he got one hell of a surprise. He opened his eyes, looked to his side, and there he saw his own doctor in a recovery bed. The man must have thought he had awakened in The Twilight Zone. The look of shock and confusion on his face was like nothing I have ever seen since.

A Full Liquid Diet

ANOTHER MORNING, DR. BLALOCK CALLED me on the phone, and he asked me if I could come up to his office. He told me that he had some films that he wanted me to see. I had been working with Dr. Blalock for quite a while by then, but he was a very formal man, and a strong sense of decorum usually governed our conversations. This morning he was much more relaxed than usual.

He asked me, "Charles, what do you think of those x-rays?"

I looked them over and it seemed pretty obvious to me, "Well, that poor devil has a tumor in his rectum."

"*I'm* the poor devil!"

"Oh, well," I said, "perhaps this is the balloon from the catheter."

"No," he said, "you're right. I've got a tumor. I've been passing blood and mucous. I'm going to have to have it removed."

"Well, we'll arrange to have it removed."

"I know it might involve an abdominal perineal-resection. Therefore we'll need to have two surgeons. Now whom do you think we should invite to help you take care of me?"

I had a feeling that he wanted to have Dr. Edward Stafford do the perineal portion, and have me do the abdominal half. So I said, "I think the best surgeon for this kind of thing would be Dr. Stafford."

He agreed and he asked me if I would mind speaking to Dr. Stafford, "I'd like to come in the hospital on Sunday. No one will know I'm coming in, and I'd like to be operated on first thing Monday morning. I don't want you to tell a soul after you leave here, except obviously, Dr. Stafford."

Well, I was feeling pretty good about myself. Hell, I'm the chief resident and Dr. Blalock has just called me and asked me to operate on him, and take care of him, and admit him to the hospital, and do all this behind the

119

scenes. Not many people ever have the opportunity to take care of their professor. I was thinking to myself, Charlie, you are really hot stuff.

But then he said, "Now I know I'm going to have to be on a liquid diet."

And I said, "Yes Dr. Blalock."

"Do you understand that I want to be on a *full* liquid diet?"

"Dr. Blalock," I said, "bourbon will be included in your liquid diet."

"Good boy," he said, "I knew I could trust you!"

Well, we had a laugh, but that brought me back down to earth pretty quickly. Instead of being the world's greatest surgeon, called upon to take care of his professor, Dr. Blalock knew that I was the most reliable person to see to it that bourbon was included in his liquid diet. Anyway, we operated on him, and he did fine, though I would soon find out that he did not have many years left.

The Fortunate Occurrence of an Unfortunate Incident on the Island of Stromboli (or How I Won My First Job at The Emory Clinic)

I FLEW DOWN TO ATLANTA in the middle of July. This was not my first trip through the Atlanta Municipal Airport, as it was known then. I had been to the airport years earlier and it was a small place. There was one little Quonset Hut and the food service at the airport consisted of a Coca-Cola machine and a hotdog vendor. Well, when I returned that July, the airport had just opened up a massive new terminal, the largest terminal in the whole country in fact. Atlanta was growing by leaps and bounds in the 1960s, socially, culturally, and physically.

Atlanta, home to Dr. Martin Luther King, Jr. was the de facto center of the Civil Rights Movement. Dr. King had been arrested a year earlier, during a lunch counter sit-in at a downtown department store. Back then, whites had yet to flee the central city en masse, and thus downtown was still the bustling center of Atlanta. Mayor Ivan Allen, Jr. came out in favor of desegregating Atlanta's public schools in 1961. A tenuous balance played out between whites and blacks, held together by a coalition of business and political leaders. This coalition helped foster the notion of 'the city too busy to hate.' It certainly was a busy city, especially so to a country boy like me. Skyscrapers were sprouting up like weeds and by the end of the decade the

CHARLES HATCHER, JR., M.D.

city would add a new baseball stadium, the Civic Center, and the Woodruff Arts Center to a growing roster of cultural institutions.

The birth of the Woodruff Arts Center, which grew into the city's premier cultural institution, is a sad story. In the spring of 1962, the Atlanta Art Association made a trip to Paris. Among the group's members were some of the city's foremost art patrons. After spending a month in Europe, they boarded their chartered Boeing 707 for the trip back across the Atlantic. The air traffic controllers at Orly assigned them the shortest runway at the airport. The plane was completely sold out and everyone had done a lot of shopping so the plane was heavily loaded, at its passenger capacity, on the shortest runway. They just could not get the plane up in the air in time. One of the motors failed and the pilot attempted to abort the takeoff. There were only 3,000 feet of runway left as the pilot began to apply the brakes and raise the flaps. His tires evaporated and one of the plane's wings dipped and hit the ground. The plane skidded off the end of the runway, over a field. The fuselage careened into a stone cottage, exploding in a ball of flame. All on board died except for three stewardesses who had been sitting near the rear of the plane.

News raced across the wires, stunning Atlanta. The city had not just lost 106 of her citizens; the city had lost many of her prominent art patrons. Newly-elected Mayor Allen rushed to Paris to oversee the salvage operations. A consensus emerged in the stunned and saddened city to erect a fitting memorial to those who perished—an art museum. Mr. Robert Woodruff donated $4 Million dollars, which was used to construct The Atlanta Memorial Arts Center (The gift had been made anonymously, and only later was the center renamed The Woodruff Arts Center).

The Emory campus is a few miles northeast east of Downtown Atlanta, in historic Druid Hills. Much of the original land of the campus had been owned by Asa Candler, who was developing The Coca-Cola Company. The neighborhood was Atlanta's second suburb. Fredrick Law Olmstead of Central Park fame planned portions of the exclusive community and it was in these bucolic surroundings that I arrived on campus, giddy with anticipation. Perhaps it was because I was so excited, but for whatever reason, I did not get myself properly acquainted with the structure of the Emory University School of Medicine and The Emory Clinic. I had arranged my visit with Dr. J. D. Martin, the Chairman of the Department of Surgery.

Dr. Martin was pleasant throughout the interview, but it was obvious that he had no great interest in having me join his faculty. We talked about a variety of subjects, and then he said something that surprised me.

"Dr. Hatcher," he said, "you seem to be a nice young man, so I am going to level with you. We are going to have one position open in the Department of Surgery next July, but I am saving that for my son-in-law, Harland Stone. You know Harland."

I did know Harland, and thought him to be a nice young man. I had met him a few years earlier, up in Baltimore.

"I'm going to see that Harland gets the break he deserves."

I saw little point in continuing the discussion. I thanked Dr. Martin for his time and returned to Baltimore the following day, and well, I wouldn't have given you a plugged nickel of my ever being at Emory after hearing what I had just heard.

Back in Baltimore it occurred to me that I had once taken a course in American History with Dr. S. Walter Martin (no relation to Dr. J.D. Martin), back when I was a junior in Athens. Dr. Walter Martin was now the President of Emory University. He was a devout Methodist, and Emory University, if only so in name, as it sometimes seems, was and still is a Methodist-affiliated institution. I had a feeling that he would remember who I was. I had made an A+ in his class. I had also missed the final exam when I came down with the measles. He gave me the final exam at a later date, just the two of us. I was a good student, and we got on well. We talked for a while that afternoon. Better still, I was sitting in his classroom the day that Ingrid Bergman ran off with Roberto Rossellini on the Island of Stromboli. Dr. Martin, an active Methodist churchman, was filled with such righteous indignation that he could not bring himself to lecture from his notes that afternoon. Instead he delivered a scathing condemnation of Ingrid Bergman's morals, or lack thereof. I knew right away that I would mention that day in my correspondence, as a means of rekindling his memory of me. So I sent off a letter to President Martin. I recalled that day in class, and then I mentioned that I had been somewhat surprised and disappointed that Dr. J.D. Martin did not see an opening for me on his faculty in the near future. I added that I was sorry I had not had a chance to drop by and say hello.

President Martin responded quickly. He apologized for the disinterested reception that I had received. He assured me that Emory University took pleasure in my interest in a faculty appointment, stating that I was exactly the type of doctor that the university was looking for. If I would make another trip to Atlanta, he said that he would see to it that I be would given a warm and cordial reception, and another interview. Finally, he explained to me that after conferring with the Dean of the Medical School, Dr. Arthur Richardson, he had discovered that The Emory Clinic was not structured entirely along departmental lines, rather there were independent sections in the major surgical subspecialties, such as cardiothoracic surgery. Thus, the man I really needed to see was Dr. Osler Abbott, the Professor and Chief of Cardiothoracic Surgery, not Dr. Martin, who was the chairman of the department of surgery in the medical school and chief of the general surgery section at The Emory Clinic.

So I returned to Emory and I had a good interview with Dr. Abbott. He was warm and pleasant and he stated that he was quite pleased by my interest in joining his division. He assured me that he would do the best he could to work out the necessary details. Despite this, I felt the odds were still stacked against me. I flew back to Baltimore over the weekend, and first thing Monday morning Dr. Blalock summoned me up to his office.

"Well Charles, how did you like Emory?"

"Well, I like Emory," I said, "but I don't think they want me down there. I don't think they have a place for me."

"I didn't ask you that Charles; I asked you if you like Emory."

"I like Emory."

"Would you like to go to Emory?"

"Of course I would," I said, "but I don't think that there's a position available. The Chairman of the Department, Dr. Martin, seems to be very reluctant to have me join the Department at the same time as is his son-in-law."

"Just tell me yes or no."

"Of course I would."

He buzzed his secretary, Ms. Frances Grable. "Get J.D. Martin on the phone," he told her.

Dr. Blalock received a call from Dr. Martin a few minutes later. I was somewhat amused by what I heard, and I also learned a great deal about power politics in American medicine. What I heard was this:

"J.D., how are you? This is Al...Yes, fine thank you. Say J.D., Charlie Hatcher was just down at your shop this past week, and he tells me that he would like to join your group."

At this point Dr. Blalock listened for a minute or so, as Dr. Martin protested that he had no money, no lab space, and really no great prospects for me. Dr. Blalock looked straight into my eyes and said into the receiver, "J.D. *those* are details. You work out the details. Charlie will be there on the first of July, OK?...Yes, thank you very much. Nice to talk to you J.D."

Well, there it was; everything was settled. Dr. Martin did not seem to want me at Emory, not because I wasn't deserving of a place, but because he felt that he did not have a place for me, which is a big difference, but he had a great deal of respect for Dr. Blalock. As you may have already gathered, Dr. Blalock was quite the prestigious surgeon. In American medicine, prestige equals power. And power had spoken. Well, it was on these pretenses that

I left for Georgia and Emory the following June, and you might say that I was looked upon as a rattlesnake; a rattlesnake that Dr. Blalock had just thrown in Dr. Martin's nest.

Section Five: Back Home to Georgia and My Early Years at Emory

A Personal Word

From the beginning, I learned never to let my emotions show or be detectable in my voice in the operating room. Everyone on the surgical team keys on the operating surgeon, and until that individual manifests fear and uncertainty, the team can function in a routine fashion. The more desperate the situation, the more the surgeon needs the effective help of his assistants.

Ice Water In My Veins

AFTER DR. BLALOCK'S CALL TO Dr. J.D. Martin, a number of things happened. Dr. Osler Abbott and I worked out the details of my appointment. Dr. Elliott Scarborough assisted by smoothing things out. Dr. Scarborough was a surgical oncologist of great repute, but more relevant to my employment situation, he was the Director and CEO of The Emory Clinic. There were three points that I needed to clear up with him before I departed for Atlanta: 1) Could I have patients sent directly to me, or would they be sent to a chief or one of the senior surgeons, and only then be subsequently passed on to me; 2) Being a young father, I wanted to know how soon I could become a partner in The Emory Clinic and share in the productivity and profitability of the clinic. Non-partners were paid only an annual salary; and 3) I wanted to know if there would be any limitations placed on my personal income, after I had contributed my share of the revenue to the Dean of the School of Medicine.

Dr. Elliott Scarborough

On the first count I was assured that I would have however many patients sent to me as I chose to accommodate. Later on, this question of patient assignments would become a contentious one, but at the time I enthusiastically accepted their assurances. In regards to the second point, I would be eligible for partnership after twelve months, which was more than reasonable. Finally, there would be no limits on my personal income. With those answers I was so excited to get down to Emory that I never thought to ask what my initial salary would be in the year before partnership. Dr. Blalock inquired about this, and I was embarrassed to tell him that I had not brought up the matter of my starting income.

"I'm sure that it will be fair and satisfactory," he said, "but you should *at least* call to confirm that."

I promptly rang up Dr. Scarborough. He informed me that the maximum starting salary at The Emory Clinic had been $12,000 per annum. In my case, however, I would be afforded $13,000 per annum, the highest starting salary to date which, of course, was July, 1962.

All was not rosy though. Dr. J.D. Martin appointed me an Instructor in Surgery, when a position of Assistant Professor would have been far more typical for an American medical school. I think that this was Dr. Martin's way of showing his lack of enthusiasm about my presence at Emory.

I arrived in Atlanta over the first weekend in July; I called the Division of Cardiothoracic Surgery, just to check in. *Just to check in?* How wrong I was. The nurse I spoke with informed me, rather matter-of-factly, that I had been scheduled to perform a total correction of tetralogy of fallot on a teenaged college student at 8:00 a.m. Monday morning, my first day at Emory. It was another first morning and one more first morning surgery appointment.

Dr. Abbott assumed with my Hopkins background on Dr. Blalock's service that I would feel entirely at home with the surgical procedure to correct tetralogy of fallot. I visited the patient at Emory University Hospital on Sunday afternoon, and during my visit I confirmed the diagnosis. I agreed with the decision that total correction was the procedure of choice, and that the timing for corrective surgery was appropriate. This, my first procedure, went extremely well, and it was only after I had completed the surgery that someone mentioned that I had just performed the first total correction of Tetralogy of Fallot in Georgia.

The following day I went over to the Atlanta Veteran's Administration Hospital (which sits at the edge of Emory's campus) to do a pericardiectomy for constrictive pericarditis. The chief of the medical service and the chief of cardiology at the VA Hospital met me in the operating room. They welcomed me warmly to their hospital, but pointed out that they had never done this type of procedure in their facility. In fact, the only reason the procedure was being done that morning was because I was now on the staff. I realized that all responsibility was being shifted to me, and that if there were difficulties, no blame could attach itself to anyone else on the hospital staff. I was to assist the chief resident in general surgery at the VA, Dr. Doyle Haynes, with the procedure. Dr. Haynes would later join the surgical faculty at the Emory University School of Medicine, then work at a clinic in East Alabama, and finally return to lead the department of surgery at Emory-Crawford Long Hospital. His career, as well as mine, could have easily been very different had things played out differently that morning.

In lay terms, this is what was wrong with our patient: his pericardium, which is the sack that contains the heart and a portion of the great vessels, had been inflamed. In time, scarring and calcification replaced this inflammation. The constriction of the pericardium compromises intracardial pressures and reduces cardiac output. In this patient, the calcification was dense, and particularly so along the right heart and over the outflow track of the right ventricle. Doyle was quite skilled, but of course not at all familiar with this procedure. In dissecting the calcium deposits over the outflow track of the right ventricle, he made a tear in the thin myocardium. It developed that we had no vascular suture with swedged-on needles, only French eye needles which had been threaded with fine silk. He made a figure eight suture, but he tied it a bit too tightly. The stitch tore through the myocardium, enlarging the hemorrhage site.

Although he was essentially my age, I turned to him and said, "Son, in a few minutes you are going to be in more difficulty than I am certain I can get you out of. Would you like me to close this myocardial laceration for you?"

He was tremendously relieved. We quickly swapped places at the table. I was able to close the laceration and terminate the hemorrhage, but in the process I produced sufficient irritation to the heart to produce a ventricular fibrillation. I massaged the heart manually, and with a steady voice asked if a defibrillator was present in the operating suite.

"No, but there is a defibrillator in the cath lab."

I quietly said, "Get it."

The defibrillator was brought up. With a single electrical discharge, the patient's heart rhythm returned to normal. I made a final inspection for any bleeding points, and then closed the chest in a routine fashion with two chest tubes in place. The patient was alert and partially awake on the stretcher before we left the operating room. I was so relieved by this successful outcome that I was tempted to suggest that he be wrapped in a cashmere blanket and that I be sent the bill.

I have often turned over the question of how different my career might have been had that patient not survived. From the beginning, I learned never to let my emotions show or be detectable in my voice in the operating room. Everyone on the surgical team keys on the operating surgeon, and until that individual manifests fear and uncertainty, the team can function in a routine fashion. The more desperate the situation, the more the surgeon needs the effective help of his assistants. To be critical of an assistant in these circumstances can compromise their effectiveness just when it is desperately needed. Under extreme circumstances, it may even be desirable for the senior surgeon to assume the role of first assistant to use his superior knowledge to obtain exposure, or for the strategic placement of surgical instruments.

The situation that morning could have descended into chaos, but it did not. I could have lost that patient, but I did not. The nurses and the other doctors in the hospital whispered amongst themselves that I had ice-water in my veins.

A Wonderful Opportunity

EMORY UNIVERSITY IS PERHAPS MOST famous for its relationship with the Coca-Cola Company. For nearly a century, Coca-Cola executives have donated vast sums to the University. The Emory Clinic enjoyed a special relationship with Mr. Robert Woodruff, one that was quite personal.

In the late thirties, Mr. Woodruff's mother developed cancer. Mr. Woodruff was troubled by the lack of quality treatment readily available in the Southeast. Seeking to remedy this situation, he traveled to Memorial Sloan Kettering, in New York. There he met Professor Ewing, Sloane Kettering's Chairman of Surgery. He asked him if he had any young men who would like to come down to Atlanta to work at a cancer clinic, which he would endow. Dr. Ewing introduced him to Drs. Elliot Scarborough and Robert Brown. They had been classmates at Harvard Medical School and they had gone through the residency at Memorial together. They came down in the late 30s and established the Winship Cancer Clinic.

At the end of the year Dr. Scarborough called Mr. Woodruff. He told him how many patients they had treated, what they thought the cure rate was going to be, and so on and so on, and then he announced how much cash they had in the bank. The sum was larger than the amount they had started with. Mr. Woodruff was very intrigued that they could do all that they had done and be solvent. Mr. Woodruff had been providing the Medical School with operating funds for years. He now saw a medical endeavor that could support itself.

By 1953, Mr. Woodruff decided that the thing to do would be to expand the clinic into a multidisciplinary institution. He challenged the university: he would give the money for the building if they would let the clinic be organized as a private partnership. There was a lot of discussion about this proposal. The Medical School did not want it to be structured that way and the Medical Association of Georgia was uneasy about the fiscal angle of this arrangement. The Medical Association actually brought a lawsuit against the clinic, claiming illegal corporate practice of medicine. At the time, this was considered a no-no. In the end, nothing came of the lawsuit.

There were seventeen members when the clinic was founded—all of them full-time faculty members of the clinical Departments of the Medical School. A physician joined and served for a certain period of time as a member of the clinic and then the other doctors would elect you to partnership. You were expected to make your payments, which included fees to the school for the facilities and equipment that you used, and some further contribution to the medical school department to which you belonged. You were also expected to spend the equivalent of one day a week in teaching and research.

When Mr. Woodruff established the clinic he had donated funds to construct a new wing of the A Building, which is now known as the Scarborough Building. I think it cost about $9 million dollars to do this. He insisted upon the clinic's financial independence, allowing its members to pursue profit. In return for this, the university would make no commitment to the members' income. In this way, the medical school could afford to pay the people who needed to be paid, while those who could support themselves through their practice would be asked to do so. Through the one day a week equivalent mechanism the clinic staff would teach or do clinical research.

Over time we realized that part-time researchers were not that effective. In the same way, someone who is in the lab most of the week is not particularly effective when he comes out to the clinic for one day. We drifted more and more to people who were into *either* research or clinical work. Reflecting this reality, we had to establish three tracks in the medical school: 1) the academic track; 2) the clinical track; and 3) the research track. Someone who has a keen research mind ought to spend his or her time in the laboratory, just as an excellent clinician ought to spend his or her time with his or her patients. Those on the academic track were still expected to do a bit of everything. This was not a simple process, and I'll return to the implementation of these three separate tracks later.

Dr. Hugh Woods, dean of the school of medicine, was also the first clinic director. Dr. Scarborough became the second clinic director. He was a fine person, very knowledgeable, and an excellent doctor. In a short period of time, it was apparent that these two positions should be separated. Dr. Scarborough was very close to Mr. Woodruff, and it was he who introduced me to Mr. Woodruff when I first arrived in Atlanta. He was an active manager and he had a relationship with the dean of the medical school that, at times, could only be described as rough. Because of some early conflicts over manpower and who would pay for that manpower, Mr. Woodruff successfully pushed for the director of the clinic to report directly to the Vice President for Health Affairs, bypassing the dean of the medical school entirely.

The thoracic and cardiovascular surgical service at Emory originated with the arrival in Atlanta in the late 1940s of Dr. Osler A. Abbott and Dr. Robert Major. It became apparent that these two men could not work together, and when the opportunity arose, Dr. Major accepted a position at the Medical College of Georgia, while Dr. Abbott remained on at Emory, becoming one of the founders of The Emory Clinic in 1953.

Dr. Osler Abbott was Canadian by birth, the son of a Bishop in the Anglican Church. He graduated from Princeton University, and the Johns Hopkins University School of Medicine. After his General Surgery residency in Cincinnati, he trained in Thoracic Surgery under Dr. Evarts Graham in St. Louis.

Dr. Abbott came from an extremely distinguished medical pedigree. He was the nephew of Sir William Osler, who still stands as one of the greatest figures in all of modern medicine. Among his many accomplishments, Sir William is best remembered for developing bedside teaching. Dr. Abbott's mother, Sir William's sister, served as hostess for Sir William, and indeed Dr. Abbott was very proud of the pieces of furniture and personal items that he had inherited. Among these items was a portrait of Sir William, which he had received upon his uncle's death. I mention all of this because I believe that Dr. Abbott's name and background placed him under some strain—he felt that he was required to become a preeminent surgeon and physician in a class with his uncle, which was no small feat. Perhaps striving toward this end, Dr. Abbott seemed rather absorbed with his reputation and his place in the *big picture* of surgery.

Dr. Osler Abbott

Dr. Abbott became Chief of the Section of Thoracic and Cardiovascular Surgery at The Emory Clinic. He recruited Dr. William Van Fleit, and later Dr. William Sewell to join the new section. In 1961, both of these men resigned from the Emory faculty to relocate their practices.. Dr. Van

Fleit reestablished his practice in South Bend, Indiana, while Dr. Sewell moved to Guthrie, Pennsylvania. With the departure of these two faculty members, Dr. Abbott was threatened with inadequate manpower to meet his clinical responsibilities. Dr. William D. Logan, a former resident of Dr. Abbott's at Emory, had just returned from a year in London with Lord Russell Brock and had established a practice in downtown Atlanta. Dr. Abbott convinced Dr. Logan that he should close his office in town and join him at the University, which he did in September of 1961. Dr. Logan was a very likeable fellow and we had a very nice relationship from my earliest days at Emory.

Over the years, I came to know the departed Dr. Van Fleit quite well, and we became good friends. In his terminal illness, Dr. Van Fleit returned to Emory under the care of Dr. Willis Hurst. He had developed severe heart failure due to cardiomyopathy, but unfortunately was not a candidate for cardiac transplant. As for Dr. Sewell, we crossed paths infrequently, and I never had the opportunity of coming to know him personally.

It is interesting to note that the departure of these two members of the faculty, only months before my arrival, presented me with a great opportunity. Within a week or so of my arrival in July, 1962, both Dr. Abbott and Dr. Logan left on vacations. They were exhausted after months spent compensating for the departures of Drs. Sewell and Van Fleit. I was a little surprised at this, and called Dr. Blalock to discuss my new situation.

"Dr Blalock," I said, "you wouldn't believe it, but these guys have gone on vacation, and I'm all alone here at Emory."

I expected a bit of sympathy perhaps; I got none.

Dr. Blalock chuckled and said, "What a wonderful opportunity!"

That was one way of looking at the situation.

"You know you can do the work, and now you don't have to worry about adjusting to your new partners, so do all you can, as well as you can, while they're away."

That's The Way It Is:
A Lesson In Politics

I WAS OFF TO A good start. Prior to leaving Hopkins, Dr. Blalock had offered me one last piece of advice. He warned me to be selective in the patients I subjected to surgery, it was not necessary for every cardiology patient to die in the operating room. Further it was important that I obtain good results in those early days of my career and of heart surgery in general. Dr. Edgar Fincher, the chief of neurosurgery at Emory offered similar advice. He told me that in his first year at Emory he had rarely operated upon malignant brain tumors, fearing that the field of neurosurgery and his career needed to be better established before he undertook such high-risk and rather hopeless cases.

With some protective selection and extremely good fortune it was possible for us (the Cardiac Surgery Section) to achieve 96 successful outcomes out of our first 100 cases. Similarly, we succeeded in nine out of our first ten cases in our valve replacement series, which was the most demanding cardiac procedure of the era.

When Celeste and I arrived in Atlanta we came with our young daughter Marian. The three of us moved into a rented home on North Decatur Road, a few minutes from Emory's campus. I was a young doctor and I was very excited to be in Atlanta, at Emory.

Immediately after my arrival at Emory I was visited by Dr. Eugene Drinkard, pastor of Glenn Memorial United Methodist Church, who offered his support and counsel with my career as a heart surgeon, a field that he suggested would be filled with temptations of many sorts!

My family and I have been lifelong members of the Methodist Church. I mentioned my father's devotion to the Attapulgus Methodist Church during the depths of the Great Depression. I was baptized as an infant and welcomed officially into the church at age 12. In college and medical school I attended First Methodist Church in Athens, Georgia, and the First Methodist Church in Augusta, Georgia. In Baltimore while on the Hopkins house staff, I transferred my letter from the little church in Attapulgus to the Lovely Lane Methodist Church, one of the wonderful old churches of American Methodism, where Charles Wesley and Thomas Asbury had held the fabled Christmas Conference. Upon my move to Emory University, I joined the Glenn Memorial Methodist Church, the quasi-official Methodist institution of the University, and was a member of that fine institution until my retirement.

The Emory Clinic was nine years old when I arrived, and there were less than fifty doctors working there—and I thought this was a huge place. Within a short period of time we were doing things that had never been done before at Emory.

Soon I confirmed all that I expected from my brief visits to Emory over the past year. I had been presented a wonderful opportunity, and I was delighted with every colleague I met at The Emory Clinic. The Cardiology service was a very strong specialty. Internal Medicine was also well regarded. Dr. Willis Hurst was the Chairman of the Department of Medicine, and himself an outstanding cardiologist. Dr. R. Bruce Logue was the Chief of Cardiology at The Emory Clinic, and the Chief of Medicine at Emory University Hospital.

Drs. Bruce Logue and J. Willis Hurst

On one of my initial interviews at Emory, I was introduced to Dr. J. Willis Hurst. I was very flattered that he should grant me this interview. He had just undergone a hemorrhoidectomy, and he was placed in a hot Sitz bath and draped completely with a large white sheet, only his head exposed. We had a rewarding visit, and I always appreciated his making this personal effort to meet me and encourage me to come to Emory.

Dr. J. Willis Hurst

Drs. Hurst and Logue enjoyed the admiration and respect of all the Fellows and Residents, and the utmost respect from our referring physicians. They were flexible and always willing to consider new forms of therapy or new surgical procedures. I came to rely on Dr. Logue, especially in those first few months. He gave me the opportunity to operate on his private cases from the very beginning. This was one way that he expressed his confidence in me. He backed this up with his recommendations to referring physicians. Dr. Blalock had warned me against taking on too many hopeless cases early in my career, and Dr. Logue assisted me in selecting those patients who would indeed benefit from surgery. As his confidence in our section's abilities grew, we were paradoxically rewarded by being sent sicker and sicker patients for surgery.

Dr. Bruce Logue

One of the first things that I noticed about The Emory Clinic was that all of the partners were outstanding clinicians. I admired them tremendously, and friendships were easily made and maintained. Nevertheless, I felt that the doctors at Emory did not give themselves adequate accolades for their or skill or achievements. Having worked and studied at the Johns Hopkins Hospital, The Peter Bent Brigham Hospital, and the Walter Reed Army Medical Center, I felt that the doctors at Emory easily matched up to the outstanding staffs at these institutions. I felt that this was something to be proud of, and I became somewhat of a cheerleader for The Clinic. I think my comments and demeanor helped contribute to improved institutional attitudes and feelings of self worth among the doctors. People want to work with winners, and whether or not people want to work with you—whether that means winning grants, securing donations, or simply caring for patients in a competitive healthcare marketplace—can make the difference between an average hospital and a good hospital, and a good hospital and a great hospital.

I felt that a vague sense of masochism prevailed among my colleagues. Nowhere was this more apparent than in the weekly mortality and morbidity conferences. These conferences were the only conferences held with any regularity in the department of surgery. While the conferences were extremely worthwhile, the attitude among many participants seemed to be that by exclusively discussing errors, clinical misadventures, and mistakes in public, one could achieve an intellectual catharsis.

I remember Dr. Abbott came to me one time, wondering if I wanted to join him in writing a book on the complications of cardiac surgery. I told him that I certainly did not, that I didn't want to be known as an authority on complications in cardiac surgery.

The rationale for mortality and morbidity conferences is unassailable, but I felt that those meetings should be balanced by some discussion of successes and new and improved forms of surgical therapy. I brought this up with members of the department of surgery, and most of them understood my position. I had been at The Emory Clinic for a year when I brought this up, and in that time I had never had the occasion to discuss a single successful case. Although our mortality rate was quite low, there were of course a number of cases for the mortality and morbidity conferences. Our medical students and house officers received much of their instruction in these conferences, and I think this situation was leading many of them to develop negative and distorted views of cardiovascular surgery. I proposed that the conference be divided between the mortality and morbidity cases and cases indicative of clinical success. The department of surgery supported this new approach. Further, our trainees voiced their pleasure with the dual conferences.

I suppose that I was somewhat naïve in my expectations during those early months. I sincerely thought that I had been recruited to jumpstart the open heart surgery program at Emory, which was in its infancy when I arrived. It was time for a crash course in personal politics.

Dr. Abbott had been trained as a thoracic surgeon, and with the dawning of cardiac surgery he had shifted his interest toward cardiac surgery, as he considered these activities more appropriate to his professional persona. Similarly, Dr. Logan had been trained by Dr. Abbott, with an additional year as a Registrar at Guy's Hospital in London.

The cardiac surgery program was good, but not great. I felt that I could help the program achieve its goal of excellence. I had been trained at an institution where cardiac surgery was emphasized, an institution that attracted some of the best and the brightest young doctors in the country, if not the world. My arrival presented an opportunity for the cardiovascular surgical service to do things that had never been done before at Emory.

In my eagerness to show that new cardiac procedures could be performed at Emory, I accepted as many cases as possible. I worked tirelessly in the operating room and on the floors. With the support of the cardiology staff, my operative schedule quickly became disproportionately large. Perhaps because I was so busy, I failed to notice the concurrently increasing resentment of Drs. Abbott and Logan. I thought that my successes were for our Section and for Emory. In retrospect, I realize that the two of them did not always see my personal success as success for the group.

I was shocked when, a few months after my arrival, Dr. J.D. Martin called me into his office. He informed me that Dr. Abbott felt that my large and still growing cardiac surgical service was inhibiting the development of his and Dr. Logan's careers. In essence, I was being damned for being successful. The irony of this was not lost on me; I truly believed that I had been recruited to do specifically what I had been doing.

Dr. Logue, as Chief of Cardiology, became aware of this situation. Dr. Abbott had proposed that we assign cardiac surgical cases in a rotation among the three of us. Dr. Logue adamantly refused to consider such a system. He felt that cardiology reserved the right to send any patient to the surgeon they felt most qualified to manage each particular case. At the same time, he was aware that I was coming up against entrenched authority in the department of surgery, and that this situation if not ameliorated somewhat, could lead to significant future difficulties for me.

He called me into his office and expressed his confidence in me.

"Charles," Dr. Logue said, "Osler and Bill are beginning to resent you, and we're going to have to be careful to see that patients are sent to all three of you. I assure you that you'll always receive the most patients, but we think for your sake we should perhaps send more patients to Osler and Bill. If there is anytime you become aware of a particular patient in the hospital, and you would like to operate on that patient, just let me know. We'll always send you anyone that you wish to operate on."

I thanked Dr. Logue for his support, but I said, "Well, I can see how this is going to develop. The highest risk patients are going to be sent to me, but in the interests of peace and harmony, you're going to send more patients to Dr. Abbott and Dr. Logan, and these will have to be the lower risk patients—so I assume that I'm not going to be receiving any more straightforward cases in the future?"

Dr. Logue laughed and said, "I'm afraid that's the way it is."

Four Men

As I SETTLED IN AT the Thoracic and Cardiovascular Division, I came to understand that there were four individuals who would directly affect my career. All were capable individuals, but they differed markedly in their personalities and styles of supervision. Heading the division was my immediate supervisor, Dr. Osler Abbott. Dr. Abbott was trained as a thoracic surgeon, and cardiac surgery had developed after he had entered the practice of academic surgery. He considered this new field to be his group's prerogative, and he was eager to establish a reputation in cardiac surgery. His busy practice precluded extensive laboratory work, so he picked up his knowledge of cardiac surgery by visiting major centers where he could directly observe pioneering operations, and by attending surgical meetings where he could watch films and discuss these emerging surgical techniques. He then added some of these procedures to his own surgical armamentarium. It is my belief that the cardiologists at The Emory Clinic knew that he had limited experience or background in these procedures and thus they rarely expressed confidence in him when he attempted an operation he had yet to perform.

I also believe that if Dr. Abbott had limited himself to thoracic surgery he could have achieved preeminence in the field—but there was too much glory in cardiac surgery in those years for him to accept what he considered a lesser role. I came to feel that though I had been recruited to provide additional expertise in cardiac surgery, Dr. Abbott would have preferred for my professional development to have amounted to more of a subplot to his own career.

Dr. Abbott wished to be known nationally and internationally, and on occasion was known to accept notoriety in the absence of fame. At one national meeting of a distinguished medical society, he rose to discuss all but one of the papers on the program—a feat never equaled before or since. Nevertheless, after that day, everyone knew who Osler Abbott was, and thus I suspect he considered that his stunt had been worthwhile. The Southern Thoracic Surgical Association established an award in his honor, The Osler Abbott Award; this award is given annually to the member or guest providing the most verbose discussion of a paper or papers. Dr. Abbott explained this as a joke.

"All in good spirits," he said, chuckling.

The members of the Southern Thoracic did have great affection for Dr. Abbott, and he enjoyed their annual meetings.

My second chief was Dr. J.D. Martin, Joseph B. Whitehead Professor and Chairman of the Department of Surgery at Emory. Although he had been less than enthusiastic about having me join his department, Dr. Martin proved himself to be an extremely fair and honorable individual within the scope of his own personal vision. He told me directly that he didn't believe cardiac surgery to be a viable specialty.

"Charles," he warned me, "Don't you go and do anything wild that will bring discredit to this department."

Dr. J.D. Martin

He eventually came around. In the meantime, aware that working with Dr. Abbott was not always easy, he gave me his advice, support and protection on a number of occasions.

On the academic side of Clifton Road (The Clinic is on one side of Emory's main thoroughfare; the college and most of the professional schools are on the other side), I was responsible to Dr. Arthur P. Richardson, the Dean of the School of Medicine. Dr. Richardson, a pharmacologist by training, had resented the establishment of an independent Emory Clinic and seemed to have little regard for surgery and surgical subspecialties. He lasted as one of the longest serving deans in the nation. This was due in part to his diplomatic skills. He was known to reverse his position on an issue whenever disaster loomed without ever providing an explanation or suffering embarrassment. From a practical standpoint, I felt that he was a successful dean because the financial independence of The Emory Clinic spared him from having to distribute the clinical practice monies among the several clinical departments and divisions. Most deans who become involved in the distribution of clinical practice income tally up a new set of friends and enemies with each annual disbursement. Mathematically the enemies come to outnumber the friends after the third or fourth such disbursement. All too often the lifespan of a typical dean is about three to four years. With no such danger inherent in his position, Arthur remained above the fray, and enjoyed a remarkably long tenure as dean.

Finally, I was responsible to Dr. Elliot Scarborough, the Director and CEO of The Emory Clinic. He and Dr. Robert Brown had established the Winship Cancer Clinic at Emory prior to World War II. He was the personal physician and confidante of Mr. Robert W. Woodruff, who was a unique and major donor to The Emory Clinic and medical activities at Emory in general. In the early days there had been considerable friction between Dr. Scarborough and the Dean of the Medical School, as well as between The Clinic and organized medicine in Atlanta and throughout Georgia. Questions over how far an institution could blur the lines between for-profit medicine and academic medicine were just beginning to be tested. In this environment, Dr. Scarborough became rather secretive, and he urged his physicians to maintain low profiles, which would minimize the hostility of the Fulton County Medical Society. He urged a modest lifestyle, and took the position that an overly generous income was inconsistent with the mission of The Emory Clinic.

During my interview with Dr. Scarborough, I had found him to be charming, gracious, and the embodiment of a southern gentleman. At one point he asked me if there were anyone on the staff of The Emory Clinic whom I knew personally. I replied, "Dr. Billy Hagler in Ophthalmology is a good friend of mine."

He made a face and asked me how I knew Billy.

I told him that we had belonged to the same medical school fraternity.

He stared at me with a disapproving look on his face, and asked, "Would you say that Billy Hagler is the kind of person you have as a personal friend?"

I was unaware of any difficulty that had attached itself to Billy, although Dr. Scarborough seemed to be encouraging me to minimize or negate my friendship with him. I decided what the hell, and said, "Yes, I like Billy Haggler, and I would say that he is a very good friend of mine."

Dr. Scarborough broke into a broad smile and said, "I like Billy Hagler too."

I realized that I had just been tested to see if I would forsake a friendship in certain circumstances. I think I passed the test.

Dr. Scarborough was quite aware that working with Dr. Osler Abbott might be difficult. Others had had problems in similar situations. I knew that Dr. William Hopkins, one of the doctors who founded The Emory Clinic, had resigned a few years earlier. Dr. Hopkins was quite embittered by the way the partnership had allowed Dr. Abbott to treat him. Dr. Hopkins entered private practice at St. Joseph's Hospital in Atlanta, and had a long and distinguished career with that institution.

Every now and then, Dr. Scarborough would drop by unannounced and ask me how I was getting along. My usual answer was that I was getting along well and enjoying myself tremendously. On one occasion, however, I did mention that Dr. Abbott and I did not always see eye to eye. I quickly added that I would continue to do everything I could to prevent friction between us. As a result of that casual comment, Dr. Scarborough apparently called Dr. J.D. Martin, my surgery chairman and told him that I was having problems with Dr. Abbott. The first I knew of this was when I received a page from Dr. Martin.

When I answered, it was obvious that he was quite upset.

"I will thank you, Dr. Hatcher, not to discuss department of surgery business with Elliot Scarborough. If you're having any problems in thoracic and cardiovascular surgery, you come to me. Do you understand?"

I assured him that I hadn't 'gone' to Dr. Scarborough, that any I remarks I may have made were informal, and only the result of a direct query by Dr. Scarborough. Nevertheless, I realized that there was some strain in their relationship, probably because of the overlap in their authority.

I had been at Emory for a little over two years when Dr. Scarborough dropped in one afternoon, and having exchanged pleasantries he said something startling.

"Charles," he said, "you and I are going to get along fine. It takes me a while to determine what someone wants. But once I know, it's easy for me to get along with them." Then he smiled and said, "I know what you want."

"What, Dr. Scarborough?"

"You want to take my place."

I attempted to demur, and suggested that such an ambition would be immodest for me. Dr. Scarborough strolled out of the office, but as he reached the door, he turned round and said, "Charles, I can't promise you that you'll someday take my place, but I can tell you that from where I stand, no living person has a better chance."

I was elated by this comment to say the least, but only a short time later, Dr. Scarborough was admitted to Emory Hospital. A diagnosis of carcinoma of the pancreas was made. He deteriorated rapidly, and died a few weeks later. Had he lived, my circumstances may have been quite different.

Progress: Mechanical Valves and Pacemakers, Oh My!

THE YEAR I ARRIVED IN Atlanta was one of great technological advancement. It was a fortuitous circumstance that I arrived when I did—if you were going to be a young heart surgeon, 1962 was an awfully good year to start. I arrived during a watershed period, affording me access to technologies that were just becoming available, allowing me to do things for people that could not be done before then. If I had arrived just a year earlier, I would not have made nearly as big a splash, and if I had arrived a year or two later, a lot of the things that I did would have already been old hat.

The newest generation of heart-lung machines was a breakthrough technology. These units were far more reliable than previous models, allowing one to be more aggressive in their use. The administration of Emory University Hospital did not want to invest in a heart-lung machine for me. The hospital had a heart-lung machine that was sort of a Rube Goldberg contraption, and though it seemed to work, I did not want to have to rely on it in the operating room. So, right away I requested a new heart-lung machine for our division. The hospital rebuffed my request; the Women's Auxiliary wound up buying the machine for me.

That same year, the first mechanical heart valves became widely available, and my training and background permitted me to take advantage of the improved artificial valves. Up until then we had no reliable valves—only five or six prosthetic valves had been implanted in the country. Remembering Dr. Blalock's advice regarding hopeless cases, I was quite choosy with my early valve replacement patients. It is essential that a surgeon have good results treating his or her first patients for a particular condition; only with those results will physicians refer the surgeon better and better patients.

As a result the mortality rate will continue to decline. The converse is also true; if the surgeon has poor results, the patients that physicians will refer for surgery will be closer and closer to death's door. Once the surgeon is in a situation like that, it can be quite difficult for him or her to pull back. Anyway, we never found ourselves treading down that path, and instead valve replacements became commonplace in our division.

In those days, an aortic valve replacement was the most difficult operation being attempted. The reason for this is that you must interrupt the flow of the blood moving through the coronary arteries while you are operating on the aortic valve. This was not necessarily the case in a mitral valve replacement, which made that procedure a bit easier to perform. Aortic valve replacements carried the highest mortality rate in the group.

One of my first successful aortic valve replacement surgery cases was a young woman who had survived bacterial endocarditis. That the surgery was a difficult and risky one is not the only reason that I remember her; I performed the surgery the day that President Kennedy was assassinated. I removed her valve and replaced it with a Starr-Edwards ball-valve. This artificial valve was a recent invention, having been approved for human trial in July of 1960. She did well following surgery, but then, on about the fourth or fifth day, she spiked a fever. We came in to examine her and we discovered that she had some infected fluid in her wound. This could be catastrophic. Dr. Logue was quite distressed because he had never seen a patient recover from such a situation. It was a little bit tough but I did not think that this was the end of the world. I opened up the wound and irrigated it thoroughly, and packed it with antibiotic-impregnated sponges. I changed those sponges twice a day and within five or six more days she was ready for secondary wound closure, and a few days later she was discharged from the hospital.

At any rate, Dr. Logue and his colleagues were convinced that I could do aortic valve replacements, and the moratorium on these procedures was removed.

As I recall, I was successful in nine of the first ten patients undergoing aortic valve replacement. Further, 96 out of my first 100 surgical patients made it through surgery. Thereafter, the valve replacement program at Emory was off and running. We made much of our reputation doing aortic valves and Dr. Logue let us know how proud he was of our efforts.

During one of those early days, Dr. Scarborough called me up to his office and asked me, "Charles, what in the world is being done in New Zealand for cardiac patients that you can't do here in Atlanta?"

Assuming that he was thinking of tissue valves, I said, "I suppose you're speaking about Professor Brian Barrett-Boyes' use of homograph valves rather than mechanical valves, which may have a beneficial effect in reducing episodes of thrombo-embolism."

Dr. Scarborough explained that Mr. Robert Woodruff had become aware of the wife of a good friend of his, Mrs. Leonard Rensch, who had been referred to the Green-Lane Hospital in Auckland, New Zealand, for just such a procedure. Apparently Mrs. Rensch was seen annually at Johns Hopkins, and on this occasion she had been seen by a physician who was a neurologist. Rather than decline her care and refer her to a cardiologist, he went to the library and read the reports comparing tissue valves and mechanical valves. With just the right amount of medical expertise he was able to say something to the effect of, "I believe the tissue valves may have a small advantage, and since you can go anywhere, why not go see Professor Barrett-Boyes?" What he meant by, "you can go anywhere" was that her husband was a man of quite substantial means. Her husband, Mr. Leonard Rensch, had served as President Truman's Press Secretary, had arranged the famous Kennedy-Nixon Debates, and was at the time of his wife's surgery, Chairman of Cox Broadcasting.

Mr. Woodruff was quite upset that in spite of my arrival at Emory, his good friends were still traveling to the farthest ends of the world for cardiac surgical procedures. So, Dr. Scarborough advised me to travel to New Zealand, or elsewhere, but to quickly master the technique of tissue valve implantation. Well, I was aware that Mr. Donald Ross of London (surgeons in England are called *Mister* rather than *Doctor*), was also performing the procedure, and feeling that the experience I would receive upon a visit to either place would be comparable, I decided that I would rather spend a few days in London.

I visited Mr. Ross in London, and shortly thereafter began to use tissue valves, in addition to mechanical valves, in our replacement series. In the meantime, Mr. and Mrs. Rensch traveled to New Zealand. They became quite close with Professor Barrett-Boys during their trip, and suggested that I might like to invite him to be a Guest Professor at Emory. Professor Barrett-Boys would eventually be knighted for his service as one of the outstanding young cardiac surgeons of the British Empire. Later, Sir Brian visited the Mayo Clinic, and while he was there, Mr. Rensch generously offered to fly him down to Atlanta on the Cox corporate jet. I remember my young son asking how he should address our guest. I suggested that he call him Sir Brian, and he and Sir Brian got along famously.

The pacemaker was another breakthrough device that had recently become widely available. Dr. Abbott did our first pacemaker implantation, but because of my training, the cardiologists were more comfortable sending me their pacemaker cases, and I wound up doing about 90 of our first 100.

The implantation of epicardial cardiac pacemakers quickly developed into a more or less routine procedure. Nevertheless, pacemakers were a very exciting topic and people were constantly inviting me do talks on them, at kickoffs, luncheons, Georgia Heart Association meetings, and so on. I had a little tray that I would bring with me with functional pacemakers and valves and models of arteries, and I would pass them out amongst the crowd, which everyone seemed to enjoy.

I remember one afternoon, in those early days, a phone call with a salesman at Medtronic, the company that invented the world's first wearable artificial pacemaker. We had been on the line for a few minutes, when all of a sudden he said, "You aren't that bad."

Not having any idea what he was talking about, I said, "Excuse me."

"You really aren't that bad."

A little more confusion followed, but then he explained himself. Medtronic had been looking to hire an actor to perform and narrate pacemaker implantation training videos, but he thought that I would be perfect for the role. My voice, apparently, wasn't that bad. I flew up to their headquarters in Minnesota. Medtronic had set up a soundproof room and this is where we recorded the audiotape. The script was printed on felt-backed pages, so the microphones would not pick up any rustling noises. The script girl handed these thick sheets of paper to me one by one. And thus, my brief recording career began.

• ◆ •

The story of a patient I will refer to as M.B. presents a resume of the development of surgery for Tetralogy of Fallot. When M.B. was a young child of some three or four years, she was recommended to Dr. Blalock at Johns Hopkins as the first surgical candidate he had seen from Georgia. The WACS at Fort McPherson, in Georgia, had led a fund drive to sponsor M.B.'s trip to Baltimore. Dr. Blalock performed surgery on the side opposite the arch of the aorta, as was his custom. He found she had a very small pulmonary artery, and he simply could not do an anastamosis to such a structure. He closed her up and informed her mother that M.B. was not a candidate for surgery, and that in all likelihood she wouldn't survive childhood.

M.B. and her mother returned to Georgia. While remaining deeply cyanotic, she survived childhood. She developed into a very intelligent girl who, although physically unable to attend school or function outside of the home, was able to carry out all of her schoolwork and graduate from high school. About the time she graduated, her family and her attending physician became aware that I was now practicing cardiac surgery in Atlanta. The fact that I had trained with Dr. Blalock made me the surgeon of choice to conduct the reevaluation of M.B.'s situation.

We found, by pulmonary anteriogram, that M.B. had a very hypoplastic pulmonary artery on the side on which surgery had been attempted. Her larger, more normal pulmonary artery was on the opposite side. I felt that a shunt could be performed to the larger pulmonary artery; the heart-lung machine made this procedure feasible. The maintenance of her circulation by the heart-lung machine had not been possible in the 1940s, when Dr. Blalock had performed the initial procedure. A subclavian pulmonary artery anastamosis was established, which means we divided the subclavian artery, brought it down with a gentle curve, and implanted it into the side of the pulmonary artery. M.B. pinked up beautifully and experienced a significant increase in her tolerance for exercise. She was able to leave home and seek employment for the first time in her life. As the years passed, we hoped that the increased pulmonary flow from the subclavian pulmonary shunt would result in additional growth in the pulmonary vascular bed. We were delighted when our studies confirmed that the hypoplastic artery had shown a significant increase in size, and that her vascular bed now made a total correction feasible.

M.B. underwent a third operation years after the shunt procedure, and the total correction of her tetralogy was quite satisfactory. Throughout all the years that have passed since, M.B. has never failed to send me an annual Christmas card, which I am so happy to receive, and which I appreciate so very much.

•◆•

At both Emory University Hospital and Egleston Children's Hospital one condition after another, congenital and acquired, came under successful surgical attack. Our surgical volume steadily increased through the 1960s and the early 1970s.

In 1967, the world was stunned and amazed by the news that Dr. Christiaan Barnard had successfully performed a cardiac transplantation at the Groote Schurr Hospital in Capetown, South Africa. Many had assumed that cardiac transplantation was in the offing, but we expected Professor Norm Schumway at Stanford University to achieve this milestone. Dr. Barnard was well aware of Dr. Schumway's work, and by working in South Africa, he freed himself of many regulatory restraints, allowing him take larger steps, faster. Dr. Barnard later stated that he had not bothered to duplicate the work (or perform similar work) that Dr. Schumway had done in the laboratory. He explained this away by informing the world that he had developed rheumatoid arthritis and felt that he had a limited time to perform his surgery. At any rate, his first patient, a man named Louis Washkansky, died eighteen days after the transplantation, as expected.

His second patient, Philip Blaiberg, lived for quite a number of months, and this success forced the cardiac surgical community to take a long hard look at the procedure. The National Research Council called a meeting in Washington, D.C. of 100 professionals: surgeons, cardiologists, ethicists, lawyers; anyone who should have a voice in the national debate about this procedure. It was contemplated that a crash program, akin to the Manhattan Project, might be in order for cardiac transplantation.

I was privileged to be invited to this conference. We were afforded the opportunity to inspect the hearts removed from Dr. Barnard's patients. As the conference convened, word came that Dr. Denton Cooley had performed a cardiac transplantation in Houston, Texas. This patient's original heart was sent to Washington as well. We inspected the original hearts to see what kind of irreparable damage would justify this new and dangerous procedure.

We could not reach a unanimous decision regarding a proper course of action, and it was left for each institution to make its own decision about whether or not to undertake a cardiac transplantation program. I felt that kidney transplantation would offer a better model for the improvement of immunosuppressive therapy, which I believed would be required before we could perform successful cardiac transplantation. We expanded Emory's renal transplantation program, but we did not elect to perform our (and Georgia's) first cardiac transplantation until 1985, when there had been significant improvements in immunosuppressive therapy.

There had been so much media and lay interest in cardiac transplantation that I actually had to appear on local television in Atlanta to explain our reasoning. Dr. Barnard became an international celebrity, consulting with the Pope at the Vatican and dating Gina Lollabrigida while he was in Rome. It grew even harder to defend our conservative position when Dr. Denton Cooley and a dozen or so of his cardiac transplantation patients appeared on the cover of *Life Magazine*. Sadly, every patient in that photograph was dead within a year.

•◆•

In 1970, I can look back on another major milestone. That year I performed the first coronary bypass surgery in Georgia. My patient was a man from Tallahassee, Florida, which is actually only thirty miles or so from Attapulgus. He was so grateful, that after the surgery, he decided that he wanted all of his friends in Tallahassee to have the opportunity to have coronary arteriograms taken, so that if they needed, they could head up to Atlanta to have someone in our section perform the bypass surgery on them. An arteriogram is an x-ray image of the blood vessels, and with one, you can see if the patient has an aneurysm (a bulge in the blood vessel wall), stenosis (a narrowing of the blood vessel), or a blockage.

He asked me what it would cost to set up a catheterization lab at the Tallahassee Hospital, and I told him the bill would come to about $750,000 dollars. So he gave the Tallahassee Hospital the money to build a cath lab, and, rather unexpectedly, they immediately hired themselves a cardiac surgeon. Things did not work out as my patient had foreseen—the hospital did not send me any patients, which is what he had hoped for, and he confided in me that if he had known that it was going to be like this, then he might not have made the gift in the first place.

This is the nature of modern medical practice in America. Later on, as I assumed more and more administrative duties, I would have to contend with similar efforts by other hospitals in Atlanta. I never complained—this is just simply how it is. There is though an unfortunate downside to this constant striving by smaller hospitals to be more than they are. I remember, many years later, I was down in Attapulgus and my mother mentioned something rather startling to me.

"Charles," she said, "you know they're going to do cardiac transplants in Tallahassee."

"No, No," I said, "they do coronary bypasses."

"No, they say they're going to be doing transplants."

Well, they got a lot of publicity—this small, regional hospital could do anything that the national teaching hospitals could do—and they did about fifteen or twenty transplants. Unfortunately, their experience did not permit the institution to remain approved to receive available donor hearts.

We did well with the coronary bypass procedures, but it was not without great and delicate effort. We needed to win over the cardiology community and we did this by keeping a sharp eye on our mortality rate. Remember, the patients who are candidates for this type of surgery are at great risk of having heart attacks. In fact, this was probably the sickest group of patients you could contemplate at the time. We were very selective with our early patients, and from then on we got better and better patients referred to us. Well, we took the extra steps and precautions and we saw the result of those efforts in our low mortality rate—in a series of 1000 consecutive coronary bypass patients we lost only two. It bears repeating—our mortality rate was *two tenths of one percent*!

The cardiac surgery section, which should have been the riskiest unit at the hospital, had managed to set the standard for mortality rates. The example we set spread to other departments, helping raise up the level of excellence throughout the entire hospital. When Medicare decided to review the hospitals in the country performing heart surgery, we had the best mortality rate of any major hospital that had done more than 1000 surgical procedures. This achievement was not lost on other members of the local medical community. I can remember receiving a phone call from a cardiologist at the Medical College of Georgia in Augusta. His brother needed to have coronary bypass surgery and he decided to bring him to see me in Atlanta. He explained his reasoning to me.

"Dr. Hatcher," he said, "the boys in Augusta are doing well and I'm proud of them, but their mortality rate is three or four percent. I know what you're mortality rate is and even though we're talking about little numbers, I couldn't help but see our rate as ten times greater than yours."

Tension Mounting

YOUNG SURGEONS GENERALLY BECOME MEMBERS of the candidate group of the American College of Surgeons. Once they have finished their training and have been out of Medical School for ten years, they automatically become eligible for promotion to Fellowship. I received a notice from the College that ten years had expired and that I was now eligible for Fellowship. I had to fill out a handful of forms and express my desire to join the College, which I promptly did.

Some months later, I was informed that I had not been approved for Fellowship. Amazed and baffled, I immediately went to Dr. Martin to discuss this unexpected situation. He smiled, and said something to the effect of, 'This all could have been avoided if you'd come to me and gotten my approval for your plans to join the College.'

It did me no good to explain that I hadn't initiated the application, rather I had responded to a request directly from the College itself. I apologized for any inappropriate action that I may have taken. I learned another lesson in politics and I was approved for Fellowship the following year.

As the months passed, Dr. J.D. Martin regarded me with less and less suspicion, and we slowly became closer and closer friends. He realized that I respected him, and that Harland Stone and I were good friends, and that I represented no threat to Harland's career. He began to invite me down to his office for late afternoon chats over glass bottles of Coca-Cola. I received steady promotions making Assistant Professor in a minimum number of years of service, and subsequently rose to the position of Associate Professor of Surgery (Cardiothoracic Surgery).

Dr. Martin personally proposed and sponsored me for membership in the Southern Surgical Association, his favorite Surgical Society. The same year that I was proposed, Dr. Martin also proposed Dr. Richard Amerson, who was the most senior of the general surgeons.

Dr. Martin held a position on the council of the Southern Surgical Association, and he felt it was within his ability to elect both Dr. Amerson and me for membership in the same year. At the council meeting, a Professor and Chairman of another Department, also a council member, pleaded that his nominee—in his fifth year as a proposed member—be selected. If he were passed over again, then he would have to be resubmitted for the entire process at a later date. He asked that he be shown courtesy for his faculty member rather than Dr. Martin getting two of his faculty members accepted into the society in the same year.

When Dr. Martin returned from the meeting he gave me greetings from a number of friends who had been in attendance. I found out that Dr. Amerson had been elected. Dr. Martin didn't say a word about my candidacy, but I imagined what had happened, fairly accurately. I felt that Dr. Martin had done the proper thing under the circumstances. Later, I learned through another surgeon knowledgeable of the circumstances that Dr. Martin had said that I deserved to be elected, but that if I were elected and Dr. Amerson were not, it would have hurt him. Dr. Martin didn't believe that he would have been able to get over the perceived slight, whereas Dr. Martin was confident that I would understand the situation. He was so confident in fact, that he never mentioned any of this to me. Fortunately I never mentioned any of this to him either, and I was elected to the Southern Surgical Association the following year.

• ◆ •

On one of my first visits to Atlanta, we drove down Lullwater Road on our way to the hospital, and I said, "Now this is just beautiful."

It was only later that I found out that I had driven down one of the finest streets in the city. Lullwater Road was very, very close to the hospital, and I realized that it wouldn't just be a beautiful place to live; it would also be a very convenient place. If paged in an emergency, I could be at the hospital in less than five minutes. My son Charles, III, was also on the way, and we would need a larger house when he arrived. After a year of renting a small bungalow near Emory, when I saw a house on Lullwater with a 'for sale' sign in the front yard, I decided to make an offer. It so happened that I saw the sign the day it had been put up in the yard. I called my broker and asked him to get in touch and work it out. We went over that afternoon, and after a bit of haggling, we bought the place in 1963.

Lullwater Road is a street that is one mile long, and it was laid out by Fredrick Law Olmstead. The houses are elevated on both sides of the wide street, and the neighborhood was developed in the late 1920's by Asa Candler, the Coca-Cola magnate. One year after coming to Atlanta, I bought the house at 1105 Lullwater Road, which we still occupy today.

After we moved in, Celeste gave off another sign that things were not well, which I now recognize in hindsight. Though Celeste had a lifetime of experience with antiques and beautiful furniture, she found it very difficult to make decisions regarding the furnishing of our home. Mrs. Edith Hill, a well known local designer, assisted us in this process. She had designed the interiors of the Piedmont Driving Club in Atlanta, and the Eisenhower cottage at the Augusta National Golf Club in Augusta, Georgia. After a period of several months of exasperation, Mrs. Hill called me and said that if the house was to be furnished properly I would have to become more actively involved. I enjoyed working with Mrs. Hill, and the interior of our house took shape over the next two to three years.

When we moved to Atlanta, Marian was about two years old, and during the next year she began to ask for a baby brother. It so happened that Charles, III, made his appearance at this time, and for several years Marian thought of him as her baby since she had made the request and her request had been so quickly addressed. Marian's birth had been planned when the end of my surgical training was in sight, and Charlie's birth four years later (in 1964) was designed to avoid having two children attending college at the same time. Such old-fashioned family planning is atypical among young couples today.

Celeste's obstetrician for this pregnancy was Dr. Armand Hendee, along with his associates at The Emory Clinic. When she went into labor Dr. John Bottomy was on call and he managed her delivery. I kept little Marian with me in my office, where she contented herself with emptying the drawers and cabinets within her reach, as she made her way around the office. When the time came, I was summoned to the delivery room. Outside, the nurses and doctors proudly presented a healthy little boy to me. I inquired as to who was looking after his mother, and was somewhat chagrined to realize that everyone had come out to present the little boy to me; no one was in the delivery room with his mother!

The little boy was named Charles Ross Hatcher, III, after my father and me. His first few months were quite uneventful. In his second year, when he had learned to talk, his personality changed completely, and he became a very happy, playful baby.

In due time, Marian attended the Kindergarten of the Glenn Memorial United Methodist Church, and grammar school at the nearby Fernbank

Elementary School. The Fernbank bus picked her up at our driveway; when Marian was little, and I felt the same about Charlie, I believed that a long ride to school each day would be difficult. At the same time I was determined that they should ultimately attend the Westminster Schools, which are located in northwest Atlanta. Marian enrolled in Westminster in the 6th grade, and Charlie followed the same course four years later. Westminster is a demanding school academically, and I monitored the children very closely to see that they were not placed under undue stress. Both children thoroughly enjoyed Westminster, and handled the work without difficulty.

For several years Marian rode to a school with a neighbor whose daughter was also enrolled at Westminster. I had always been critical of parents who gave their children an automobile at an early age, but the technicalities of her transportation during those years prompted me to wake her up on her 16th birthday dangling a set of car keys over her bed. Marian could then drive herself and Charlie to school until graduation, and later Charlie could drive himself.

•◆•

Over the next several years following Charlie's birth, I enjoyed the complete and unfailing support of the cardiology staff, and contended with episodes of resentment of Drs. Abbott and Logan. One day, in a moment of candor, Dr. Abbott asked me if I realized that my air of confidence was resented by some of my surgical colleagues. He continued, declaring that 'the rest of us are cautious in our predictions of outcomes, and reserved in our surgical recommendations. You always seem to assure the cardiologists that you can take care of the problem, whatever it is.'

I laughed to discharge the tense atmosphere a bit, and said, "Well, Dr. Abbott, I try to be as cautious as I need to be, but when I know that I can do something, I feel free to say so."

My approach to Dr. Abbott was to appreciate his finer qualities and do all that I could to respect his position as Chief of our Service. He was perhaps his own worst enemy. His less desirable traits were superficial; the deeper you probed his character and personality the more you appreciated his traditions and values. Despite my best efforts, it was often impossible to seize an opportunity or make a desired surgical advance without seeming to step on Dr. Abbott's toes. In such circumstances, I was always very cautious and usually discussed the proper course of action with Dr. Martin or Dr. Scarborough.

While I was yet the young assistant professor, a situation occurred which embarrassed me and certainly must have embarrassed Dr. Abbott as well. The cardiovascular surgery division at Emory had applied for a Cardiac Surgery Training Grant a few years before I came to Emory. They applied for this grant under a program funded by the National Institutes of Health. NIH made a site visit, and then rejected the application. Shortly after my arrival, Dr. Martin and Dr. Abbott informed me that they were planning to reapply for the training grant. I participated in the preparation of the grant application, and along with the others, met the site committee during their visit. Again, the grant was not approved.

Disappointed and somewhat perplexed, Dr. Martin called a source at NIH and inquired as to what the problem was. Apparently he was informed, off the record, that they would have approved the training grant if I had been listed as the principal physician in charge. Dr. Martin called me to his office and informed me that he wished to immediately reapply for the training grant, this time in my name. I questioned what effect this would have on Dr. Abbott, but he reassured me that Dr. Abbott had agreed to these circumstances. Henceforth I would assume directorship of the residency program as well as the cardiac surgery training grant; in this way they could be integrated and managed efficiently. There would be no change in my academic rank or titles, in order to minimize Dr. Abbott's potential embarrassment, but I was given full authority to govern all aspects of the training program. For a young doctor, with only modest academic achievements on my curriculum vitae, this was really a big deal.

NIH dispatched another team to make a site visit, and the contrasting details of how I managed this visit elucidated the stark differences of opinion on the proper way to present a service to a site committee. The two previous grants had been based largely on the clinical materials available, and the necessary meetings had been held in spartan environs. Dr. Abbott had taken the team to lunch in the cafeteria at Grady Memorial Hospital. He reasoned that you had better look like you need money if you are standing there with your hands out, and there are few places that look like they need money in Georgia more than Grady Memorial Hospital. I had a different opinion. As I mentioned earlier, no one wants to invest in a loser, and a grant is, in a sense, an investment. NIH obviously does not expect a fiscal return on the dollars that they give you, but they do expect you to accomplish a specific task, and someone who *looks accomplished*, seems more likely to accomplish that task than someone who does not.

We held our meetings in the Whitehead Room, a lovely wood-paneled and exquisitely furnished room at Emory University Hospital. This room had been endowed by Mrs. Joseph Whitehead Evans at the time she funded the Whitehead Professorship, and I believed it to be the best meeting space on the entire campus. We enjoyed our meals, which were catered, and I attempted to project a service already successful and destined to become more so with the passage of time.

During their visit, the NIH team stayed at the Emory Inn, which is on campus. Now they were not supposed to make any contact with me outside of the scheduled appointments, but, a fortunate act of nature caused them to break that rule. There was a storm and the Emory Inn lost power. They called me and said, "Look Charlie, we're cold and we don't have any food up here—can you help us out?"

I told them that I would arrange something, right away.

I had recently been inducted in to the Capital City Club, which has a location in Downtown Atlanta. I called them and explained my situation. The Club was already closing up for the night, but they assured me that they would keep the dining room open for us. They kept a waiter and a chef on, and told me to bring my guests downtown. We drove down and had a private dinner at the Capital City Club.

The grant was approved, and it provided significant enhancements to our traditional residency program. I never knew the exact nature of Dr. Abbott's reaction at this turn of events, but I was delighted that we had obtained the grant, and went out of my way to seek his advice and counsel whenever I had the slightest pretext to do so.

I knew it was only a matter of time before this arrangement—Dr. Abbott in charge of the division of cardiac surgery, and the residency program under my control—would lead to conflict. Sure enough, a second episode soon occurred, which was even more awkward than the awarding of the grant itself.

Dr. Abbott was a frequent international traveler. He was always pleased and impressed when, during his travels, young men in host departments would express their desire to come to Atlanta to train with him. One such young surgeon was from Turkey. Dr. Abbott arranged his appointment following introductions at a banquet, and upon arrival we all found him to be a gentle and polite individual with a significant language problem and limited surgical experience. Within a short time, he realized that he was in over his head. He voluntarily withdrew from our program.

Several years later, he reapplied to the program. He was not competitive with the other candidates. Apparently though, he had called Dr. Abbott, who told him that he would be welcome back to the program at any time. When he received notice from me that he had not been accepted, he called Dr. Abbott seeking clarification of his situation.

Dr. Abbott responded as he had hoped, stating, "If I say you are accepted, you are accepted." If this had not made things perfectly clear, he continued, adding, "You may disregard any correspondence you have received from Dr. Hatcher."

When Dr. Logan and I became aware of this situation, we were quite distressed. I had a meeting with Dr. Martin, who immediately understood the awkward position in which we had been placed. He picked up the telephone and called Dr. Abbott in my presence.

"Osler," he said, "you know you're not to involve yourself in this way in the residency program. Charles is in charge of the residency program, and you may not override his decisions."

After a few moments listening to Dr. Abbott, he concluded, "Well, I suggest you call the young man immediately and tell him that you made a mistake—that he has not been accepted. And I want you to see that this type of thing does not happen again...Yes."

And he hung up.

Dr. Abbott and I never discussed this situation. I knew he had been embarrassed by the experience, and I felt for him strongly. Fortunately, nothing like that ever happened again.

Dr. Abbott could be a charming and gracious man, but his strong personality and professional ambitions inspired strong feelings about him; you either liked him a great deal, or you disliked him a great deal. There were considerable numbers in each camp. At first he was pleased to have me join his division. He took me around campus and introduced me to pertinent colleagues, invariably mentioning that I had been one of Al's (Dr. Blalock's) residents at Johns Hopkins. I remember being introduced thusly to Dr. Edgar Fincher, Chief of Neurosurgery at Emory.

He immediately scoffed, "Damn, we don't need any more surgeons! What we need are more operating rooms! Nothing personal, son."

From that moment, Dr. Fincher and I became fast friends. He was a frequent advisor, helping me launch cardiac surgery in Atlanta as he had launched neurosurgery a few years earlier. Years later when I visited Scotland as a Visiting Professor at Edinburgh, Dr. Fincher arranged for an old colleague of his from the Mayo Clinic, Sir James Lermont, to host a luncheon for me. Sir James had been knighted after performing a sympathectomy on King George VI, and he told me rather jokingly that he didn't accept the Knighthood for the sympathectomy, which he regarded as a rather simple operation, rather he accepted it for all that he had been put through having to live at the Palace for several weeks before and following the King's surgery.

Many years after my visit to Scotland, Dr. Fincher became terminally ill. He was incapable of raising his secretions, and this death rattle was most disturbing to Mrs. Fincher. The staff at the hospital recommended that I perform a tracheotomy to control these secretions. I explained to Dr. Fincher what I needed to do.

He sighed and said, "All right, Charles, if you'll promise me that that's the last thing that you'll do."

Through the tracheotomy his nurse maintained a satisfactory tracheal-bronchial toilet, much to the relief of Mrs. Fincher and the other members of his family.

In the late 1960s, Dr. Abbott had an illness that took him out of the office for a period of several weeks. Dr. Logan immediately went to Dr. Martin and asked to be named Acting Chief of Thoracic and Cardiovascular Surgery during Dr. Abbott's absence. By that time, Dr. Martin was well aware of the tensions in our section. He had also come to rely on me as a strong supporter of the department of surgery, and someone he counted as a friend. Thus, he refused to take action. Dr. Martin told Dr. Logan that the two of us should work together as there would be no need to appoint an acting chief for such a short time.

Later, in 1970, Dr. Abbott flew to Milwaukee to undergo surgery. Dr. Dudley Johnson performed a coronary bypass, utilizing the internal mammary artery. Post-operatively, he experienced severe pericarditis, requiring him to take large doses of steroids. Dr. Abbott returned to Atlanta and he began to behave rather inappropriately, which we attributed to his steroid therapy. He also suffered from delusions of grandeur, believing that that the President of the United States needed him to lead a worldwide tour to assess cardiac surgical facilities in foreign countries. He flew up to Washington, D.C., and spent several days milling about the White House, waiting for an appointment that would never come.

At long last, Dr. Martin and the Administrative Committee of The Emory Clinic decided that they could no longer ignore this situation. At a meeting of the Administrative Committee, Dr. Willis Hurst reminded everyone that in Dante's Inferno, there's a special circle of Hell reserved for those who fail to speak up in times of moral crisis. Dante actually wrote that the dead souls of those who are neutral in times of moral crisis are damned to reside outside the gates of hell. Abhorrent to God and Satan alike, these souls are therefore worse than Hell's greatest sinners. Despite this common misconception, Dr. Hurst had made his point.

Dr. Hurst, who had seen Dr. Abbott wandering aimlessly and inappropriately on stage at a national meeting, felt that almost everyone was aware of the situation with Dr. Abbott, and that he should be directed to take a leave of absence. Dr. Hurst felt we could no longer ignore the fact that Dr. Abbott was ill. He feared that the care of patients would deteriorate.

Dr. Martin agreed that it was time to appoint an acting chief, and he asked me to assume this responsibility. Although I knew that Dr. Logan might not be pleased with this action, I detected no hostility on his part, and we enjoyed working together without the stresses produced by Dr. Abbott's illness. However, every time things seemed to settle down a bit, Dr. Abbott would return and produce confusion. This situation could not last.

No *Deadwood* in this Department

IT BECAME APPARENT TO ALMOST everyone in the department of surgery that Dr. Abbott, at the relatively young age of fifty-nine, needed to be urged into retirement for health reasons. The staff came to this consensus about the same time that Dr. Martin was set to retire as chairman of the surgery department, March 1, 1971. A few days prior to this, Dr. Martin witnessed Dr. Abbott throw a tantrum in the operating room.

My personal cases were always scheduled in room two, the largest operating suite at Emory University Hospital. This was because of the heart-lung machine's special requirements, and the additional monitoring equipment, which was essential to cardio/pulmonary bypass surgery. Dr. Abbott's cases not requiring cardio/pulmonary bypass equipment, which made up the vast bulk of his practice at the time, could be performed in a much smaller operating theatre, and he was frequently assigned to room seven, or a similar suite.

For whatever reason, he decided that he could no longer tolerate this situation. I was working in the larger operating suite that morning, while he, 'The Professor,' had been assigned to a smaller room. Apparently he pitched a fit in the operating room, while his patient lay on the table. The circulating nurse dropped into my room to inform me how upset Dr. Abbott was. Upon completing my case, I immediately set out for the room where Dr. Abbott was operating. I told him how sorry I was that he felt he had been given an inferior room. I attempted to explain to him that the reason I had been allocated room two was because of the nature of the surgery scheduled, and certainly not for any personal reason.

He drew himself up and said, "Dr. Hatcher, I am not now and never will be interested in any of your excuses."

I made no comment to such a remark and turned to leave the room.

Just outside the door, I bumped into Dr. Martin, who had overheard the entire exchange. The nursing staff had already alerted Dr. Martin of Dr. Abbott's behavior.

He put his hand on my shoulder and said, "Charles, you're a real gentleman, and I promise you that I'll take care of this situation."

The next day Dr. Martin informed me that he planned to relieve Dr. Abbott of his duties and name me chief of the division of cardiothoracic surgery in the Emory University School of Medicine, and chief of the section of cardiothoracic surgery at The Emory Clinic. Dr. Martin said, "I suppose there might be some comments made about my taking this action only a day or two before I retire, but I wouldn't enjoy my retirement if I knew that I had left you in your current situation."

Dr. W. Dean Warren had been selected to succeed Dr. Martin as Whitehead Professor and Chairman of the Department of Surgery, and Dr. Martin informed him of the action he planned to take. Dr. Warren gave him his complete support, and told him that if he had not taken this action, then he, in fact, would have done the same upon his arrival in Atlanta.

Dr. W. Dean Warren

Dr. Abbott was not pleased with this turn of events, but in his heart of hearts he must have realized that he was not well, and consequently not competent to continue in his position of responsibility. He publicly objected to my appointment on behalf of Dr. Logan, taking the position that I should be named the chief of the division at the School of Medicine, and that Dr. Logan should be named the section head at The Emory Clinic. While this compromise might seem appealing, it was impractical and unrealistic. No one could be in charge of an academic division without control of the monies produced by the complimentary clinical enterprise (the section at The Emory Clinic). Of the two positions, only the clinic section head was subject to discussion and vote. Everyone conceded that I was the proper choice to be the academic leader of the division at the school of medicine. This was the situation heading into the monthly meeting of The Emory Clinic's Administrative Committee, which was presided over by The Emory Clinic Director, Dr. Robert Brown. Each section head served on the committee.

At the time, I, of course, was not yet a member of the Administrative Committee. Dr. Abbott continued to perform this role until the committee had taken action on my proposed appointment as section head. I remember sitting in my office all alone while the Administrative Committee was in session. At the conclusion of their meeting, I was informed that I had been confirmed as chief of the section of cardiothoracic surgery by a vote of twenty-two to one. Dr. Martin called me forthwith and offered me congratulations. He also gave me a piece of advice that has stuck with me.

"Charles," he said, "I know you are inclined to be extremely fair, and you have a natural instinct to make adjustments on their behalf. This would be a mistake. Be firm, clear the decks, and rebuild the division with people whom you recruit."

This advice was not just practical to that situation; it was a bit of wisdom I relied upon in future years as I became involved with many delicate personnel decisions. My instincts are to seek out a consensus. Lead by consensus is better for everyone involved. Sometimes a consensus is not possible, and a leader needs to recognize when that is the case. Fortunately, this situation took care of itself without my direct involvement.

Dr. Logan promptly moved on, accepting a cardiothoracic surgical position at Atlanta's Georgia Baptist Medical Center.

Dr. Abbott accepted an early retirement. Unfortunately, Dr. Abbott was only fifty-nine at the time of this action. I had noticed a pattern in his long and frequent absences. A partner in The Emory Clinic retains full privileges of partnership for the first three months of an illness. If incapacitated longer than three months, the partner is placed on medical disability, and his or her income is transferred to our insurance carriers. I felt that at least part of Dr. Abbott's reluctance to remain on a leave of absence, and his return to work almost exactly after a three-month period, indicated that at least some of his apprehensions were financial in origin. Recognizing this, I proposed to Robert Brown that he advise Dr. Abbott to take his Social Security benefits at age sixty-three, and that from his current age until then, The Emory Clinic and Section of Cardiothoracic Surgery would divide payments made to subsidize his insurance. This plan proved acceptable to all concerned.

•◆•

I quickly realized that I had been given tremendous responsibilities. I also had been afforded a rare and unique opportunity. The Division of Cardiothoracic Surgery would be mine to rebuild from scratch. I would be able to personally recruit the type of individuals whom I considered ideal for our specialty at Emory. There would be no egos to satiate and no personal aspirations standing in the way of our collective progress. There would be no *deadwood* in my division.

I only say *my division*, because for the next year, I performed every cardiothoracic case at Emory University Hospital and the Egleston Hospital for Children. Fortunately, two capable young men had just completed our residency program, and although they were not licensed to practice in the state of Georgia, they were very capable of assisting me in the management of all types of cases. Drs. Zafrullah Khan and Dr. Kamal Mansour had been outstanding residents—highly intelligent and technically gifted, they were absolutely invaluable during this period.

Section Six:
Leadership, Recruitment, and the Next Right Thing

A Personal Word

We recruited an excellent team of doctors, built up a core of accomplished technicians and skilled assistants, and grew our service to one of the nation's largest. During that time I showed a lot of people what it meant to treat people graciously toward the end of their careers. I also began to see a trend – the personal element of medical care was missing. It's so easy to keep a patient's friendship and devotion; all you need to do is take the time to keep them informed. A patient is more than a patient, he or she is a customer, and unless you recognize that, it is difficult to improve upon customer service.

Don't Mind Him

ONE OF THE LAST THINGS that I did before my promotion to division chief was to help recruit someone to replace Dr. J. D. Martin as Chairman and Whitehead Professor of Surgery. Dean Richardson appointed a faculty committee to conduct the search. He also instructed them to make an evaluation of the surgery department. The search committee consulted with Dr. Rollo Hanlon, who was then the Executive Director of the American College of Surgeons.

Ultimately the committee submitted a list of five names. Dr. W. Dean Warren was the top candidate, and he came to Emory for an interview at a time when I happened to be in Puerto Rico, giving a lecture to the American College of Surgeons.

When I got back to Atlanta, I heard that Dr. Warren had been here, and that he had been offered the surgical chairmanship and had turned it down. I could not understand this. I felt that there must have been something wrong with the presentation, or perhaps, whoever had conducted his tour of the facilities had not touched upon the right points. I could not imagine why any academic surgeon would not want to come to Emory as the Whitehead Professor and chairman of the department of surgery!

Dr. Martin had called to tell me the news. He said to me, "There are five names on the list and you're the only local candidate. So, let's pull in all of our IOU's and get you the chairmanship."

"No," I said, "I'm uncomfortable with that. If the committee and the dean want Dr. Warren, then I don't want to be their second choice. I'm not that hungry. I'd rather help them get Dr. Warren."

He asked me how I proposed to do that.

I knew Dean through Hopkins. He had taken an early part of his surgical training there and completed his residency at the University of

179

Michigan in Ann Arbor. He was an outstanding person, and I respected him as a fellow surgeon of the finest caliber.

"Well," I said, "I know Dean and I'll call him and invite him back up here. I'll tell him that somehow there were errors on our part."

I walked over to Dean Richardson's office, and asked him if it were true that he and the committee preferred Dr. Warren to be the chairman.

"Yes, Charles," he said, "It's true. He's been a chairman and a dean and an acting vice president at the University of Miami. We're not saying that at some point in time we wouldn't prefer you as the chairman; it just looks like Dean Warren would be a better fit right now."

"Then let me help you get him."

"What do you propose to do?"

"I propose to call him and invite him back up here."

"Well," he said, "I'm going to be out of town next week."

"Well that may even be better—you'll run no risks if I'm unsuccessful."

"The committee will want to be involved in the visit."

"No," I said. "Their job was to advise you on the best candidates available and they've done that. I'm going to help you get him, but I'll attend to this myself."

So I called Dean Warren and said, "You must've gotten the wrong impression." I asked him to come back up to Emory.

"If you think so," he said, "then I'll be glad to do that Charles."

He came up to Emory the following weekend, on a Friday. I set it up so that I met him at the airport. I brought him directly to Dr. Martin's office, as I do believe that not having done so the first time was a mistake.

He had not been introduced to Dr. Martin on his initial visit. I thought this was wrong on two counts. First of all, it was a slight to Dr. Martin. Second, I thought that this had made a bad impression on the man whom they hoped would fill Dr. Martin's shoes. I jokingly said, that's like walking past a brick wall with an old man up against it and a firing squad lined up, and the committee saying, 'Oh no, don't pay any attention to that, he's just the guy who had the job before you.' How you treat people who are going out the door is obviously a factor in how the new person is going to judge you; he knows that he will eventually be that man. At any rate, I took him to meet Dr. Martin and the conversation went well.

I then took him around The Emory Clinic and the campus and introduced him to everybody whom I felt he should meet. I arranged a luncheon for him at the Capital City Club, and asked the president of the university to join us. I asked Dr. Garland Herndon, the Vice President for Health Affairs, and personal physician of Mr. Robert Woodruff, if he would take Dr. Warren down to Ichauway Plantation on Saturday afternoon. I hoped that he could spend the night there with Mr. Woodruff, and that Mr. Woodruff might talk about his plans for The Emory Clinic and Emory University Hospital. He went down to the plantation and Mr. Woodruff told him that he was planning on making a gift of roughly $35 million dollars for the new G-Wing to the hospital. Finally, I asked Boisfeuillet Jones to give him a call, representing the Woodruff Foundations, letting him know how interested he would be in having him at Emory.

We had a written acceptance from Dr. Warren early the next week. We had our man, and everyone was happy.

I still believe that I made the right choice regarding the chairmanship. One is always impaired if you are local and you are not an early consensus choice. As second or third choice, I don't think that I would have had the backing and the support that I would have required to do the job. By making a point of bringing Dr. Warren and Dr. Martin together, I showed a lot of people that I believed in treating people graciously as they neared the end of their careers. Furthermore, I think that the way I stepped up and helped rescue Dr. Warren's recruitment, possibly at my personal expense, left a good taste in people's mouths.

Number One Draft Picks

WHEN IT CAME TO RECRUITING young surgeons to the Division of Cardiothoracic Surgery, I like to say that I got the number one draft pick every year. There were a number of reasons for this. Atlanta was a young, growing city. It was an attractive place to come to work and to live. Emory was on the move, striving to become more than just a regional university. I was considered a younger guy – 40 years old when appointed chief of the division – which appealed to a lot of my future colleagues.

Our division would eventually include three former Harvard residents and three former Hopkins residents, along with some fine doctors from a few other prestigious medical institutions. Doctor Abbott, Dr. Logan, and I had all worked very hard to grow the section into one of the best, but both of them were gone now. It would be up to me to recruit the kind of surgeons whom I believed would not merely maintain our level of success. Rather I hoped to fill the ranks with men who would collectively achieve an unparalleled level of excellence in our field.

Upon my elevation to division chief, Dr. Abbott retired. Doctor Logan accepted a position at the Georgia Baptist Hospital here in Atlanta. I had two young men available to me who had just completed their residencies under my mentorship. They were Dr. Kamal Mansour and Dr. M. Zafrullah Khan, neither of whom was an American citizen nor did they have licenses to practice in Georgia. I asked them to stay on with me for the next year as "super-residents." They could help me with anything but they could not take personal professional responsibility or submit charges for services rendered.

We also had Dr. Peter Symbas, a cardiothoracic surgeon trained by two of Dr. Blalock's earlier residents, Dr. William Scott at Vanderbilt University and Dr. Rollo Hanlon at St. Louis University. I considered Dr. Symbas a very valuable faculty member. He served as Chief of Cardiothoracic Surgery at Grady Memorial Hospital.

Dr. Roger Sherman and Dr. Peter Symbas

We didn't do as much surgery at Emory as the three of us had done the year before, but we came pretty close to the section's previous mark. We didn't lose any initiative. I operated day and night, knowing that assistance would be coming the following July.

There was a pediatric cardiologist at Emory – Dr. Dorothy Brinsfield. She had worked very closely with Dr. Logan. She was a bit uneasy about my having to carry the pediatric load largely by myself for a year, but I went out of my way to take special care of her patients. When the results were tallied up, we had a very good year. Our mortality rates remained low and we didn't suffer a significant decrease in the number of patients operated upon. Doctor Brinsfield would not forget our success.

At the same time, I had begun to recruit. Doctor Ellis Jones had come to speak to me the first week I was at Emory, back in 1962. He was a rising senior in the Medical School. He wanted to work with me in the lab that summer. He also hoped that I would eventually recommend him to Dr. Blalock for an internship at Hopkins. He was a good student. I liked Ellis very much and was prepared to help him as best I could.

When I left Hopkins, Dr. Blalock told me that he was prepared to offer me an internship every year for an Emory student whom I thought could handle the Halsted Program.

"You can count of their appointment," were his exact words. He also informed me that he had also extended this offer to only a few of his former chief residents. With this assurance, I called Dr. Blalock. They interviewed Ellis a few weeks later. Sure enough, he got the internship.

Like me, Ellis needed to go into the military. I was very lucky in being able to assist him in attaining an appointment at the Walter Reed Hospital. After he had been at Walter Reed for a year, he got a notice that he was being sent to Vietnam. General Westmoreland's massive troop buildup had recently begun. Ellis called me and said, "I've just got these orders calling me to Vietnam. What are we going to do?"

"*We* aren't going to do anything, Ellis," I said.

"In peacetime I'm happy to use whatever connections I have because nothing is on the table. But once you receive orders saying that your country needs you in Vietnam to take care of wounded soldiers, you're going to have to go to Vietnam. I'm not about to attempt to get you out of *that*."

I told Ellis to get in touch with me when he got back home from Vietnam. He went over to Vietnam, served his country honorably, and then came back and completed his residency at Hopkins. He finished up in the spring of 1973. He came to Emory to work with me that July. I was glad to have Dr. Jones. He quickly helped shoulder some of the burden.

Doctor Blalock passed away in 1964. Ellis was only able to train under him briefly. Nevertheless, having made it through the Halsted Program, I had full confidence in Ellis' ability. Indeed, he went right to work.

Doctor Jones became one of our most active and successful adult cardiac surgeons. At the beginning of his career, he also operated on quite a number of children with congenital heart disease. We later added doctors to the service who focused exclusively on congenital heart disease. Doctor Jones reduced his portion of the pediatric work to concentrate on his adult patients.

The pediatric cardiologists seemed to have a bias against surgeons who operate on both adults and children. They relate better to surgeons who limit their work to children and who were able to spend most of their time in the then Egleston Children's Hospital and were therefore more accessible and available. This I accepted as a fact of life. I adjusted our faculty accordingly.

Emory Cardiac Surgery Team
Back: Dr. Robert Guyton, Dr. Joseph Miller, Dr. Joseph Craver, Dr.
Willis Williams; Front: Dr. Kamal Mansour, Dr. Ellis Jones, Dr. Charles
Hatcher, Dr. David Bone

The next two young men I recruited were Drs. Joe Craver and Joe Miller. Both joined the division in the summer of 1974. Dr. Miller took his general surgery residency at the Mayo Clinic. He then did two years of cardiothoracic training with me. I was glad to have him remain at Emory.

Doctor Joe Craver took his general surgery residency at the Massachusetts General Hospital. He then took his thoracic training with a good friend of mine and former Blalock resident, Dr. Harry Muller, at the University of Virginia. I remember that Harry called me and said that he had a guy who was "really good" whom I "really need to take a look at." Doctor Craver came down to Emory. I saw that Dr. Muller had been right in his appraisal of the young man. During the visit he kept on telling me how good he was! When we were through, we stopped in front of the terminal at the airport. Before he got out of the car, he turned to me and said, "Dr.

Hatcher, I know you're tired of my telling you how good I am. But sir, I really am that good!" I laughed and said, "I'm pleased to offer you the job. I can deal with that kind of confidence." Doctor Craver more than fulfilled his own expectations of himself at Emory.

Around this time, I assisted Dr. Mansour in obtaining his citizenship so that he could qualify for a Georgia license and practice on his own in Georgia. I sponsored his application and I promised him that if we were successful I would give him a position in the division. Everything worked out.

By that time I had put in so many pacemakers that we had someone coming in with a failing pacemaker or "end-of-life" battery just about every day or night. Pacemakers, far more reliable now, needed to be replaced every several months back in those days. Doctor Mansour more or less took over my pacemaker replacement service. In time he proved to be an excellent technical general thoracic surgeon and went on to pioneer a number of procedures. Back during those early years I remember him most as being so helpful to me in handling all those pacemaker replacement cases.

As he developed his early practice, initially at the then Crawford Long Hospital of Emory University, Dr. Craver expressed the strong desire to move out onto the main campus and take an office on the floor with Dr. Jones and me. At about that time I was trying to develop general thoracic surgery as well as cardiac. I asked Dr. Miller – and subsequently Dr. Kamal Mansour – if they would undertake the development of general thoracic surgery at Emory and limit their practice to thoracic surgery. I felt that being committed even partially to cardiac surgery in those days was such a consuming task that thoracic surgical patients might be added to the schedule at the end of the day. Possibly the emphasis placed on their care might not be comparable to the care provided the cardiac surgical patients.

Drs. Miller and Mansour understood my motives and accepted the opportunity presented to them. They both limited themselves to thoracic surgery and in time developed a very splendid service which proved to be of great value to our private patients and to the excellence and diversity of our cardiothoracic surgical program.

In a short time, I would also spin off pediatric surgery and recruit surgeons who limited themselves to this field. Doctor Jones and I discontinued our very active work in congenital heart disease. Pediatric patient care and teaching were probably best in the hands of individuals who were not involved with the adult program, spending most of their time in the Egleston Children's Hospital on the Emory campus while continuing to see their patients and families in The Emory Clinic.

Doctor William Fleming had taken his cardiothoracic surgery training with Dr. James Malm at Columbia Presbyterian Hospital in New York. He was recruited on the basis of strong personal recommendations from Dr. Malm, an old friend and colleague noted for his work in pediatric congenital heart surgery. Doctor Fleming joined our division on January 1, 1971. While we developed pediatric cardiac surgery as a specialty, it was necessary that Dr. Fleming have an additional assignment. Accordingly, he was made Chief of Cardiothoracic Surgery at the Atlanta Veterans Administration Hospital. This limited his work at The Emory Clinic and on the Emory campus at the Egleston Hospital for Children to pediatric cardiac surgery. In the summer of 1976, Dr. Fleming moved on to another academic health sciences center in the Midwest where he served as chief of the service for many years.

In 1976, in the wake of Dr. Fleming's departure, I brought Dr. Willis Williams to take over pediatric cardiac surgery and to serve as Chief of Surgery of the Egleston Hospital for Children. Willis took his residency at the Massachusetts General Hospital and the Boston Children's Hospital, serving as chief resident in both pediatric surgery and cardiothoracic surgery in both institutions. Willis served under the mentorship of the renowned pioneer in both pediatric and cardiothoracic surgery, Dr. Robert E. Gross. This outstanding training made him an ideal man to kick-start our pediatric service. Right away I could see that he was a very, very good pediatric surgeon.

In July, 1977, I was successful in recruiting Dr. David Bone, another Halsted Resident from Johns Hopkins who was in practice in Tulsa, Oklahoma and not entirely satisfied with his opportunities there. The cardiac surgery program at the Carlyle Fraser Heart Center at Emory-Crawford Long Hospital had developed to the point where Dr. Bone could be located at the hospital full time. He was extremely successful in his practice and was highly regarded by his medical colleagues. With the Emory University rules in effect at the time, Dr. Bone, then an assistant professor, had to be promoted to associate professor within five years or his appointment could not be renewed. This would have required additional commitment to the academic program including more publications. Unfortunately, Dr. Bone was not willing to make these adjustments, preferring to concentrate on his clinical practice. He accepted a position in a non-academic setting at St. Joseph's Hospital in Atlanta where he contributed mightily to the development of their cardiac surgical program.

Doctor Bone's departure resulted in the loss of approximately two million dollars in billing at Emory-Crawford Long Hospital. This came up at a meeting where someone asked, "How in the world did we lose David Bone?"

"We didn't lose David Bone," I replied. "We pushed him out because he hadn't written any papers."

"My God," the chairman of the board said. "You could have hired a Ph.D. to follow him around and let him dictate his papers *for two million dollars!*"

Another recruit, Dr. Jim Sink, had been a resident at Duke with Dr. David Sabiston, whom I knew from Hopkins. David strongly recommended Dr. Sink. I recruited him for a position we had at the Atlanta Veterans Administration Hospital. Jim was a fine surgeon, but he was not the type of man who was content to stay there for too long. He soon found more lucrative work and left us.

Doctor Doug Murphy was another bright man we lost, albeit under very different circumstances. Doctor Murphy did his general surgery residency at the MGH. He then continued his training with us. I kept him on when he finished his residency to develop our cardiac transplantation program in the mid-80s.

We spent a large sum to set up a tissue typing lab. We sent Dr. Murphy to Stanford to visit with Dr. Norm Shumway. When I felt that we were finally ready, I invited one of the surgeons from Stanford to stand by as we performed our first cardiac transplant in 1985.

We had chosen to remain on the sidelines when Dr. Christian Barnard of South Africa announced in 1967 that he had performed his first heart transplantation. Doctor Cooley in Houston followed up this work in the states. In the mid-70s, cyclosporine, an effective immunosuppressive drug, was developed. The evolution of cyclosporine into a usable drug was a major step forward, but it would not be approved by the FDA for the prevention of transplant rejection until 1983, following a long series of animal and human trials. As cyclosporine became commercially available for clinical use, survival following cardiac transplantation changed overnight. I decided it was now time for us to begin doing cardiac transplants. With Dr. Murphy heading up the effort, the division performed Georgia's first cardiac transplant in 1985.

We had invested time and not a small sum of money to get the cardiac transplant program up and running. Things went well for a year or so. Then, without any warning, we found ourselves without any cardiac transplant program whatsoever. I was quite dismayed to find out that St. Joseph's Hospital in Atlanta had recruited Dr. Murphy and his team. I had no idea that he was unhappy or that he planned to leave. It turned out that

St. Joseph's had made him an extremely attractive offer which he couldn't refuse.

Doctor Murphy has been quite successful with his group at St. Joseph's and several other local hospitals. I was saddened when he accepted the position at St. Joseph's. At the same time, I was quite busy by 1987, having accepted many responsibilities outside the division. I now recognize that I failed to nurture Dr. Murphy's career as he had expected.

The result of all this was to divide the number of transplantable donor hearts available in Atlanta between two institutions. I suspended our service for six months and immediately began recruiting someone to replace Dr. Murphy.

I enticed Dr. Kirk Kanter to Emory. Within a year or so we had returned to and exceed our previous transplant volume. In the end everything worked out well for us. Doctor Kanter was a fine man and an excellent surgeon. He had done his medical internship at Emory and then completed his surgical and cardiothoracic training at Johns Hopkins. He also studied transplantation and congenital heart surgery for a year in London. When he returned to Atlanta after a brief period at St. Louis University, he was quite ready to go.

In 1980, I helped recruit two extremely talented men to Emory – one, an accomplished pioneer in his field; the other, fresh out of his residency.

Doctor Robert Guyton, a young resident at the time, ultimately would succeed me as Chief of the Division of Cardiothoracic Surgery. A graduate of Harvard Medical School, Robert did his internship and residency at the Massachusetts General Hospital. When he was in the final year of his residency, he came down to see me about a possible job at Emory. We were very keen to have him join the group. He was the son of Dr. Arthur Guyton of the University of Mississippi, author of the physiology textbook used by most medical schools in the country.

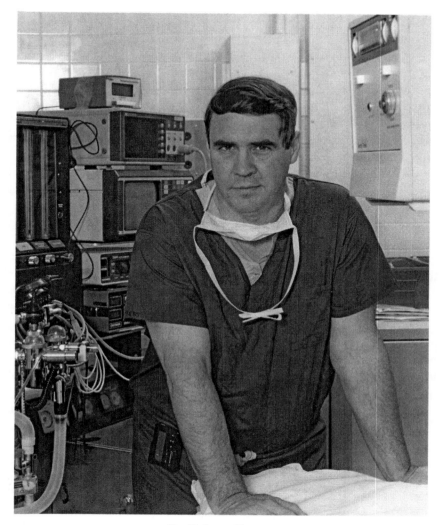

Dr. Robert Guyton

Friends of mine who were professors at the MGH let me know about Robert's performance there, informing me what an outstanding doctor he was. We were not above employing attractive devices to interest him in Emory. He made his tour. We returned to my office. On my desk I had a stack of charts, about eight high.

"Bob," I asked, "Do you know what that stack of charts is?" He shook his head, "No."

"Those are the records of everybody who died having heart surgery at Emory last year."

"Oh."

I nodded.

I felt like the staff at Harvard would never say anything negative about me or Emory. They were far too elegant to do that. However, I was sure that they would say something like, "Bob, Dr. Hatcher's a nice guy and Emory's a nice school, but it's going to interrupt your research work if you go down there. You'll have to establish a new laboratory, but if you stayed on here with us you would have the same lab and the same techs and you could just keep on with what you're doing without interruption."

So I asked him, "Bob, tell me about what you're doing. Can you give me a list of the technicians and what they do and a list of the equipment you would need?"

He gave me the information. I went down to Emory-Crawford Long Hospital to see Wilton Looney and my other friends at the Carlyle Fraser Heart Center. I told them that we wanted to get Dr. Guyton to come down there, but he would not come unless he had a good lab. I figured that we were going to have to invest about a half-million dollars to set up a lab that would be the equal of his space at Harvard. Mr. Looney understood my desire to bring Dr. Guyton to Emory. He gave us the money. We bought the building that housed the John Smith Chevrolet dealership across the street from the hospital. With major renovation, we converted it into a laboratory. We then purchased all the equipment like that he was using at that time at the MGH. We recruited a team of technicians.

Doctor Guyton made another visit to Emory. This time, I told him that we had his lab set up for him. He accepted the position and arrived in Atlanta on January 1, 1980, ready to go to work. He performed his first experiment on January 15; exactly as he would have had he stayed in Boston. Initially, Dr. Guyton based his work at Emory-Crawford Long Hospital at the Carlyle Fraser Heart Center. He established a nice clinical reputation, recruited a number of fellows, and has been very active in his laboratory.

I stayed on as Chief of Cardiothoracic Surgery longer than I otherwise would have, I believe. I had it in the back of my mind that Dr. Jones and Dr. Craver were at the same level and so intensely competitive that it would have been impossible for anyone to choose one over the other. Doctor Willis Hurst would alternate using Dr. Craver and Dr. Jones to operate upon patients referred to him. There did not seem to be a way for either one to become chief without the other leaving Emory. I thought that if Bob could be given a little more time to develop, he might emerge as an appealing candidate. By 1990, I thought that he was ready for evaluation and I could step down. I had served in this role for 20 years – one year as acting chief and 19 as chief. By this time I was serving in two other quite demanding roles, both of which we will get to in time.

I met with the chairman of the department of surgery and the dean of the medical school, telling them that I thought it was time for me to step down. I asked them to promise me three things.

First, my successor would be chosen from within the group. I had spent too much time recruiting these men – my number one draft picks. To pick an outsider to be their chief would be very divisive as well as an academic insult. Several might well leave Emory.

Second, I wanted them to interview everyone in the division individually. I did not want them to just have a group meeting. I wanted each man to have his chance to voice his choice for the best man to succeed me.

Finally, after I left the room, I did not want to be involved in the search in any manner.

It became apparent very quickly that there was consensus favoring Dr. Robert Guyton. His appointment as Chief of the Division of Cardiothoracic Surgery was approved by the Emory University School of Medicine and The Emory Clinic.

The Department of Medicine recruited Dr. Andreas Gruentzig to join the Emory faculty in 1980. Doctor Willis Hurst, Chairman of the Department of Medicine, and Dr. Spencer King, then Director of the Cardiac Catheterization Laboratory in the Department of Medicine, were able to entice Dr. Gruentzig to Emory.

Doctor Gruentzig, a German citizen, first performed coronary arterial angioplasty in Zurich, Switzerland, in 1977. He was a creative genius and a charming man, destined to become world famous.

Doctor Hurst pointed out in a later conversation with me, "Since angioplasty would have competed with coronary bypass surgery, it was necessary to have the support of the cardiac surgeons if we were to recruit Dr. Gruentzig. Charlie, you especially, and all of your staff reassured Dr. Gruentzig that you would welcome him and work with him. Your reassurance and ability to work with a competitive technique was a major contribution to Gruentzig's recruitment."

Running Out of Options

AFTER I BECAME THE CHIEF of Cardiothoracic Surgery I began to spend a little more time on social activities. I became a Rotarian. I had been invited to join the Capital City Club before my promotion, and soon I was a member of the Piedmont Driving Club as well. These were things that you did if you wanted to advance in Atlanta.

Joining these sorts of clubs allowed me to meet a lot of non-medical people in Atlanta, which helped grow my social circle. Coming from Attapulgus it was very nice to be in Atlanta, and to join these social groups.

While I was making exciting progress at the clinic and socially, all was not well at home. In the late 1960s, Celeste began to manifest signs of schizophrenia. She had her first breakdown in 1969. It was Christmastime and the family was together, at our house in Atlanta. In the middle of the day, just before lunch, she floated out of the house, looking for an air pump at a gas station, to fill a basketball. This was strange enough; things only got worse the following day. She woke up and from there she was like a record grinding down. She was supposed to have been in the kitchen, helping to prepare that day's lunch and dinner, but she simply could not. She seemed to be slipping off into a profound state of depression.

This was very troubling, especially with so many people around the house, including my daughter Marian, who was old enough to know that something was wrong. I decided to take her over to the Emory University Hospital. The chief of psychiatry admitted her to his unit for about three weeks. He then decided that she was too close to home not to be at home, so we moved her back to the house, and brought in a psychiatric nurse to care for her. She seemed to be losing touch with the day-to-day minutiae of reality. I asked her on one occasion if she wanted beef or pork for dinner, and an hour later she had yet to come to an answer. Another time I found her in the kitchen eating breakfast for dinner.

Feeling as if things were not getting better, I took her to be checked out at four different institutions, including Sheppard Pratt in Baltimore. She was seen by many psychiatrists, and they all reached more or less the same diagnosis—schizoaffective disorder.

I believe that my son, Charlie, may have sensed that his mother was not entirely stable, because he never really bonded with her. He bonded well with my parents, and during his mother's first major psychiatric episode he spent an entire summer with them on the family farm in Attapulgus, having a wonderful time doing all the things that little boys enjoy.

We had always had a cook and a maid, but with Celeste still in Baltimore, I realized that I would need someone to take care of Charlie, who was now in kindergarten at Glenn Memorial, like his older sister before him. "Son," I said, "You know I'm very busy at the hospital, but I'm going to go with you to class today and I want you to point out your favorite teacher."

So I went to his school and he pointed to one of the young women, and said, "That one, that one, Jody!"

I introduced myself to Miss Joanna Wood, and then said, "I'll just keep this real short. Charlie's very fond of you, and tells me that you're a wonderful teacher. Would you consider moving into our home and looking after Charlie? I'm quite busy at the hospital, always on call, as you know."

"Oh," she said, "I'd be pleased and honored."

We worked out the details, fixed a bedroom and bathroom for her, and she moved in. This worked out very well. We used to say that Jody was the housekeeper and the housemother; she quickly became a part of our family.

Jody enjoyed taking the children to one of my nearby clubs, and particularly enjoyed the Sunday buffets. She was a small woman who had some difficulty twisting her neck, so that she pulled out of a parking space without regard to passing traffic. This quickly resulted in three or four fender-benders. I received a nervous call from my insurance agent, who assured me that he didn't wish to intrude on my personal life, and that whatever I wanted to do I could do. But, he continued, I had apparently placed a car at the disposal of a Miss Joanna Wood, and that she had had a fender-bender a month since using the vehicle. I laughed at the implied suggestion that I had given a car to a girlfriend, explaining the situation. Thankfully we were able to teach Jody to handle her physical handicap without colliding with other cars as she backed blindly into the street.

About six months later Celeste returned to Atlanta. She had checked herself out of Shepherd Pratt. I found her in the driveway, and she said, simply, "They can't help me." We started some local care, and things were difficult. Jody had been invaluable to me and the children; but when Celeste returned to the household, friction quickly developed between the two of them. The job became very awkward for Jody, and we both agreed that she would seek other employment. The same happened with our cook, who regarded the kitchen as her domain. She felt that she was cooking for me the things that she knew I liked, and that she did not need Mrs. Hatcher's input. In a short time, she too tendered her resignation, declaring the working conditions unacceptable.

Despite this turnover in staff, we really were dependent on our domestic team during those years. Mary Birdsong and Jewel McClain were now too old to work a full schedule, so they divided the week into three days of service each. Hector was our yard man, a retiree from a prominent landscaping company in Atlanta. He was extremely good with planting and pruning, but as he grew older his strength did not permit the heavier yard work. So, we brought in Patrick to help Hector. After their first day working together I came home to ask Hector what he thought of Patrick. Very seriously he said, "Well now Doc, I can't tell you whether Patrick goin' to make it or not."

I understood and asked him to do the best he could and to be patient. Sure enough, Hector brought Patrick along to the point that he soon was no longer needed on full-time basis. He retired completely to live with a sister in a small town in the Atlanta suburbs. Twice a year, in the spring and fall, I invited Hector back to help us with the seasonal planting and pruning, and to give his advice to Patrick. Fortunately, we had a new cook by this time, and she was able to offer Hector a bedroom in her home during these visits. We did this for several seasons, until Hector called me from the bus station when he arrived in Atlanta, and while speaking to me, someone stole his suitcase. He called me back a few moments later, very sad and depressed. I tried to sympathize with him about the loss of the clothes that he and his sister had so neatly prepared for these visits, assuring him that I could get him other clothes within hours. But he said, "No sir, I just don't feel like it now. I'm hurt, and I'll just go back home."

Hector died a week later.

Years passed and Patrick, too, grew older. I had employed him for one day a week, and he worked the other days of the week for various families on the street. He was very straightforward in saying that he worked for me, and he just gave these other people extra days when he had them. I appreciated his loyalty, and looked after him until he, too, was too old to work. One by one the other families let him go, because of his inability to care for their lawns as they wished. When he could no longer work at all, I told him I would send a check every month, around the 15th, knowing that he would receive his Social Security check around the 1st of the month.

I did this for several years, calling from time to time to check on him and confirm that he was still alive. I was not certain that I would be informed about his death, since that would mean the checks would cease. Well, I misjudged his family—they called me when he was terminally ill, called me when he died, and refused to accept any more checks.

Willie Haynes was the final member of our extended family. He had worked since he was a lad for an older relative of ours in Atlanta, serving as her driver and butler. During those years he occasionally drove for me, and we enjoyed each other very much. His employer, Mrs. Edna Thornton, had spoken with me about Willie on a number of occasions. She had seen to it that he owned a nice, little cottage. She also gave him an automobile. She planned to leave him well fixed in her will, but she wanted him to continue to drive for me, and for me to continue to look after him.

I promised her that I would, and had the opportunity to honor that promise when Willie had a stroke, which confined him to bed. His wife, Johnny Mae, was a very small woman, and could not possibly have managed a paralytic the size of Willie. I was able to arrange for nurses and therapists to visit and provide care management for Willie in his home through my associations with Grady Memorial Hospital. Shortly after Willie's death, Johnny Mae had to be admitted to a nursing home; we called on her from time to time, and tried to make sure that she was looked after properly.

I mention these associates as extended family, knowing that many cannot comprehend the relationships that existed in the south during that era between the white family and the black caretakers and employees. Many years had passed since my childhood in Attapulgus, years that saw the achievements of the Civil Rights Movement and the growth of the south, and Atlanta in particular, into a modern, international city, but like other southern families, we proudly and dutifully cared for those who worked in our homes, just as our parents had. As alien, backward, and perhaps even patriarchal this may seem to a northeasterner or a Californian, consider the typical relationship between well-to-do families in those regions and their often recently immigrated housekeepers, and ask yourself who is better off.

In the South relationships with your staff are more personal, but at the same time we were slow to give up on the notion of supporting the people on the bottom so long as they 'stayed in their place.' It is a delicate balance, but as I said before, when comparing this difference between the North and South, declaring which arrangement is better is not as clear a decision as many would believe.

I grew up with the same feeling of responsibility for these people as my father had shown as an example to me. The children and I were close to every one of the members of this extended family. They all considered themselves, and were treated as extended family. As such, when Willie grew too old to remain my driver, a young man by the name of Richard Bonner came to me and said, "I want Willie's job when Willie can no longer drive for you."

I liked Richard, and gave him the opportunity to drive me on a number of occasions. I never needed, or felt I could afford a full-time chauffeur, but by allowing people such as Richard to remain employed elsewhere, and to have them work for me as needed, I felt fortunate to have the best of both worlds. Soon after I retired, Richard left The Emory Clinic to start a business -- "The Handyman Can" -- and took jobs as they became available. I give him work whenever possible, and he still drives for me if his schedule will permit. I can count on Richard to be available if and when my increasing age makes more personal care necessary.

We have similar relationships with our staff in Attapulgus. Shortly after my father died, Mrs. Annie Mae Bouie arrived at the house and indicated that she would like to work for me.

Annie Mae's parents, Catherine and Sylvester Russell, and Annie Mae herself had known me during my childhood. For a time, her father had been employed by my father on the farm. Annie Mae recalled many kindnesses shown to her and her mother by my parents. Perhaps Annie Mae was thinking of those times when she expressed the desire to work for us.

Annie Mae maintains the South Georgia home in our absence, and frequently provides extra help when we have guests. She is a delightful person, and we frequently say what a wonderful world it would be if there were more Annie Maes. She has now taken care of us for over twenty years, and we look forward to having her in our extended family for many years to come.

•◆•

One day, in those years following her first episode, Celeste made an abortive suicide attempt. She took some pills and came down and announced, with a sort of gleam in her eye that she had just swallowed the pills. She knew what would happen next, that I would take care of her and see that she came to no harm. I put her in the car and sped over to Emory Hospital. Her stomach was pumped out quite thoroughly. She recovered promptly, but we kept her under observation in the ICU. While she was in the ICU, I was upstairs performing the state of Georgia's first coronary bypass.

After this, the chief of psychiatry at Emory decided that it was time to commit her to a psychiatric hospital. I did not like the idea of this at all. We were running low on options, but I was determined to pursue every treatment available before I committed her to a hospital for the rest of her life. At this time there were not many of today's pharmacological treatments yet available; instead we turned to electroconvulsive therapy. I took her to see Drs. Cleckley and Thigpen in Augusta. She underwent treatment for two days. I then received a phone call. It was Celeste, and she wanted to know if I would like for her to join me for the Masters Golf Tournament that weekend. The shock therapy had worked. It was as if it had kicked the needle back into the groove.

Several years passed after this without incident. In 1976, around the time I was taking a major step forward at The Emory Clinic, Celeste took a manic turn. She became aggressive, often out-of-line, and she was generally unmanageable. Dr. Thigpin prescribed lithium, but she refused to take it and lose her manic high. Up until then, things had been quite difficult for the children, but we had managed to work them out. This was the turning point. In her manic state, she came to the conclusion that she should have never married or had children. She grew convinced that by getting married and having children, she had forsaken a life of great accomplishments. She asked me for a divorce, and offered me custody of the children.

Charlie, III, was 14 by this time, and so he, like his older sister, under Georgia Law, could choose which parent would have custody. I was pleased to have the children continue to live with me.

As if things could not get any worse, just about the time Celeste left the house for the last time, she had a breast biopsy taken, and it came back positive. I made sure that she had good doctors tending to her care, and that she never saw a bill for her treatment, which unfortunately was unsuccessful. She did fine for over a decade, but eventually there was a reoccurrence of the cancer and this time she succumbed to the disease.

When we got the divorce it was not acrimonious; it was necessitated by her condition. We had one lawyer, and she paid half of his bill and I paid the other half. She went on her way, but before she left, I told her to work out a budget, which I would pay. I approved it and added a little to it, because

I believed it would be unfair to her for the children to receive everything from me. We were divorced in 1978, and at the time I truly believed that I would never remarry.

I was the first person in my family to get a divorce, so naturally I worried a bit about what my mother and father were going to say. I called my mother and she said, "Charles, we can't believe that you stuck it out this long. Now what can we do to help you"!

•◆•

When Celeste had her first nervous breakdown in 1969, her mother had lamented the negative effects that this would have on my career. I assured her that this would not necessarily be so. I had structured my career on my own, and while it would have been nice to have had a marital partner involved, I felt I could stand alone if need be. I mentioned the excellent staff I had available at home, and most of the time we had a tolerable degree of friction between family and staff.

When in the late 70's her disease took the direction of mania, it was she who announced her desire for a divorce. Her parents called on me, and urged me to agree to the divorce, stating that they knew that I would not have initiated such action, but since she wanted a divorce, this was the best course of action for me. During those trying years I became the director of The Emory Clinic, and I had been divorced for several years when I was selected as the vice president for health affairs and director of the Robert W. Woodruff Health Sciences Center.

Years later, when I met and married Phyllis, I came to know how much a wonderful wife can mean to her husband and his career, and we have often joked about what we could have accomplished if we had been working together all these years as a team. Phyllis has a Bachelor's and Master's Degree in Interior Design, and has made every effort to see that we have a beautiful home and a loyal staff. She has become actively involved with the personnel of the health sciences center, and is universally admired by all of my associates.

•◆•

Marian was very close to her mother during these years, and naturally her mother's instability caused her difficulties. I knew that I had to be supportive of her mother, whenever circumstances permitted; otherwise her situation would have been untenable. By the same token, I knew that

I was the only person Marian could appeal to when her mother made an irrational or illogical decision. I tried to be as stable and reliable as possible, to offset her mother's dramatic mood shifts. As Marian became a teenager, I arranged for Dr. Dorothy Yeager-Lee, an adolescent psychiatrist at The Emory Clinic, to be her female adviser and confidante. Dorothy performed this role beautifully. It was very comforting to know that she was available to Marian.

Marian graduated from Westminster and determined that she would like to attend an all-girls school. She selected Randolph-Macon Woman's College, in Lynchburg, Virginia. She had a very enjoyable college experience in Virginia. She spent a couple of months at home after graduation. We both felt she should have her own place, so I purchased a two-bedroom condominium close to Emory's campus for her. Marian was very happy during this time, leading an active social life.

She then met her husband-to-be, George Thorpe, Jr., whose father and mother were friends of mine. They have been happily married for over twenty years now, and live in Washington, Georgia, where they are very involved in community activities, and travel extensively. Marian has developed into a lovely, witty, sensitive young lady. We have grown closer over the years.

• ◆ •

Charlie followed the same pattern of schooling as Marian, transferring in his instance from Fernbank to Westminster in the 7th grade. I must say I was extremely fortunate with both children, never receiving a call from a teacher about misconduct or disappointing performance. They were both very healthy kids who rarely, if ever, missed a day of school, or had to be taken to a physician. I have been extremely proud of my children all of their lives, and have always loved them dearly.

Charles, Marian and Dad on vacation at the Cloister

During those years in which I was largely responsible for the children's Christmas presents and plans, I developed a system that limited the gifts that they were to receive, but guaranteed that they would receive the items they most wanted. Starting in early December, I asked each child to prepare a list of five presents, and state them in order of preference in case Santa Claus could not afford or find every item. Over the next several days there was a great deal of fun and activity relating to changing the priorities of these items. The final list had to be completed by December 15th and forwarded to Santa Claus, or to me as his surrogate. I would take the list and share it with my secretary, Mrs. Alice Scott, who was quite helpful in locating the items requested. The limit of five presents was selected to avoid personal selfishness in requesting an excessive number of items, and at the same time to let Santa Claus show generosity in spite of the fact that he had so many children on his list. In almost every instance, we were successful in getting the children the items that they strongly desired, but within the limits which I felt were appropriate.

I followed a similar system with birthday presents. Although several presents might be forthcoming, the basic present for each child, and particularly so as they grew older, was to expect $10 dollars for each year of age on their birthday. In time, this amount would become significant; i.e., as they have now entered their forties. With each monetary gift, the children are encouraged to buy something they really want, and this can be supplemented by smaller gifts to which I am attracted during the year.

In the summers, I traditionally took the family to Sea Island, Georgia, where I rented a house in the Cloister Complex for the month of August. A new house staff always came to work at The Emory Clinic on the first of July, and I felt that I should be in Atlanta to help settle them in the service, before taking off on vacation. We frequently remained at the beach until after Labor Day, and were usually joined for a week or so by my parents.

Charles, III learns to skeet shoot

Marian and Charles became of age, and learned many of their social skills as guests of the Cloister. Their lessons included swimming and diving, dancing, skeet shooting, golf, and being dropped off for dinner with the counselors who saw to their table manners, eating habits, and social behavior. I considered myself very fortunate to provide them with this wholesome and traditional environment.

Both Marian and Charlie accompanied me to various medical meetings – alone or together. Marian and I were at such a meeting in California when our home in Atlanta was burglarized. Fortunately, all furnishings and sporting items had been photographed, officially appraised and insured, but we lost many items of sentimental value. On another occasion, Dr. Willis Hurst, Chairman of the Department of Medicine, organized a trip to Athens and the Greek Isles to honor several partners and colleagues on their retirement. This trip was organized as a post-graduate teaching course in cardiology for about 100 doctors. Charles, III greatly enjoyed this experience with our medical group.

As Charlie approached graduation at Westminster his advisor called to ask me to stay out of his application process, to let him handle it on his own. I did, and after he considered a number of schools on his own, Charlie came to me and said that he had narrowed his choices down to Duke, the University of Virginia, and Princeton. I was single at that time, and Charlie and I were very close, Marian having been away for a full four years. Emory University had offered Charlie an early admission acceptance, and as a child of a full-time faculty member, he would be entitled to a full scholarship. Nevertheless, I felt that he should be separated from me during those formative years. So, I discouraged him from remaining at home or living nearby to attend Emory. He ultimately announced that he had decided to attend Duke, as he could drive home on the weekends to see me, whereas at Virginia or Princeton he could only fly down for short visits. I was secretly pleased by his decision, and ultimately gratified that he enjoyed Duke and performed well there.

Charlie majored in Political Science and Economics, participated as a member of the wrestling team—as he had at Westminster—and became President of the Phi Delta Theta fraternity. Willie and I drove him up to Duke, and four years later we returned to bring him home.

During his final spring at Duke, his fraternity planned a trip to the Caribbean, and naturally Charlie wanted to go. I told him that I thought he should spend that spring break interviewing for jobs. Doing so would put him a step ahead of the pack come graduation. I was able to schedule interviews for him with the Coca-Cola Company, the Genuine Parts Company, and two of our leading banks, First Atlanta and the Trust Company of Georgia. Charlie had worked for two summers with the President of First Atlanta; they were quite pleased that he decided to continue that association.

The banking industry has undergone much upheaval during Charlie's career. After going through several buyouts and mergers, he finally took a position with a smaller community bank, where he has been extremely happy and productive.

At Duke he had courted a young lady, Leslie Williges, and after graduation she moved to Atlanta to begin a career with Invesco. Charlie and Leslie were married in 1989, and the happy marriage has produced three lovely children, Charles, IV, Caroline, and Catherine. We remain extremely close, and I am very proud of him; and I think he sincerely appreciates having me as his father.

Institutional Growth

IN THIS ERA, THE CORONARY bypass program was the real focus of our activities. We had been operating on patients who needed valves and pacemakers, and the children with congenital heart disease, but of the pool of patients who needed heart surgery, the vast majority of them suffered from coronary artery disease. We had made our own sporadic little attempts to revascularize the heart, but with indirect techniques—we had tried to abraid the heart to promote adhesions between the myocardium and the pericardium. At the Cleveland Clinic, Dr. René Favaloro, Dr. Don Effler, and others began to make significant advances. Dr. Mason Sones was the first to use coronary angiograms—putting a catheter in the coronary artery, injecting dye, and taking tiny pictures of the coronary circulation. If there were a blockage they would then use a saphenous vein or internal mammary artery to bypass the blockage. They did this for the first time in 1967, and we started three years later, while I was still the acting chief of the section.

Dr. Craver and Dr. Jones performed a large number of these bypass procedures. Both of them quickly came into their own, as I expected they would. In fact, during one period, Dr. Jones performed cardiac surgery on 350 consecutive patients without a single death. This was a great accomplishment and I had a clock engraved for him to memorialize the streak. Now these 350 cases were not just coronary bypasses—I think a number of our colleagues could have done that—the streak included valve replacements, aneurysms and everything else we were doing at the time.

I would say that from 1971 to 1976, we grew the service into one of the ten largest in the country. We rapidly grew our bypass program and we continued to improve the techniques we utilized in our valve replacement series. And it was not just quantity—the quality of our results remained excellent. We were able to accomplish this for a number of reasons, but I think the chief factor in our growth was the success of my recruitment of young surgeons. I wanted the doctors who joined me to be my partners, not just my assistants. This might sound like common sense, but as I have already said, cardiac surgery was at the forefront of medicine in this era, and thus the leaders in the field became quite prominent. Egos often played a role in hiring decisions.

About the time I took over the residency program, I realized that when a service is lacking in manpower, it can be quite tempting to appoint fellows. A lot of people did just that, recruiting doctors from the Middle East, Pakistan, India, and other foreign countries. We were authorized to train three cardiac surgeons per year—I think there were perhaps three or four other programs allotted three residency positions each year based on their patient volume and variety of material. Nevertheless, we still had trouble getting all of the work coming to us done in a timely fashion. Everyone was clamoring for us to recruit fellows, but I said, "No, let's not train fellows, because they'll end up in the job market, instead of going back home, and we don't need to put our stamp of approval on somebody who just came through and worked for us for a year." I also did not want to contribute to a "brain drain" of less developed countries.

Instead I proposed that we hire some physician's assistants, a new category of medical worker, pioneered at Duke by Dr. Eugene Stead. Emory's physician's assistant program was started by Dr. Willis Hurst a few years later. The physician's assistant would work for us, but they wouldn't become cardiac surgeons. That approach really tested you. If you appoint a fellow, his salary is taken care of by the hospital's house staff program, but if you hire a physician's assistant, you've got to pay him, or her, out of your office income. I felt like we put our money where our mouths were by hiring P.A.'s. I believe we were the first cardiac surgery service in the country to do this. I delivered a paper on our use of P.A.'s in cardiac surgery at a meeting of the Society of Thoracic Surgeons. P.A.'s were used in this era mostly by general practitioners, because they could help G.P.'s stretch the number of patients whom they could see on a given day. I said, "This is the exact opposite of how it ought to be. If you're going to have someone who's not a doctor, he or she needs to be with a specialty group, doing repetitious work over and over again."

Working for a general practitioner, in an office, is probably the most demanding job you could put on a P.A.. He or she has all this responsibility, seeing patients with all sorts of different diseases and maladies. I proposed that moving P.A.'s into a specialty, in the way I had on our service, made much more sense. The paper was well received, though it cost me the two

P.A.'s I had at the time. Someone who heard the speech came through Atlanta soon after and offered both of them twice what I was paying them. I quickly recruited some replacements, and since then, we've always had a large program.

At the time, Georgia state law dictated that no doctor could have more than two P.A.'s. Under the law, the doctor and the P.A. were professionally married. The P.A. works in union with a particular licensed doctor with a particular job description. Not every one of our surgeons operated every day, but we wanted the extra P.A.'s to help out in the operating room with whoever was in surgery that day. I decided to go see Mr. Arthur Bolton, Georgia's long-serving Attorney General.

"Now be very careful," he said, "I want to approve what you're trying to do, but we have to be very careful of the questions you ask me, because almost everything is going to be *no* unless we've worded it perfectly."

So we spent all afternoon working through scenarios, such as: *If one P.A. is employed by someone of the same specialty who is a legal partner of the doctor to whom he is assigned and his protocol is exactly the same… would it be possible for him to assist surgery for the partner?*

After fighting through if clauses and sub-clauses, and so on, we finally arrived at a suitably worded question, to which he could provide me with an answer *yes*. This was a rather important precedent, and now it's quite common at Emory to have P.A's working for a particular group, such as general surgery, or neurosurgery, or, of course, cardiothoracic surgery. Dr. Willis Hurst, Professor and Chairman of the Department of Medicine at Emory University established a P.A. training program shortly thereafter. He originally ran it out of his department office. As it succeeded, Dean Richardson took it over as part of the Allied Health Division of the Medical School. This program is now ranked in the top five in the nation. With the establishment of this program, we were eventually able to hire P.A.'s who had come through our own program. With the decision in hand, we built up one of the finest teams of P.A.'s you could ever hope to employ.

I wanted the very best people available to operate our heart-lung machines. A degree in the field is similar to one in physiology. Ohio State ran the country's first program in profusion technology, and I recruited one of their graduates to head up our pump team. We recruited more and more people, and at one time I think every member of the team had graduated from Ohio State's program. Our team was so good that it attracted the attention of the other local hospitals. People were always trying to hire away our profusionists, but there is one episode that I can remember more so than the rest. Georgia Baptist Hospital had been trying to lure several of our profusionists, and they seemed rather determined, so I called in the director of the team, and asked him, "Who is the weakest of the ten that you have on your team?"

"No, no, no," he said, "we don't think any of them are weak."

"I know that," I said, "but, if push comes to shove, which one would be your weakest."

So he gave me a name.

"OK," I said, "the next time you give raises be sure he gets the smallest increase!"

The news of the raises quickly got back to the profusionist in question and sure enough, he bolted for Georgia Baptist Hospital. I knew that Georgia Baptist Hospital was not going to stop their recruiting efforts, so I figured the best I could do was pass on to them the individual I preferred to lose.

So, we recruited an excellent team of doctors, built up a core of accomplished technicians and skilled assistants, and grew our service into one of the nation's largest. I realized that we were doing so much clinical work that Ellis, Joe, and the rest of us might be criticized for not analyzing and publishing the results of the work we were doing. It appeared to some people that we might be taking on cases just for the money. I thought that this criticism was unfair, that we were doing important work, performing surgery that had not been done before in Georgia. If we were a bit busy, there could have been far worse problems. Nevertheless, I decided to address this possible complaint—I took some of the money earned by the service and had a computerized database set up. This way, every piece of information, for each patient, would be recorded in a single place. It became very easy to publish papers, because all of the necessary data was now in an easily accessible, digital form.

Today, this seems like a no-brainer, but that was hardly the case back in the 1970s. Up until this point, all of our records had been written out longhand, and stored in filing cabinets. We were actually the first section at Emory to setup a computerized database. Everyone was trained to use the software and the pump technicians would have the forms filled out within an hour of leaving the operating room. We hired a statistician to help us analyze our data and we brought on a manuscript typist to further speed up publications. Basically, I wanted to do whatever I could to make it as easy as possible to publish papers, as the research and casework were already being done.

Everyone in the division published scientific papers, all of which appeared in peer-reviewed journals. As an example, over the course of my career, I personally published nearly 200 papers. My professional reputation and the division's reputation grew in stature during this time.

As a result, I was appointed to the American Board of Surgery in 1980. I served on the board for the next seven years. During my tenure, we faced the issue of recertification. I did not favor a dreaded and potentially punitive reexamination, but spoke strongly for making the recertification process a positive experience, requiring that all candidates demonstrate proficiency in the new knowledge which had come to be accepted in our specialty since original certification. Another major issue for the Board during my membership was financial. Only a small number of residents complete their training in cardiovascular surgery each year. Yet you wish to make the examination fair and up to date. Trainees about to enter practice could only pay a modest amount for their examination, not an amount that would cover the administrative cost of the Board and the cost of examination development and the certification process. At that time I served on the Finance Committee of the Board, as did Dr. Frank C. Spencer of New York. Frank and I dictated a letter which we sent to all previous diplomats of the Board explaining the situation and asking for their assistance. The response was quite gratifying and the Board received over a million dollars in gifts. These monies permitted the establishment of an endowment fund which could supplement the examination fees and put the Board in a stable financial position for the future.

•◆•

Mr. Carlyle Fraser was a prominent Atlanta businessman, who presided over the Genuine Parts Company for over two decades, dying prematurely in 1961, after suffering a heart attack.

One morning in the early 1970s, Mr. Fraser's son, Jack, walked down the driveway to get the mail. He did not return. His family looked out the window some time later, and they saw him unconscious in the driveway. They called an ambulance and he was rushed to Piedmont Hospital. The staff at Piedmont explained that they did not have the capability to take care of him. He was brought over to Emory, where I was busy at work, in the operating room. Dr. Logue came in and told me that Jack Fraser was in the hospital. He asked me how soon it would be until I finished. I told him that I would be closing my patient in a few minutes.

I joined Dr. Logue at Jack Fraser's bedside. I agreed that he had suffered a massive pulmonary embolism. He was in shock, and his blood pressure was very low. He was hanging by a thread. Mr. Wilton D. Looney, the successor of Carlyle Fraser at Genuine Parts, and a friend of the Fraser family, stood with the family. I turned to Mr. Looney and said, if they can just keep him alive until I can get him to the operating room, then I'll take care of him. He was impressed by my courageous attitude, as he would tell me later.

We had Jack positioned upright, and we were giving him oxygen. I infiltrated his groin with enough Novocain so that he would not feel any pain. I put him on bypass, under local, and then we opened up the chest. We removed a perfect cast of the pulmonary vascular bed. We pulled out the major clot and the clots from all of the little branches. We then closed the chest and groin. He recovered completely. This impressed Wilton and the Fraser family very much. They had been devoted to Crawford Long Hospital for some time and now they were offering to bring me down to Crawford Long, in order to establish a cardiac surgery unit there. They would provide the endowment, but I would be in charge, and everything would be private. This would have resulted in considerably increased personal income to me, and the freedom to work outside the bounds of Emory University.

After consideration, I declined this most generous offer. I told them that I didn't think that this was the way to go. If they wanted something that would stand the test of time, it needed to be a part of Emory University and a part of Emory-Crawford Long Hospital. The center they had proposed might be outstanding only as long as I lived, and then we wouldn't know what might happen. If the center were established as a part of the University there would be other excellent people waiting in line when I retired.

They were very happy with my proposal and we opened the Carlyle Fraser Heart Center in 1975. Since then, Mr. and Mrs. Looney and the Fraser family have raised over $20 Million dollars for the Center. This unit is certainly the premier service at the Emory-Crawford Long Hospital, and indeed it is the hospital's calling card. The Fraser Heart Center is still located in Midtown, in the new Medical Office Tower, which opened in 2002.

•◆•

The Hospital, which was to become Emory University Hospital Midtown, began as the Davis-Fischer Sanitarium at 323 Crew Street in Atlanta in 1909. The hospital was an immediate success and rapid expansion demanded a new and larger facility which was constructed on Linden Avenue in 1910-1911. In 1931 the hospital was renamed Crawford W. Long Memorial Hospital to honor Dr. Crawford Williamson Long (1815 -1878), a physician from Jefferson, Georgia who is credited with the discovery of ether anesthesia and the initial application of this technique to surgical patients. Others, including Dr. W. T. Morton, a Boston dentist, claimed this discovery, and it was some years before Dr. Crawford Long was finally given credit for the discovery, and in 1926 his statue was placed in the Hall of Fame in Washington, D. C. Following the death of Dr. Davis, Dr. Fischer continued to direct Crawford W. Long Memorial Hospital which came to include an independent medical unit within the hospital, which was known as the Jesse Parker Williams Hospital. Discussions began with Emory University in 1938, culminating in the January 21, 1940 transfer of the property to Emory University. In April of 1953, Dr. Wadley Raoul Glenn became the director of the hospital and served for many years as hospital CEO until his death from cancer in 1985. In time, the relationship to Emory University was recognized in the official name of the Hospital, i.e., Crawford W. Long Memorial Hospital of Emory University. The Emory University Trustees created the Woodruff Medical Center in 1966, of which Crawford W. Long Memorial Hospital of Emory University became a component. In 1985, Emory trustees created The Robert W. Woodruff Health Sciences Center as a successor to the Woodruff Medical Center in order to recognize the unique personal contributions of Mr. Robert W. Woodruff, and to more appropriately recognize the contributions of the school of dentistry, the school of nursing, and other health professions. Presently the institution is officially named Emory University Hospital Midtown, and has expanded its campus and facilities to serve an enhanced role within the health sciences center.

Sir Lancelot

THE CARDIAC PROGRAM WAS VERY successful during the mid-70s—we were seeing more and more patients each year, and I was adding one or two young cardiovascular surgeons to the team every year—and this was not lost on the other doctors at The Emory Clinic. They also saw that I had structured the section so that everybody profited equally within a year or two of joining the group. Perhaps I or some of the other longest serving doctors in the section earned five percent more than the rest, but we were all roughly within a few dollars of each other. It also spread around the clinic that everyone in the section was quite prosperous.

Dr. Robert Brown had founded The Emory Clinic, along with Dr. Elliot Scarborough. Dr. Hugh Wood, Dean of Emory School of Medicine, was the first director of the clinic. Dr. Scarborough had become the CEO and Director, while Dr. Brown had served as the Associate Director. When Dr. Scarborough died of pancreatic cancer, Dr. Brown stepped up to the plate, as everyone expected he would. Dr. Brown's assumption of control was a smooth one—the man was a gentleman in every sense of the word, exceedingly polite and genteel, and I never knew him to raise his voice in any discussion or debate. If you asked me to name a finer person at Emory, I could not. It is possible that he was a bit too nice to be entirely effective in this administrative position. Dr. Brown shied away from controversy, and I believe that certain elements of Emory University and The health sciences center took advantage of this fine gentleman to strengthen their position vis-à-vis The Emory Clinic.

Dr. Robert Brown

Dr. Brown served for some ten years as the Director of The Emory Clinic. As he approached the then mandatory retirement age of 68, the clinic partnership prepared to select his successor. This would be the first time in the clinic's two decade history that the partners would be free to choose a successor. Our Administrative Committee met and we decided to form a Search Committee, which would be led by Dr. Dorothy Brinsfield, from the Department of Pediatrics. Dr. Brinsfield would go on to serve as an effective Associate Dean of the School of Medicine. Members from The Emory Clinic's major sections joined Dr. Brinsfield on the committee.

The Committee reached a decision, and they dispatched Dr. Brinsfield to come see me. I was somewhat surprised and certainly flattered when she stated that there were a large number of doctors who would like for me to become the clinic's director. I was a bit taken aback by this situation, since my surgical practice was extremely busy, as well as extremely profitable for the clinic.

"Well look," I said, "I'm probably the busiest surgeon we have, and I contribute a significant amount of billings. I don't think it would be a wise thing to take me out of the lineup."

She quickly assured me that I would be able to remain the chief of cardiothoracic surgery and that I would be able to see as many patients as I deemed fit. I would be asked to provide leadership, and improve our finances; toward that end I could hire as many assistants and business managers as I needed. She stated that she, as well as many of the other doctors, hoped that I could do for the other sections what I had done for my own. Again, I was flattered, and after some reflection, I made a suggestion.

"Let me see how much time it will take. I'll start helping Dr. Brown with the work and over the next several weeks I can see what it will be like."

Dr. Brinsfield agreed that this was a wise course of action. I found that I enjoyed this period of work with Dr. Brown. The duties were pleasant, and not unduly time consuming. When Dr. Brown became stressed about a particularly difficult situation, I would join him and lend a hand with problem resolution or personality readjustment as needed. I also realized how quickly I would be able to make some of the changes and reforms that I and others had sought in how the clinic was administered.

I hoped to become a forceful and articulate voice for the clinic within the greater university. I tested the waters, to see if others were keen to this notion. I said to some of my colleagues, "I'm not as much a gentleman as Dr. Brown."

And to this, the common response was something along the lines of, 'If he were any more of a gentleman, we might be flat broke.'

With everyone seeming to want someone who would be a bit more forceful, I declared to Dr. Brinsfield and her committee my willingness to take on the directorship of the clinic. The committee had graciously declined to interview, or consider any other candidates during this trial period of sorts; they allowed me the time I needed to make my personal decision. I indicated my willingness to serve, and my nomination was put to the partnership for a vote at the next quarterly meeting. There were no other candidates—the vote was for Dr. Hatcher, *Yes* or *No*. I was especially proud when the ballots were unanimously marked *Yes*. I remember a senior member of the clinic passing me a note which stated simply – apparently you can fool all of the people, all of the time!

I assumed the chief executive responsibility in 1976, feeling that I had a strong mandate to reform clinic operations. I felt fortunate that there had been no controversy, and no blocks of negative opinion among my peers. I will always remember those early years as director of The Emory Clinic as being the most pleasant and productive of my entire academic career.

•◆•

I did not wish to move from my office in cardiothoracic surgery; I had come up through the ranks, and I felt that a large administrative office might strain my relationships with the other partners. So I made the director's office available to Mr. Barney Chisholm, the business manager of the clinic, and I kept my office in the section of cardiothoracic surgery. We quickly went to work and made some changes in clinic operations.

In my first year on the job, we doubled the income at the clinic, and within a decade we had quadrupled billings. The clinic was soon providing millions of dollars to the medical school each year, which greatly helped its financial situation. It was not that we were so much smarter, rather we just got things organized and applied some common sense business principles. In the past, if you wanted to pay your bill when you had just been seen as a patient, you would be told, 'Oh, no, you'll ultimately get a bill from the clinic.' In the face of this I said, "I'm inherently suspicious of any business that can't accept money when people want to pay for services they've received." If someone wanted to pay, I said that we needed to make sure they could pay. Within a short time we were accepting cash, checks and credit cards.

•◆•

Surviving Founding Partners –
Photograph taken late 1970s-Early 1980s
Dr. Bernard Hallman, Dr. Sam Wilkins, Dr. Bruce Logue,
Dr. Charles Hugheley, Dr. Willis Hurst, Dr. Robert Brown,
Dr. Spalding Schroder

When the clinic was established in 1953, it was decided that the director would receive compensation for his administrative duties equal to 125% of the average income of the full partners. The business manager, then Mr. Chisholm, would receive 75% of the average income of the full partners. Since I had a very productive practice in cardiac surgery, and had no intention of significantly reducing this practice over the next several years, I asked Mr. Chisholm to credit the section of cardiothoracic surgery $100,000 dollars to compensate for the time I spent in clinic administration, knowing that I would have easily billed that amount in the hours I now spent in my role as clinic director. This financial plan also allowed me some additional resources with which I could compensate Mr. Chisholm and other key members of the clinic business office.

In one of my earlier discussions with Mr. Chisholm, I recall asking what we did with our cash flow as it passed through the clinic.

"We have a checking account at the C & S Bank," he replied.

"I know that we have a checking account, but what are we *doing* with the money as it passes through the system?"

"Well," he replied, somewhat confused, "we put the money in the checking account at the C & S Bank."

I realized that there was no short term investment program for the clinic cash flow, so I did not pursue the conversation further. But, over the next year, I made sure that the clinic became very aggressive in the short term investment of its funds. For example, some significant income could be produced by investing these monies during the extra day or two they were not needed. By the end of my first year on the job, we had made enough money just from cash flow management to cover a large percentage of the business office's administrative costs, as well as some of the clinic's other administrative costs. This left more profit for the clinic partners, something everyone appreciated. One of the nicest compliments I ever received was from the wife of a partner, who when asked when I became head of the clinic, replied, "I can tell you the exact day, I only have to look at my husband's checkbook!"

There was one investment proposal that I would have liked to implement, but never had the chance to. The idea first occurred to me a few years before I became director. As the Bretton Woods system collapsed and Nixon began withdrawing us from the Gold Standard, I argued that we should use the clinic's reserves to purchase gold. The Nixon Shock in August of 1971, coupled with The Smithsonian Agreement, resulted in gold's transformation into a floating asset. From 1970 to 1971, gold climbed from a hair under $35 dollars an ounce to $43.50 dollars. I approached Mr. Chisholm and suggested that we invest all of the clinic's reserves in gold.

"Oh no no no, Dr. Hatcher," he said. "We can't take that risk."

"What do you mean risk? I guarantee you gold is going to go up as Nixon takes us off the standard."

"I know, but we might be swindled. How do we know that it's real gold? How do we know that it weighs the amount they say it does? Where are we going to keep it?"

Well I invested some of my personal funds in gold. By the end of 1972, gold had already reached $64 dollars an ounce. And then it really started to move—by 1980, the price of gold had climbed to over $675 dollars an ounce. I did well for myself, but if he had let me invest the clinic's far more substantial reserves, I would have made every single doctor at the clinic quite rich.

Another major reform I implemented was a new productivity driven compensation system. For the younger and more aggressive partners, this was very exciting. If you billed a certain amount of money, you were going to make a certain amount of money, after overhead and some adjustments. The key was that there was nothing arbitrary about it. Total billings were adjusted to collections using the collection percentage of each particular Section.

If someone came to me and said they didn't think they were making enough, I would say, well let's look into this right away. I would call the business office and have them bring me a sheet, which would have a list of this doctor's billings, collections, indirect expenses, and direct expenses.

The indirect expenses were allocated expenses of clinic activities and payments to the dean of the School of Medicine. Direct expenses would be travel, books, dues to societies, and equipment. Everything on this second list would have been requested by and personally signed for by the individual partner. Collections minus these two sets of expenses gave us a target for proper compensation. If this number was not very close to what the partner had produced, then the situation had to be corrected. Usually the sheets were correct. Often the doctors had forgotten to account for money put away into retirement accounts, or failed to realize that expenses billed to the clinic had to be paid for by someone. When this occurred, I said, 'And just *who* is this clinic that you thought would pay for this?' Sometimes the doctor was simply ahead of our collections, questioning why charges he had sent in last week had not shown up yet, failing to understand that they would take a couple of months to work through the system.

There were cases where the doctor was correct. At the outset of each year we had to estimate what people would produce. If a particular doctor did more than anticipated, the numbers would be thrown off. We adjusted these numbers quarterly, but if a doctor came in wondering, I always offered to check the sheets. If there was an error, I would say, for example, 'Well you're right, you've produced $10,000 more dollars this quarter than I'd anticipated, congratulations!' I would turn to the business manager and say, 'Would you cut this man a check for $10,000 dollars,' which I would then sign and hand to him. He would leave my office with everything settled. People liked this kind of management—there was nothing arbitrary and it was very predictable. It also encouraged them to work just as hard as they wanted to work.

During that time, compensation for the partners of The Emory Clinic consisted of three elements—the monthly drawing accounts, sectional quarterly profits, and the annual general fund of the clinic. The drawing accounts were analogous to monthly salary, based upon our projections. Every quarter the partners received money in what we called a *60/40* arrangement: Sixty percent went into a general clinic fund to be distributed equally among all of the partners at the end of the year, while forty percent of the section's profits remained in the section to be distributed among the partners of that section. In December all monies available to the clinic were paid out, and we started over with a zero balance. Based upon the previous year, adjustments to the drawing accounts were made in January. Throughout the year, we made quarterly adjustments, upward if productivity exceeded our projections, or downward if productivity dropped. Typically, when a partner suffered a decrease in productivity, only a short meeting was required.

"If you're spending your time and effort as you wish, that's perfectly satisfactory. We can do one of two things. You can see more patients at the clinic and increase your billings, or I can adjust your drawing accounts down to the lowered expectations."

Almost no one ever accepted the latter course of action; most offered to improve their billings and promptly did so. As we monitored the clinic's finances quarterly, no one was allowed to end up in a deficit situation for the entire year. There were of course cases in which a chairman or section head felt that a particular individual was overemphasizing clinical work, at the expense of teaching and research. When a chairman asked that such an individual receive less compensation from the clinic I would point out that a faculty member neglecting other duties in favor of clinical practice was their responsibility. It was not my responsibility to *inadequately* compensate someone for work they had actually done.

The partnership agreement at the time called upon each doctor at the clinic to contribute twenty percent of his or her time to the School of Medicine and its departments. I came to accept a financial contribution in lieu of a temporal contribution for those individuals who concerned themselves almost entirely with clinical practice. I gave approval for a chairman to shift one day's productivity to the department for teaching and research. This system permitted us to take full advantage of our excellent and active clinicians, and at the same time provided adequate support for the school's teaching and research efforts. Once everyone understood this system, my relationships with the partners became almost entirely pleasant. I helped them look into the system whenever they doubted whether the clinic was compensating them properly, but I also made sure that they understood that no one took arbitrary actions, which could affect their income. If they had large billings and collection, they would receive a large income. The converse was also true—but the playing field was entirely level.

• ◆ •

I have always felt strongly about several principles of management. First, if you cannot answer "yes" to a request, the second most desirable answer is a quick and emphatic "no." Do not offer to think about a problem. Do not agree to consider it again at a later date. Do not offer any type of encouragement which makes it more difficult to return to a final and emphatic "no." Second, take as long as you need to consider a problem, but when you make a decision, do not change the decision in the face of objection or criticism. Almost every time a major decision is made, someone in the organization will object. If a decision is reversed in the face of such loud objection, future decisions will also be questioned, and no decisions can be made without this undesirable process. Once I made a decision, it was not subject to change. I would inform the objecting party of the fact that I did not have time to plow the same field twice. I would then offer to consider possible assistance to them in an unrelated manner. In time, the partners of The Emory Clinic accepted my management style, and indeed related well to definite decisions promptly stated but not subject to change.

Another reform I made was to the way the doctors at the clinic saved for retirement. Each of the doctors had been left to manage his or her retirement account on their own, and there was a huge disparity between what some people were doing. Early along, I grew increasingly worried that the poor business skills of some of the doctors were eventually going to bring embarrassment upon the clinic. It was incredible how badly some of my colleagues were being taken advantage of in those days. I feared that when some of them retired, they were going to be selling pencils on the street corner.

I developed the idea that we should have managed accounts. From then on we usually offered five different investment firms, which would all invest for the doctors. Instead of just putting $5,000 dollars into your retirement account, you would take that money and buy so many shares of one of the managed accounts. This way you were more likely to be assured of a good return.

These investment accounts, which were checked out and pitted against each other, proved to be a fiscally advantageous solution. The doctors and I could tend to our medical duties, knowing that our finances were being taken care of by outstanding professionals.

The financial naiveté of my colleagues came in all sorts of stripes. I remember one doctor who had come to me. The man was a psychiatrist, and he had decided what his lifestyle cost. He then divided the number of hours he could bill into this predetermined amount in order to reach the amount he felt he should charge. I said to him that he had things backwards: He needed to add up his charges to the number of hours billed and that's what he could afford for his lifestyle.

We had another doctor who felt that he was forever entitled to his peak income, even as he grew older and performed fewer operations. I had to call him into my office when it came to my attention that he had simply begun charging more and more for the fewer and fewer operations he was still doing.

There was another doctor who lived entirely on his bonuses. He spent all of his money and couldn't send his children back to school without borrowing money because of a dip in the bonuses one particular year. This gentleman had a big house in Atlanta, a big house on the lake, and a pair of Mercedes in the driveway. He thought he was wealthy because he could afford all of these goods and services, but he was spending every penny he earned.

He wasn't the only one. Another fellow came before the Keogh Committee, to request that he take in cash the funds that were normally deposited in his retirement account. This was permitted in extraordinary circumstances. I figured he had hit some sort of bump in the road, so I said, "OK, fine, let him have his cash." The following year he made the same request. "Well," I said, "I guess the crisis must have continued. Let him do it, but don't ever let him do it again without his first talking to me."

Sure enough, the following year, he made the same request. I came down to see him and I said, "Look, this is absolutely the best investment you can make. It goes in this account and there are no taxes and you have an opportunity to let this grow."

He looked at me and said, rather plainly, "I don't pay any income taxes."

"Oh? You don't pay any income taxes?"

"No," he said, "I have a good advisor and he's got me these investments that have write-offs equal to what my taxes are."

"Yes, but the ultimate day of recapture is going to come and its going to be horrendous."

He went on and on about the efforts of his financial advisor.

"Well," I said, "You've put my mind at ease. I'm not going to worry about you anymore. Your old age is going to be taken care of. You're going to end up in the Federal penitentiary and they're gonna feed you three meals a day."

We had worked so hard to explain to these men and women the difference between wealth based upon holdings versus wealth based upon earnings—you're never wealthy if you're living on your earnings. If you stop working, then you're through. I tried to convince the doctors to transfer some of their income into assets. These pleas sometimes fell upon deaf ears.

•◆•

We held faculty meetings every month during that time. We were very interested in identifying what it took to be a successful service, and figuring out ways to achieve those things. We never discussed money as such—it was not, can we get the billings up this month, or can we charge more for this procedure—rather I would always say, 'What can we *do* to make the clinic a better service.'

A metaphor I liked was: "Our business is to plane lumber and if we plane the best lumber we can plane, there will be plenty of sawdust behind the mill, but we're not here to produce sawdust, that's a byproduct.' I thought that this was an important point to get across. Making money was not worthy of discussion in a meeting among professors. The important questions were: Are we getting our records up? Are we in touch with the referring physicians? Who's writing up this group? Who's writing up that group? Who's making presentations to which societies?

If you can answer those questions properly, you will find success. When a patient went back to work and he was asked what he thought of his healthcare at Emory, what would he have to say? My colleagues would answer, 'Of course he'd say he was happy. We're the best thing in town.'

"Well now," I said, "As we define success—in terms of outcomes, or frequency of complications—probably we would think that we're the best, but we're not patients. A lot of things about Emory aren't user-friendly. Do we have good signage? Can the patient find the doctor's office? Are they seen in a timely fashion?"

That's how a patient describes a pleasant experience at the clinic or the hospital. His doctor might have written ten papers on some subject, and even be a national officer in a prestigious society, but that's usually not what the patient cares about. He wants to be seen promptly, he wants to spend some time with you, and he wants his records sent back to his referring doctor as quickly as possible. All of these basic things that mean so much to a patient can make or break the reputation of a clinic or a hospital.

I always maintained the policy that if I were tied up in the operating room, when I was supposed to be seeing a patient, the receptionist would go to the patient and say, "Dr. Hatcher is still in the operating room, he sends you his regrets, but he wanted me to offer you the following choices: He will be here just as soon as he can be, if you can wait, if your schedule permits. If you cannot wait, then we'll reschedule your appointment, or if you want to be seen by one of the other doctors, you can see one of them right away."

Now most of the time that will diffuse any situation—just sitting there is not good, and that should never be allowed to occur. Simply being asked, most patients indicate their willingness to wait. Nevertheless, situations did arise. I can remember one time, I came over and the receptionist said, "For heaven sakes go to room two and see Mr. So-and-So, he's irate."

So I walked in and you could tell he was mad as a hornet. He looked up at me and barked, "Dr. Hatcher, I know you're an important man, *but I'm also important* and my time is very valuable! I'd like to know why I've been kept waiting here forty-five minutes!"

I looked at him and I smiled and I said, "Your time's very valuable, is it?"

"Yes!"

"Well, that's good because I can remember when your entire life wasn't worth a plugged nickel."

"What do you mean?"

"Do you remember the day your doctor put you in an ambulance and sent you up to Emory here and called me?"

"Yes."

"And I told them I'd be waiting with my team to take you to the operating room just as soon as you got here?"

"Yes."

"And I took you to the operating room and we fixed you up to such an extent that you're now here telling me how valuable your time is?

I let that hang in the air for a moment.

"What the hell do you think happened to the patients who were waiting to see me in my office that afternoon when I dropped everything to take care of you?"

He said, very firmly, "I asked a question and I got a damned good answer!"

He stood up, we shook hands and it was as if we were the best of friends. He had never thought of it like that; and a hospital cannot expect a patient to think this way. You've got to explain things to people.

To be kept waiting without any apparent reason is just the worst thing you can do to a patient. I would say that doctors today, for the most part, do a pretty terrible job of this. The personal element is missing, and it drives me up the wall, because it's so easy to keep a patient's friendship and devotion; all you need to do is take the time to keep them informed. A patient is more than a patient, he or she is a customer, and unless you recognize that, it is difficult to improve upon customer service.

I was very sensitive to make sure that no one charged an inappropriate amount. If someone made an excessive charge this would reflect negatively on the whole organization. It would also mean that there was less money available for the other people who were seeing that patient. I established a Cost Containment Committee in order to make sure this never occurred.

Senior members of the clinic served on the committee. If you wanted to change a fee from your section's approved fee schedule, then you had to come before the Cost Containment Committee and explain why you were justified. If you were about to bill some new procedure, the committee would peg it at what we considered the proper level. This way, you didn't have a dermatologist charging more for removing a mole than we charged for brain surgery.

•◆•

Just after I took over the clinic directorship I received the annual bill from the St. Paul Mercury Insurance Company. Our premium for the year was a little over a million dollars. Well you're getting into real money when you're paying a million dollars a year for malpractice insurance, so I gave them a call to see why the premium had climbed so high. I asked them to look up our loss-to-cost ratio and tell me what it was. The numbers were astounding; in twenty-five years they had paid out $125,000 dollars and here we were paying an annual premium that was over a million dollars! I said, 'I don't know anything much about insurance companies, but I can tell you that it's a good business to be in. We're going to found our own insurance company.'

So we did just that. In the meantime the CEO from St. Paul Mercury offered to cut our premium in half. This only lasted for a year, but by then we were ready to drop them in favor of the recently incorporated Clifton Casualty Company. The effort was very successful from the start. The company stabilized our malpractice losses and reduced our costs. The company was so successful, that although we founded it to exclusively serve the clinic, and it now covers many, if not all, of the Emory Healthcare institutions.

From the start I was the chairman of the board and the CEO of the new insurance company. We brought on a number of lawyers and bought umbrella coverage with a number of insurers. We were unique among insurance companies in the way we handled patients' grievances. Instead of leaving grievances to the lawyers, we addressed them directly. Most lawyers would warn you to back away in the face of a potential lawsuit, and leave things to them, because attempting to resolve things with the family might be interpreted as an implicit admission of guilt; of course the fact that handling lawsuits are their business had nothing do with their advice.

I did not want the clinic to be sued, even if we knew we were going to win. The lawyers, for their own reasons, thought that letting things play out was the wiser course. I felt that extended litigation and malpractice suits, regardless of whether we won or lost, reflected negatively on the clinic or the hospital. Nevertheless, there were occasions when an individual was determined to sue the clinic. Before trial their lawyers would usually offer to settle for an amount that was significantly less than what they were seeking to obtain in court. Most insurance company lawyers would advise you to settle at this point, reminding you that the cost of a successful defense could easily surpass the settlement sum. I never wanted to take that route. I felt that it set a bad precedent and opened us up to more frivolous lawsuits in the future.

Although we were ready to lay down arms if need be (often against the lawyers' advice), we always preferred to seek a resolution with the patient before a lawsuit was ever brought against us (also against the lawyers' advice). I saw little risk in speaking to all but a few of the patients who believed that they were wronged. I felt this way because a good number of the potential lawsuits we faced had nothing to do with malpractice; rather they were situations where the individual did not have the financial resources to cover an unexpected bill or an extended convalescence. Often, good people, when forced into a corner, seeing no other way out, will sue.

If someone had an untoward accident in the hospital, I wanted it reported immediately. Once I had the facts I could offer the patient personal restitution. In the beginning I talked to almost everybody. Of those patients, I only spoke with one who went on to sue us. Most were happy to settle for a reasonable amount. For example, I remember one patient who had a cervical spine operation done by one of our neurosurgeons. He bled postoperatively and he had to be carried back to the operating room. His surgeons reopened the wound and evacuated the clot that was causing pressure on the spinal cord. Well, he had two surgeries instead of one and he did not get to go home when we said he would. He also missed more days of work than he had expected to miss. Hearing that the operation had not gone as planned, a lawyer recommended that he sue the clinic.

I met with this man and said, "I see where you had to go back to surgery. Now you understand that that occurs—bleeding sometimes occurs postoperatively. But you didn't expect it and we're sorry it happened. Let's just say that I cancel the charges for you for that second operation.

"You were in the hospital five days longer than you had been told. We'll find out how much the charges were per day and multiply that by five. You were supposed to go back to work, but you were delayed a week. If you furnish me with some information on what your weekly wage is, we'll work that out with you. So, if we have the surgery changed, the hospital stay changed, the delay going back to work addressed, and add that all up I can have a check written for that amount right now.

"But, you understand this is not my money; this money belongs to all the doctors who make up this clinic and I'll have to have a statement from you indicating that this satisfies you and that you won't sue us later on."

That took care of everything for this patient, as it did for most. Most of these people did not *want* to sue us, they just did not see any other option, so when we gave them one, especially one that provided them with instant gratification they almost always took it.

Obviously you can only do this if you are the CEO of the clinic as well as the CEO of the insurance company, but if you can, it's very efficient.

Facing the Losses

THE SUCCESS OF ANY MEDICAL organization is dependent upon recruitment and retention of outstanding individuals. The growth and development of the institution can be, however, affected by death and disaster. During my years in medical administration I dealt with the loss of a number of outstanding individuals whose departure from the scene had a very definite effect on the organization.

The Department of Medicine recruited Dr. Andreas Gruentzig to join the Emory faculty in 1980. Dr. Willis Hurst, Professor and Chairman of the Department of Medicine and Chief of Cardiology at Emory University Hospital, and Dr. Spencer King, Director of the Cardiac Catheterization Laboratories in the Department of Medicine, were able to lure Dr. Gruentzig to Emory. Gruentzig, a German citizen, first performed coronary angioplasty in Zurich, Switzerland in 1977. He was a creative genius, and destined to become world famous.

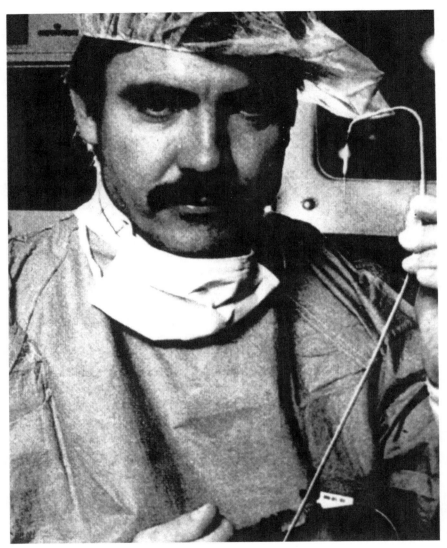

Dr. Andreas Gruentzig

Over the next five years Andreas proved to be a delightful colleague, and his national and international stature continued to grow. Andreas was an amateur pilot, instrument-rated, and as he became more affluent he acquired a Beechcraft Baron, a light-medium, twin-engine aircraft. He used this plane to fly down to a home he had purchased at Sea Island, Georgia. The plane was quite sharp looking, but known to be unforgiving. At any rate, he liked to fly, and this troubled me.

"Andreas," I said, "I'm worried about your flying. Let's get a pilot for you."

He said that he enjoyed flying and that it was his primary recreation.

"Well then any time you want to fly personally, do so; but let's have a pilot with you. When you get on a plane going someplace, and it's late, or you want to have a drink, or whatever it is—you shouldn't have all that responsibility. You don't fly that frequently."

Andreas would hear none of it; doctors have a tendency to believe that being an expert in one area makes them an expert at everything. And so in 1985, with less than 100 hours of experience with his new plane, he crashed on the way back from Sea Island, down on the coast. It was a Sunday afternoon and the weather was absolutely horrible. Andreas had ten angioplasties scheduled for Monday morning; so, in the face of advice to the contrary he took off from Sea Island to attempt the return flight to Atlanta. Sadly, when he crashed, he died, along with his wife and his dog.

Andreas was 43 at the time, and he was probably the most prominent cardiologist in the world. Losing Dr. Gruentzig was more than a major setback for the Woodruff Health Sciences Center; I feel that he had major contributions still to make to his field. Nevertheless, in the five years that he was here, he performed over 2,000 coronary angioplasties—establishing a fine program.

By the 1970s Emory had been operating Crawford Long Hospital as an independent community hospital for a long time. We eventually decided to restructure Crawford Long as a teaching hospital within the health sciences center (an interesting, and at times frustrating process that I'll discuss later). During this process we recruited a number of doctors to take up some important positions at Crawford Long. One of these recruits was a former Emory General Surgery Resident, Doyle Haynes, whom I assisted at the VA my second day back in Atlanta. At the time, Doyle was practicing in Opelika, Alabama. He accepted our overtures and returned to Emory as the chief of surgery at Crawford Long Hospital. In a few years Doyle developed Crawford Long's surgical service, and his own surgical practice to a remarkable degree. Unfortunately, Doyle was not well. One Saturday night in 1987, he called me at home. He told me that he was suffering from an excruciating headache. I told him to call Crawford Long for an ambulance, and that I would meet him in the emergency room. I drove to the hospital as fast as I could and arrived at the same time as the ambulance, but Doyle was unconscious and there was nothing I could do. We could not resuscitate him from the massive cerebral hemorrhage that had resulted from a congenital berry aneurysm. His untimely death was a major setback to our development of the Crawford Long Hospital.

Not all of our major personnel losses were due to death. Dr. Dwight Cavanagh, Professor and Chairman of the Department of Ophthalmology, was an extremely talented surgeon, and an emerging national figure in ophthalmology. I had known Dwight from his student days at the Johns Hopkins School of Medicine. He received his MD degree from the Johns Hopkins University School of Medicine in 1965, and Ph.D. in Biology/Medicine from Harvard University in 1972. His residency in Ophthalmology was spent at the Wilmer Eye Institute of the Johns Hopkins University followed by a fellowship in cornea surgery at the Massachusetts Eye and Ear Infirmary of Harvard Medical School. Early in his chairmanship he developed plans for a comprehensive eye center at Emory and became quite involved in fundraising. He maintained a very busy operative schedule, and was referred so many patients that his clinic hours frequently stretched into the early evening. I spoke to him on several occasions about the inconvenience this was causing patients, but he was so anxious to grow the service that he could not bring himself to turn patients away. One day, distracted and preoccupied with an operative schedule of fourteen patients, he operated upon the wrong eye of the final patient. This misadventure resulted in malpractice litigation and created permanent divisions within the Department of Ophthalmology. In time, Dr. Cavanagh's position at Emory became untenable, and he accepted a professorship at Texas Southwestern in Dallas. Emory conducted an extensive search for his replacement, and fortunately was able to recruit Dr. Thomas Aaberg, who served as an effective Chairman for many years. I still regard the Cavanagh affair as a major setback to the Woodruff Health Sciences Center, and these tragic events disrupted a brilliant career. Over the next several years Dr. Cavanagh was considered by the Search Committee for the top positions at Massachusetts Eye and Ear and the Wilmer Eye Institute at Johns Hopkins. Without this painful chapter at Emory, I have no doubt that he would have been picked by one or both of these fine institutions for their top position.

Profits & Tithes

EACH YEAR THE EMORY CLINIC negotiated a facilities payment to the university. Our office space was carefully calculated and then valued at the current market rate for comparable space in Atlanta. An additional twenty-five percent of the purchase price of all equipment was added and carried forward for four years before being written off. The clinic director and the dean of Emory University School of Medicine, who in this period was Dr. Richardson, handled these negotiations.

The facilities payment my first year was just over a million dollars, no small sum. I met with Dr. Richardson to conduct the transfer of these monies. I was a young and inexperienced clinic director, and Dr. Richardson was a very senior dean. When I sat down, he broadsided me. He began to object to the structure of the medical school. He stated that it was totally inappropriate for The Emory Clinic to be a separate legal entity, that it should be a part of the school of medicine. Furthermore, he declared that he felt somewhat insulted to have to negotiate the annual payment. To this day I'm not sure exactly what his purpose was in making these comments, but I assumed it was some sort of attempt at establishing his superiority over me in our relationship.

I quietly closed my briefcase and stood up. Somewhat surprised he asked me what I was doing.

"I'm not going to pay you anything. I'll take this money back across the street with me."

From the outset, I had intended as director to be a forceful voice for the clinic, though this was not exactly what I had had in mind. I had no intention of letting him walk all over me though—so I left. Needless to say, the news of this action spread around campus quickly. Within an hour or so I had a call of apology from the President of the University, Dr. Sanford

Atwood. President Atwood apologized for the way I had been treated. He also expressed his deep appreciation for the revenues generated by the clinic for the university. Apologies made, he invited me to another meeting the following day, assuring me that I would be treated with proper respect. The second meeting was concluded without difficulty, and I made the payment I had originally intended to make.

These annual negotiations over facilities payments proved to be rather tedious and somewhat unpleasant each year. Shortly after Dr. James T. Laney became President of the University, he and I agreed upon an appropriate percentage of clinic collections to be transferred to Emory University. Dr. Laney had been Dean of the Candler School of Theology before becoming the President of Emory University, so when someone asked me what I thought Dr. Laney would ask for in terms of a percentage, I chuckled and said, "I know exactly what he is going to ask for."

With raised eyebrows they would ask, "How can you be so sure?"

"He's going to ask for 10%. A tithe has special significance to a theologian!"

Sure enough Dr. Laney and I settled on ten percent of net collections as a proper payment. As a percentage would self-adjust annually there would be no need for further acrimonious negotiations. During these discussions, Dr. Laney came in one morning and said that he had prayed the night before, and that he thought ten percent was a fair and proper amount. I somewhat jokingly took exception to his actions.

"I have no problem bringing God into this situation, but I want to have him hear my position first hand. If you like, we can go to Glenn Memorial Chapel, kneel down side by side, and present our points of view. I consider it a bit unfair for you to assume that God has already approved your position as presented by you!"

We both had a good laugh over this, and the ten percent figure served us well for many years. Since the money was being transferred from a for-profit partnership to a non-profit foundation we had to be realistic in the amount we determined proper. Therefore, we asked for and obtained an IRS ruling—the uniqueness of the location of the facility, and the preferred status at Emory University Hospital of The Emory Clinic partners justified a payment that was a little higher than the prevailing commercial rent.

The Succession to the Throne in Two Parts

MY COMMON SENSE ADMINISTRATION OF the clinic impressed the university. The clinic was now contributing millions of dollars annually to the School of Medicine. Dr. E. Garland Herndon was Emory's Vice President for Health Affairs at the time. He was Mr. Woodruff's personal physician, and a good friend of his. I think Mr. Woodruff would have liked for Dr. Herndon to have been the director of the clinic, as Mr. Woodruff was much more involved in the clinic than the medical center at the time. Dr. Herndon became vice president and director of the Woodruff Medical Center in 1973. He was a very likeable man, a true man's man. He met with Mr. Woodruff daily, to keep a close check on his health. This was a great responsibility and a valuable relationship as far the university was concerned, as Mr. Woodruff was by far Emory's largest donor.

As Mr. Woodruff's personal physician, Dr. Herndon was always on call. Mr. Woodruff bought a house for him down the street from his own. Dr. Herndon would check on him every night and come over for breakfast in the morning. This was not the best thing for Dr. Herndon's personal life, but he did develop a close relationship with Mr. Woodruff.

I had first met Dr. Herndon at Walter Reed. He was a Lt. Col. in the Dialysis Unit there. Dr. Willis Hurst recruited him to join the Department of Medicine at Emory University where I got to know him better.

I can remember sitting in on a meeting with Dr. Herndon and Dean Richardson. The two of them got into an argument about something, and Dr. Herndon turned bright red. His voice began to tremble a bit.

I stepped over, put my arm over his back, and said, "Look Garland,

CHARLES HATCHER, JR., M.D.

let's adjourn, nothing's worth upsetting you this much. We'll get back to this some other time."

We adjourned, but that night I received a phone call at approximately three o'clock in the morning—Dr. Herndon had suffered a mild stroke. I am convinced that the argument was a factor in this event. It was nothing Dean Richardson specifically said or did in the meeting; rather Dr. Herndon was unusually stressed by the argument. Subsequently Garland experienced a heart attack. Dr. Ellis Jones performed an emergency coronary bypass procedure on him. After this surgery Dr. Herndon was not able to do much work. Dr. James Laney, the President of the University, became convinced that the way to work through this was to appoint someone to be the Acting Director of the Medical Center, and give Dr. Herndon a lengthy leave of absence, in the hope that his health would improve.

I was asked to come across Clifton Road and serve as the Acting Director of the Medical Center for the year. Typical foolish me, I walked over, and when they said they wanted to negotiate compensation, I said, 'Oh no, I'll be glad to take care of this. He's my friend, and I'll just do what needs to be done.' Well, I went over to his office one afternoon a week and not much happened. "I don't think this is a fulltime job," I said to Jim (Dr. Laney), "I can't stretch this to more than one afternoon a week."

"Charlie," he said, "You don't understand. Garland has been unable to work for quite some time, so people have just learned how to do business without going through that office. As soon as you have the authority, and you're functioning, you're going to be inundated with work!"

To those who do not know what a medical center is, I will take a moment here to explain the concept. In recent years it has become fashionable to designate an institution or institutions such as a hospital as a "medical center." Technically, medical centers consist of several major components such as a hospital or hospitals, a clinic, and medically related schools such as a school of medicine, a school of nursing, a school of public health, and a school of dentistry.

Deans and Directors of the Health Sciences Center
Back: Mr. John Henry, Dean Clair Martin, Dr. Ronnie Weathers, Mr. Dan Barker, Dr. Fred King, Mr. Charles Witzleben,
Mr. William Todd;
Front: Mr. Paul Hoffman, Dr. Richard Krause, Dr. Charles Hatcher, Dr. Garland Perdue

Initially, the medical institutions of Emory University were listed as the Woodruff Medical Center. By the early 1980s, in recognition of other significant health professions, and realizing that the term "medical center" perhaps gave disproportionate attention to the medical activities of physicians either as hospital staff, medical school faculty, or Emory Clinic partners, it was decided to rename the center The Robert W. Woodruff Health Sciences Center. In the 1960s, Mr. Woodruff had declined the use of his name for the medical center, preferring the family name to recognize his parents and brother, George. In the 1980s, when the plan to rename the center The Robert W. Woodruff Health Sciences Center was presented to Mr. Woodruff, Mr. Woodruff, then in his old age, thought that this was a great idea and could not recall why he had made his earlier objections.

I really did not think it was going to be a fulltime job those first few weeks at the medical center, just something I would do to help out the

241

university. The work picked up a bit after a few months, and I enjoyed doing what little work I did do, but not much changed. Eventually the university appointed an eighteen member search committee to seek out a permanent replacement for Dr. Herndon. This committee included deans and professors and trustees. Dr. Herb Karp, Professor and Chairman of Neurology, was the Chair.

They looked around nationally, and considered the CVs of nearly 100 candidates. When they finished, they reported back to Dr. Laney that I was their first choice. The clinic agreed quite strongly. Dr. Laney was not entirely sure he wanted me to be the Vice President. He was concerned that my lengthy background in private practice at The Emory Clinic might be a problem for me, and that it might be hard for me to take the university's position on some issues. He joked that he was not sure I always knew who was the Dean of the School of Medicine. If I did, it didn't matter much to me. I replied that being the CEO of The Emory Clinic was similar to being in charge of the Chevrolet Division of General Motors. I had concerned myself with the affairs of my division. If I were to be in charge of General Motors, I was certain I could rise above the division level and handle the entire company.

I never for a moment suspected that Dr. Laney's intentions were anything but what he thought best for the university. I respected him tremendously, and never doubted his basic integrity. Even in a situation of conflict between the university and the clinic, one was always reassured knowing that Dr. Laney wanted what was best for the university, and that he wished to be as fair as possible to all concerned. Over time we became good friends, but in 1983, when the committee came back to him and said that they wanted me to be vice president, I think he was a little apprehensive.

He offered me the job, but it seemed to me that he offered it under terms which he was pretty sure I could not accept. He said that he wanted me to become the Vice President for Health Affairs and Director of the Health Sciences Center, but that he also wanted me to resign from my positions as Chief of the Division of Cardiothoracic Surgery in the Department of Surgery in the Emory University School of Medicine, and as Chief of the Section of Cardiothoracic Surgery at The Emory Clinic. It was a given that I resign as Director and CEO of The Emory Clinic since I obviously would have a conflict of interest as landlord and tenant in the Woodruff Health Sciences Center.

"Well," I said, "I can't accept giving up my career in Cardiothoracic Surgery to accept an administrative position."

I thanked him and considered the matter closed. He had proposed his terms, and he could report to the Search Committee that he had offered me the job, and that I hadn't accepted it.

•◆•

Dr. Laney asked the committee to return to the drawing board. Meanwhile, I continued on as the acting vice president. The committee met over the next several months and ultimately composed another report. They handed a second list to Dr. Laney. There were three names on it. Mine was still at the top. He called me and said, "We're just going to have to work this out. The Trustees and the committee all want you to be the Vice President for Health Affairs."

We went down to Callaway Gardens for the day, to get to know each other better. We had a pleasant time down there, and when we got back to Atlanta, he asked me if I would reconsider. I said I would, and we planned a meeting. I brought along my attorney and we were also joined by Mr. Jimmy Williams, the Chairman of the Medical Center Board. I had two preconditions that I considered deal breakers—I was not going to resign from my position as Director of the Division of Cardiothoracic Surgery and my personal income was not the university's concern. We then went through a series of *what-if's*, such as, *suppose there is a dean whom Dr. Hatcher does not like but you like him? Does he have the authority to fire him? etc.* After we worked through these scenarios I accepted the offer. Dr. Laney and I went on to become very good comrades in arms.

I had been at Emory for two decades when I became the Vice President for Health Affairs. As a young doctor fresh out of my residency I never could have expected this. I had set my ambitious goals and milestones back when I was at Athens and I had basically achieved them all. So while I expected to succeed in my chosen profession, I had never even considered the notion that I would be administering an entire medical center. From a town of four hundred people to becoming the leader of 20,000 men and women—it was almost inconceivable. But it was real, and I relished the opportunity.

As I said, Dr. Laney and I, after our initial concerns, grew into the best of friends. But Dr. Laney was a strong individual, and he let me know that after all, he was the President of the University. I remember one early meeting with the other senior administrators of the university. Dr. Laney was there, as was Dr. Billy Frye, the VP of Academic Affairs, and Mr. John Temple, the VP of Financial Affairs. Well, some controversial issue came up and the three of them already had their position. This had occurred a number of times before and it was starting to look like a pattern.

"Look," I said, "This seems to be a little bit much. The three of you have already determined your positions and I'm hearing about this for the first time. Three to one is not exactly my idea of fair."

Jim said, "We've worried about that Charles; I've worried about that. But that's as fair as I know how to make it."

Section Seven:
No Scepters, Only Hard Work

A Personal Word

I never took myself too seriously. I frequently told jokes and attained a reputation as a raconteur. Certainly I never forgot who I was, or failed to appreciate the remarkable opportunities I had been given. Having come up through the ranks I did not require any of the trappings of authority. The door to my office was always open, and everyone felt free to drop by and seek my help with any problem they might have.

An International City

As I ENTERED ACADEMIC MEDICINE at Emory University I felt extremely confident in my training and my surgical ability. When elected the director and CEO of The Emory Clinic, I was initially concerned about my business training, but I found that common sense was quite valuable. I quickly learned that the staff of The Emory Clinic would be supportive if they truly believed that I was as concerned about their welfare as my own. I enjoyed this support during all my years at the clinic, and I found that the doctors, far from resenting my authority, were eager to have me take care of all manner of things in which they had little expertise or interest.

From this position of authority at The Emory Clinic, I moved into the ranks of the "power elite" of Atlanta. The Atlanta Rotary Club created a classification of cardiac surgery and asked me to become a member of the club. This gave me the opportunity to interact with some 400 outstanding Atlantans who were successful in fields other than medicine. Golf matches and quail hunts followed, and I frequently was called to consult on the care of a wide variety of prominent individuals.

My contact with the Board of Trustees of Emory University moved into high gear when I became the Vice President for Health Affairs of Emory University. I became very comfortable with all of the trustees, who usually consulted me about any medical care that might be required. I was usually asked by the chairman of the Woodruff Board to give the quarterly report of the health sciences center to the full board of university trustees. I would always speak extemporaneously, and the trustees enjoyed these reports. I came to be listed in the Atlanta Business Chronicle as one of the movers and shakers of Atlanta, and was usually referred to as the *Emory Health Czar*.

Despite all of this, I never took myself too seriously. I frequently told

247

jokes and attained a reputation as a raconteur. Certainly I never forgot who I was, or failed to appreciate the remarkable opportunities I had been given. Having come up through the ranks I did not require any of the trappings of authority. I maintained my office in cardiothoracic surgery when I was elected the director of The Emory Clinic, and made the director's office available to the business manager of the clinic. When I became the vice president for health affairs I maintained a modest office in the center of the floor, and made the corner offices available to members of my staff. The door to my office was always open, and everyone felt free to drop by and seek my help with any problem they might have.

Shortly after I became the full-time Vice President for Health Affairs, Dr. Laney called on me to help select a new dean for the School of Medicine. Dr. Richard Krause, who was the Director of the Institute of Infectious Diseases at NIH, had been on the short list of finalists for the VP position, and I suggested to Dr. Laney that we now offer the deanship to Dr. Krause; if he was good enough to be a finalist for the VP position, then he was certainly qualified to be the dean of the School of Medicine. Dr. Laney wondered whether Dr. Krause would accept the position, as he had been a candidate for a higher position within the university. I felt that Dr. Krause was better qualified to be a dean than a Vice President for Health Affairs; he was a scholarly man who had worked at NIH for many years and a purely academic position seemed more appropriate. We decided that it was worth a shot.

President James Laney

We called Dr. Krause and invited him down to Atlanta. We took him around and then made our offer, which he accepted. I felt that a committee and a big search were uncalled for in this situation, as a previous committee had thought so highly of him as to consider him for the job I eventually won.

In 1983 I dedicated Building B of The Emory Clinic. Dr. Cavanagh had overseen the project, though I did assist him during the fundraising. In the normal course of things, Dr. Herndon would have been the one to

249

dedicate the building, but because of his health, the task fell upon me. There would be other buildings to dedicate, but my first was not a project that I considered my own.

At about the same time, Dr. James Laney and the Emory University Board of Trustees made several appointments to the Woodruff Board. Mr. James B. Williams had succeeded Mr. William R. Bowdoin as Chairman, and Mr. R. Randall Rollins became Vice Chairman of the Woodruff Board. I also requested that any physicians added to the Board of Trustees of the University would be added to the Woodruff Board, and this was accomplished. Mr. James B. Williams and Mr. Randall Rollins were wonderful colleagues throughout this period. With their advice and guidance it was possible to move the health sciences center forward at an impressive pace. Few people in Atlanta could equal the position held by Mr. Williams in the business and civic life of the city. Chairman of the Board of SunTrust, Chairman of the Finance Committee of The Coca-Cola Company, board member of Rollins, Inc., Genuine Parts Company, and Georgia Pacific, he also served as board member and later as Chairman of the Board of the Woodruff Foundations. His advice was always on target, and our joint University activities extremely pleasurable.

Mr. James B. Williams

Randall Rollins continued the wonderful example of his father, Mr. O. Wayne Rollins, who had made possible the huge Rollins Research Building dedicated in 1990. Together with his mother, his brother Gary, and the Rollins family, Randall provided the financial resources which made possible the Grace Crum Rollins Building and the Rollins School of Public Health. The Rollins family would in a short time become the largest living donors to the Robert W. Woodruff Health Sciences Center of Emory University.

Mr. R. Randall Rollins

In an article in *The Chronicle of Higher Education* published September 6, 1996, it was reported that a record $295 million fund had been established at Emory University by the Woodruff Foundations. At that time the endowment may well have been the largest gift ever made in American higher education. It provided the Woodruff Health Sciences Center with financial stability as academic medical centers were faced with a "uniquely unfavorable set of pressures", a quote from the article of *The Chronicle of Higher Education,* July 13, 1994. This fund permitted Dr. Michael M. E. Johns, my successor, to develop new programs and facilities which made it possible for Emory University to continue development in an era of intense medical competition for our clinic and hospitals.

As The Emory Clinic Director, I enacted reforms favored by many of the younger doctors. I had also learned firsthand how much change (and hopefully improvement) you could affect within an organization from the top down. Our plans did not confine themselves to The Emory Clinic; one of my greatest priorities as director had been to strengthen The Emory Clinic's position vis-à-vis the university. So, it was a bit awkward to find myself working on the other side of Clifton Road, out of an office in the Woodruff Administration Building. When Dr. Laney and I had negotiated the conditions under which I would accept the vice presidency he had had some deal-breakers of his own. He held firm that I could either remain on as the director and CEO of The Emory Clinic or become the director of the health sciences center and the CEO of Emory Healthcare, but not both. The Emory Clinic, though independent from the School of Medicine, still reported to the director of the Woodruff Health Sciences Center. If I had remained the director of both, I would have become my own boss, approving my own budgets. Obviously this was out of the question. I loved serving as director of The Emory Clinic and at the time I did not want to give that up, but I understood his reservations. As a compromise, when I accepted the vice presidency, I stepped down as the director and CEO of The Emory Clinic and became the chief financial officer, The Emory Clinic's first and last physician to serve in such a capacity.

I admit it gets a bit confusing here, due to overlapping and sometimes independent institutions within the university, so I'll sum things up as they stood in 1983: I remained the chief of cardiothoracic surgery at The Emory Clinic; I also continued on as the chief of the division of cardiothoracic surgery at the School of Medicine; I stepped down as the CEO and director of The Emory Clinic to become the CFO of The Emory Clinic; and most importantly I was now the vice president for health affairs, serving in the complimentary positions of director of the Robert W. Woodruff Health Sciences Center, and CEO of the Emory University System of Healthcare. Shortly after I stepped down this name was shortened to the more consumer-friendly *Emory Healthcare*.

As I said, walking across Clifton Road was no trivial thing. It felt a bit awkward at first, but it was not as if I had been playing for one team at The Emory Clinic and now I was playing for another as the VP for Health Affairs at the University. However independent The Emory Clinic was, it was still a part of Emory University. As the vice president I sought to expand our research efforts, improve the already excellent medical school, and continue to grow the health sciences center. All of these goals, if accomplished, would surely benefit The Emory Clinic.

Dr. Garland Perdue
Director of the Emory Clinic Elected 1983

When I stepped in as VP, the Woodruff Health Sciences Center encompassed the Schools of Medicine, Dentistry and Nursing, the Emory University Hospital, Crawford Long Hospital, and the Yerkes National Primate Research Center. We were also affiliated with Egleston Children's Hospital, Grady Memorial Hospital, the Atlanta VA Hospital, and the Wesley Woods Geriatric Center.

All told, nearly 20,000 people worked within the umbrella of the health sciences center and I quickly realized that there would be decisions that I would make that would have effects outside of a particular hospital or school, and sometimes the effects would ripple far beyond the confines of the university itself. The 1984 contract renegotiation with Grady Memorial Hospital represented perhaps the largest stone tossed into the pond.

For over half a century, Emory has trained its medical students and house officers at Grady Memorial Hospital, in downtown Atlanta. Grady Hospital has a long and winding history, but by the time I arrived in Atlanta it was under the joint control of the local governments of Fulton and DeKalb, the two most populous counties in Atlanta. The counties both appointed commissioners to a quasi-public organization, The Fulton-DeKalb Hospital Authority. Under the contract that we had with the Hospital Authority at the time, Emory was responsible for all patient care at Grady Hospital. This relationship had proved beneficial for both parties.

There is another wrinkle to the finances at Grady Memorial Hospital. When funds first became available to pay for physician services provided at Grady, there was considerable discussion about the appropriateness of collecting these physician fees. It was a delicate question. The fees came from Medicaid, Medicare and other third party carriers. They were for an institution largely funded by public money for the provision of indigent care to needy citizens of Fulton and DeKalb Counties. Ultimately, the Emory-Grady Foundation and the Emory Medical Fund were established. During the years in which I was responsible for these monies, I insisted that the Emory Medical Fund be kept entirely separate from the collections of The Emory Clinic. There was obviously a duplication of collection effort, but I felt that it was essential that the monies not be co-mingled so that we could provide an accurate accounting of every dollar collected for patient care at Grady Hospital, and to further show that these funds were being spent entirely at Grady Memorial Hospital.

Mr. Roy Townsend and Dr. Charles Hatcher

Mr. Roy Townsend, longtime business manager of The Emory Clinic, assumed responsibility for the Emory Medical Fund several years prior to his retirement. Though collection of these funds have always presented somewhat of a challenge, these additional funds have augmented the Emory University and Morehouse University activities at Grady Memorial Hospital to a remarkable extent. Funding for large public institutions such as Grady Memorial Hospital has always presented significant challenges. Annual deficits have been the rule and not the exception. In 2008, in an attempt to stabilize the finances of Grady Memorial Hospital, the Woodruff Foundation pledged a series of gifts totaling $200 million if certain financial parameters could be met on the way to solvency.

The state of Georgia showed little interest in helping to fund Grady, and without the doctors from Emory, the hospital would not have been able to remain open. At Grady, Emory's interns and residents were exposed to cases rarely seen on campus. Grady is a Level I Trauma Center and as such it admits more people with gunshot wounds and serious injuries from car accidents in one night than Emory University Hospital usually does over an entire month. Whereas at The Emory Clinic and the Emory University Hospital, patients often come in for less acute care, emergency care rules the day at Grady. I felt that it was essential for our interns and residents to deal with this kind of trauma in the course of their training, and without Grady, it would be difficult to provide them with a proper amount of experience in this regard. Aside from the trauma experience, there is also the matter of why you pursue a career in medicine in the first place—to help people—and there is no better place in Atlanta to do that than at Grady. Indeed, many of my residents have told me that they regard their rotations through Grady as the most meaningful work they did during the course of their training. In addition to the residents and interns, a significant percentage of the physicians (roughly 300 men and women) on the faculty of the School of Medicine would spend all or part of their time supervising the care and teaching at Grady.

There is, as there often is, with large publicly funded institutions in Atlanta, a racial side to this story. When I first arrived in Atlanta, Grady was still segregated into white wards and colored wards. This was put to an end in 1965, but as a result, the white patients, who were already fleeing downtown Atlanta en masse for the suburbs, largely abandoned the hospital. This trend continued for many years and today less than 10% of Grady's patients are white. The city, and later the two counties, had always intended for the hospital to serve the indigent and this remains the case today—Grady, mired in a perpetual budget crisis for as long as most

Atlantans can remember, spends well over $100 million dollars a year caring for those who cannot pay for themselves.

As Emory's first contract with Grady neared its end, an important development occurred, presenting both challenges and opportunities for the City of Atlanta. In 1978, Morehouse University, one of the historically black colleges situated close to Downtown at the Atlanta University Center, announced its intention to create a two-year school of medicine.

Louis Sullivan was an outstanding colleague. He was born in Blakeley, Georgia, less than an hour's drive from my home in south Georgia. As a youngster, he was taken to Bainbridge, Georgia to Dr. Griffin for a minor illness. Dr. Griffin, a graduate of the Meharry Medical School, was the first black physician that Lou had ever seen, and it changed his dreams for the future. After graduating from medical school and securing his residency training in hematology, he was recruited unsuccessfully by Emory University School of Medicine. Just at that time, Morehouse established its School of Medicine, and Dr. Sullivan was asked to be the initial President.

This was obviously not an easy undertaking, and when called upon, Emory provided assistance. During these years when the Morehouse School of Medicine was a two-year school, Emory, the Medical College of Georgia, and several other institutions accepted their students at the junior year level. The largest number of these Morehouse transfers always elected to attend the Emory University School of Medicine if possible.

In the early 1980s, the medical schools' accrediting agencies determined to phase out two-year institutions. Morehouse was left with the difficult choice of closing their two-year school, or attempting to become a four-year school in a very short period of time. They chose the latter. Arrangements were worked out with the Emory University School of Medicine to offer the third and fourth year to those Morehouse students who wished to transfer and had successfully completed part one of the national board.

The initial contract was for a period of three years, during which Morehouse School of Medicine hoped to recruit the clinical faculty necessary to offer their own third and fourth years. Unfortunately, this could not be accomplished in the initial three year period and Morehouse asked for an extension of the contract for an additional three years. This was accomplished. Three years later, however, when I was asked for a third extension for an additional three years, I demurred. I felt that Morehouse was close enough to accreditation as a four year school to seek this status, and Emory University School of Medicine could provide the professors required by Morehouse to achieve their own fully accredited departments. This was worked out to everyone's satisfaction.

During these years, Dr. Sullivan and I worked closely together. We met promptly to address any grievances which developed in either faculty. We declined to discuss each other with the press, but held frequent meetings at which sentiments were fully expressed. I anticipated that the Morehouse School of Medicine would require access to the patients of Grady Memorial Hospital, both for the clinical teaching of medical students and to obtain their long range goal of having residency programs in a number of specialties. Since Emory University School of Medicine had a contract making Emory responsible for all patient care at Grady Memorial Hospital, such participation by Morehouse would require an amendment to the contract between the Emory University School of Medicine and the Fulton-DeKalb Hospital Authority. I urged a voluntary amendment to the contract to accommodate the Morehouse School of Medicine, and this was accomplished. There were critics, of course, who felt that two medical schools could not share properly the same public facility, and some who doubted that the Morehouse School of Medicine had matured to the point of accepting full clinical responsibilities at Grady Memorial Hospital. By this time, Dr. Louis Sullivan had been named Secretary of Health and Human Services in the cabinet of President George W. Walker Bush, and Dr. James Goodman had been named President of the Morehouse School of Medicine. In August of 1990, I was honored with an award by the Morehouse School of Medicine which I accepted on behalf of all of the faculty and staff of Emory University. Dr. Sullivan eventually returned to the Morehouse School of Medicine for several years of service as Dr. Goodman's successor as President. Good relations continue to characterize Emory-Morehouse activities, a source of pleasure and pride to both institutions.

In 1985, Morehouse was accredited to issue four-year medical degrees. As a fully accredited school, they needed access to patients, and Grady was the only public hospital in the area. On paper, there was no way they could negotiate with Grady unless we voluntarily chose to accept an amendment to our contract. I could have stood my ground, as Emory had an exclusive contract with Grady, which we had renewed for twenty-nine-and-a-half years in 1984 (This was the maximum length possible, as the Hospital Authority itself controlled Grady through thirty year contracts). Responsibility for all of the patients at Grady was extremely valuable to the Emory School of Medicine, and this was not something to be given up lightly. There were also strong reasons to accept an amendment to our contract. Times were changing and Atlanta was growing as fast as ever. The Civil Rights Movement had produced dramatic changes in the 1960s, the integration of Grady Hospital among them. As I wrote on the very first page of this book, Atlanta is a city defined by its transportation infrastructure. Overseas passenger air service commenced in Atlanta in 1971, but the year 1980 marks one of Atlanta's greatest turning points in the city's effort to remake itself as an international city. That year Hartsfield International Airport opened a massive new passenger terminal capable of accommodating 55 Million passengers a year; the world's largest terminal at the time. The new terminal hastened the city's growth as an international business center. In the early 1980s, Atlanta's leaders in government, business, and the arts were doing all they could to put to rest the demons of the city's past, and I certainly was not going to stand in the hospital door, keeping out the city's first historically black medical school.

Some of the full-time physicians at Grady did not see things this way and I got a bit of flack from them. Many of these people had spent their entire professional lives working at Grady; they felt like I was giving away the services that they had built up for years. They saw this purely from a medical perspective, and from a medical perspective they were probably correct to voice their objections. There is always a risk when you grant patient responsibility to a newly chartered medical school, but I felt that this was a risk that could not be avoided. While I was willing to give up some of our patient responsibility at Grady, there were limits on how much I would part with. After much discussion we settled on ten to twenty percent as a proper share to hand over to Morehouse in the beginning. The issue transcended medicine and I believe that doing what was best for Atlanta, in the end, was what was best for Emory.

Research

IT WAS VERY DIFFICULT FOR me to give up cardiac surgery. I had enjoyed my role in the development of the specialty. It was a particular privilege to bring several techniques to Emory University and the state of Georgia. I performed the state's first total correction of a Tetralogy of Fallot on my initial day as an Emory surgeon. Over the next several years, we performed the first successful aortic valve replacement, double valve replacement, triple valve replacement, and finally the first coronary artery bypass procedure.

As the following chapters will show, I was privileged to expand my role in administration as I phased out my personal role in cardiac surgery. I became an enabler, and took pride in providing for the needs of younger faculty members, including multiple new buildings and expanded hospitals of every sort. I am particularly proud of the new Rollins School of Public Health, which now occupies two beautiful new buildings named for Grace Crum Rollins (Mrs. O. Wayne Rollins) and Claudia Nance Rollins (Mr. Rollins' mother). These buildings are located adjacent to the O. Wayne Rollins Research Center which was my first project as Vice President for Health Affairs.

To become a nationally prominent medical center, Emory needed to do more than provide first rate clinical care; we were going to have to significantly increase the amount of research done in the schools, the hospitals, The Emory Clinic, and the other assorted institutions. Identifying separate academic, research and clinical tracks for The Emory Clinic staff was a good first step. But now I was working from a bigger desk and thus I was afforded more clay to mold.

My predecessors had not placed an emphasis on research. Despite this, the medical school was collecting millions of dollars in federal grants. I hoped to greatly increase this amount, setting an ambitious goal of $100 million in annual funded research by 1990. I wanted to build up research, without it being at the expense of our clinical care. This is almost impossible to do and care did suffer a bit as we built up our research program. This was not for naught though; we easily surpassed our goal of $100 million dollars in funded research by 1990.

When you are applying for grants, the best source of funds is NIH. It is considered the purest money you can get and you win academic brownie points for each grant that you add to your tally. If you order a list of medical schools in the United States according to NIH funding, and compare that with a ranking of medical schools, you can almost superimpose the lists. Hopkins is always number one, followed by a list of familiar names. By 1990, Emory had rocketed up from obscurity into the top thirty NIH grant winners, a position it continues to improve upon to this day. Dr. Johns, my successor as VP for Health Affairs, intensified my emphasis on research and in his first couple years in office I believe he doubled our annual research grants.

By the late 90s, Emory had grown into the number one research university in the state, surpassing Georgia Tech. This was more than a matter of simply applying for grants; rather it involved improving the caliber of the department chairmen we recruited, applying for different types of grants, and constructing new research facilities.

Following the Building B expansion, we added a wing to the A Building of the clinic, along with an addition to the University Hospital building. That in essence brought the clinical enterprise into balance. I became aware very quickly that our clinic enterprise was quite sizable and very well financed. The research enterprise was good, but small. And so, the first building that I raised money for was a research building.

Mr. O Wayne Rollins, the patriarch of the Rollins family in Atlanta played an important role at the Medical Center. Mr. Rollins was an astute businessman. He came to Atlanta to acquire Orkin. At the time Orkin was six to seven times larger than the Rollins company, but he put together one of the first leveraged buyouts. Shortly after I became the VP, Mr. Rollins called me and asked, "If I did something for you, what would be your first choice?"

I think he expected me to tell him that I wanted to build a tower at Emory Hospital for the Heart Service, as both he and his brother had had heart surgery at the clinic.

"Looking at the university's needs, we need space for research."

He asked me if I were sure.

And I said, "Yes, I think so Mr. Rollins. We have a large hospital and we have a large Emory Clinic, but our research establishment is just too small. It's a very good research establishment. If we take the number of dollars Emory brings in and divide it by the number of researchers, it's the highest in the south. If we divide it by the number of square feet of research space it's the highest in the south. It's a small group and we've got to expand that, because right now we're only competing for R01 Grants and we're doing real well with those, but they're one project at a time, and they're from several thousand to several hundred thousand. The big grants are the Center Grants, in which you have every possible person who would need to be involved in the evaluation of a particular problem funded together. With these they'll give you $10 million dollars at one time, and you determine how the money should be best spent. The object is: 1) to expand the research establishment; and 2) to add the diversity and expertise necessary to compete effectively for Center Grants."

Mr. Rollins had someone call me back a couple of days later. The building we hoped to construct carried an estimated price tag of $40 million dollars. He offered to donate $10 million dollars towards the construction of a new research building, and for that gift we agreed to name the new building after him. We secured the balance of the money and broke ground on the project. Things got underway in 1986 and the construction crews finished the building in 1990. In dedicating the building we doubled the size of our research space on campus. We gave Dr. Francis Collins, who had isolated the gene for cystic fibrosis, an honorary degree, and he spoke at the dedication. Around this time we also undertook a major renovation and expansion of the Woodruff Memorial Research Building, adding a new west wing. This was a loud, drawn out construction project in the center of campus near the undergraduate classrooms and dormitories. I remember one group of students asked if they could have just one semester go by without any construction projects. The answer was, for better or worse, *no*. In 1995, I dedicated the addition to the Woodruff research building along with President Bill Chace (who had by then succeeded Dr. Laney), and Dr. Jeffery Houpt, the dean of the School of Medicine.

One of the more controversial building decisions that we made was to ask the University to provide some land on the periphery of campus to two organizations wanting to build structures that I believed would be very beneficial to the health sciences center. On one occasion we were approached by an organization that wished to build a patient facility, at no cost to us, so long as we provided the land. I presented this to the Board, and one Trustee accused me of 'giving away the core campus.' Now this land was about as far from the central campus as possible, and further, this new Mason Transplant House would serve a vital function for the Emory University Hospitals and The Emory Clinic. Named for the Mason

261

Trust, the house provides for patients having solid organ transplantations. Mrs. Mason was well ahead of her time, as when she picked 'solid organ' transplants, this only covered kidneys. Today that category includes lungs, hearts, livers, and so on. In the end we built a very lovely home on this site. Each room has its own kitchen, laundry room, and living space, so that families can stay together when their relatives go into surgery. For this service we only charge a small fee, and ask that visitors give what they can.

The Hope Lodge, built by the ACS, is the same type of facility, for families of people undergoing radiation therapy. We managed to secure nearby land for this project, but in the process I learned another lesson in how (not) to select a project site. I had demonstrated that site in the paperwork, to the then President of the University, Dr. William Chace. Well he said, "Oh my goodness, this is going to be very visible from my back porch." I realized then that I should have waited a couple of months, as it was the middle of winter; and if I had waited, the trees would have grown in and obscured the building.

•◆•

Growing Emory into a premier national research university was not a simple matter of adding faculty and research space. There was an objective to what we were doing. It is important to note that we were not growing *just to grow.*

Clinically we wanted to take advantage of every new breakthrough our researchers made. If we had a lab researching kidney transplantations, then we wanted to eventually exploit that by expanding our patient transplant program. Often, you need to take a long-view; research by its very nature leads you to study emerging fields of medicine, the clinical applications of which are not always entirely clear. Sometimes we simply did not have the proper faculty on board to move forward with new techniques and technologies. This required that The Emory Clinic grow tremendously during the 1970s and 1980s.

Boisfeuillet Jones is a name familiar to all Emory students, as the Admissions Center is named after him. Most never figure out how to pronounce his name and simply refer to the center as the B. Jones Building. What most Emory students do not know is that Boisfeuillet was involved with the university for decades, including fourteen years in a position that became the Vice President for Health Affairs. He left this position to become Assistant Secretary of Health in the Administration of President John F.

Kennedy. In 1960 he became the President of the Woodruff Foundation. In that role he continued to serve Emory, overseeing the Foundation's famous $105 million dollar gift to the University in 1979 (at the time the largest single donation to a university endowment in history).

Back in The Emory Clinic's early days his office (The VP for Health Affairs) had done a study which found that The Emory Clinic should eventually grow to fifty-five physicians. The researchers concluded that this number would be ideal for The Emory Clinic, the Hospital, and the Medical School. Boisfeuillet brought this study up at a meeting of the university Board of Trustees. He thought that perhaps I was interested in growth for the sake of growth, as we had grown to over 200 physicians by that time. He said that we had never wanted to be the largest medical center; we wanted to be the best medical center. Well, you realized that you were in a bit of danger when Boisfeuillet became involved in any matter. I knew it would be unwise to dismiss him out of hand.

"Well Boisfeuillet," I said, "That was a wonderful study and I've referred to it many, many times, but it was done before certain things had become available for clinical practice. For example, open heart surgery—at the time of the study, when you anticipated how large the clinic should become, there had never been an open heart operation done in the entire world.

"Now, we've expanded cardiology, cardiac surgery, cardiac anesthesia, cardiac radiology, and all kinds of people have been added to take advantage of that opportunity."

And I looked around the room and winked and said, "I'd dare say the Trustees understand and approve what I'm doing since I can count a number of people in the room who've had open heart surgery."

That was the last time we heard about that study.

Though we expanded our research efforts and saw dramatic increases in federal grants throughout the 1980s, we had yet to exploit our greatest asset. The Centers for Disease Control is headquartered on a parcel of land adjacent to Emory's campus, accessible only by Clifton Road, Emory's main thoroughfare (Well, that is not entirely accurate—the helicopters float in an out of the CDC all day and night). Mr. Woodruff had purchased this land back in the 1950s, for $50,000 dollars. He gave the land to Emory University. The CDC was founded in 1946, but by the early 1950s the growing organization was seeking a new home. Dwight Eisenhower was the president at the time, and he happened to be a golfing pal of Mr. Woodruff's. During a round of golf at Augusta National, President Eisenhower mentioned that the government was looking for a new home for the CDC, possibly in Washington, D.C. The CDC's original office was already in Atlanta (located in an abandoned building on the Grady

Campus), so Mr. Woodruff proposed that he move the agency to a fifteen acre site he had given to Emory. President Eisenhower accepted the offer and the CDC purchased the site from Emory for $15 dollars. Since then the CDC has grown into a massive government agency, responsible for the public health and the safety of the American people. The CDC represented an underused asset with extraordinary potential, but like a diamond buried deep within a mine, the path to pay dirt was a difficult one.

Growth & Contraction

IN THE MID-80S THE AMERICAN Cancer Society decided that it was time to move its headquarters out of New York City. For a nonprofit organization, New York City, where they had been located since their founding, had simply grown too expensive. Their old building was right around the corner from the Waldorf Astoria Hotel, and when volunteers came to town for meetings, this is where they put them up for the night. As you can imagine, that got to be quite expensive. They evaluated a number of sites, but we were able to convince them to move to Atlanta, on a piece of land on Clifton Road across the street from the CDC. In order to do so, I promised them that Emory would build a hotel and conference center adjacent to the building site. They would save enough money on hotel costs alone to cover much of their administrative overhead.

I thought that the ACS would make a wonderful addition to campus, furthering our attempts to transform the Clifton Corridor into a national research hub. There was another reason that I wanted the ACS to move to Emory. The Winship Cancer Clinic was about to celebrate its 50th anniversary, and I could think of nothing better to honor Mr. Woodruff for his gifts than to move the American Cancer Society headquarters right down the street from the Winship Clinic.

The first thing we had to do was invite the site selection committee to visit Atlanta. By this time, my old friend LaMar McGinnis was no longer the President of the ACS, though he did remain an advisor to the society. He was one of the representatives the ACS sent to the meeting where I pitched our site in Atlanta. If you think that the scales might have been tipped in our favor, fear not, because we had a strong opponent on the committee. Dr. A. H. Letton, another former president of the ACS, was very anti-Emory. He believed that it would be unwise for the ACS to be seen as too closely attached to any one academic institution.

When he said this, I offered to excuse myself from the meeting, stating that perhaps my presence in the room was counterproductive. Everyone else in the room told me to stay put; they all thought it would be nice for the ACS to be close to Emory and the CDC.

The only snag was that we did not own all of the land the ACS would need. We tried to be pretty vague in our proposals, lest the owner of the parcel in question catch wind of our absolute need for his property. The representatives from ACS, as they should have, insisted that we mark off exactly what land we were proposing. Part of the land we needed was home to the Emory Inn, known then as the Emory Sheraton Inn. The motel was not very profitable and the Sheraton corporation had recently sold the property to a group of investors in Chicago. We approached their General Partner about buying the property.

"We have had it appraised," I told him, "and they said it's worth a maximum of $4.5 million, so we're offering $4.5 million."

He wanted $5.5 million dollars.

I went back to the Board of Trustees, who had agreed to finance the purchase. I explained to them that we needed the site, for access and frontage on Clifton Road. They said that if it were absolutely necessary, they would authorize the higher figure, but they asked that I do my best to pay less than that. Before we made a counteroffer to the group of investors, I received a very interesting phone call. A friend of mine had caught wind of the fact that the hotel was broke. He was pretty sure that they had failed to pay their taxes and it looked like DeKalb County was going to condemn the property. I was working on this project with Mr. John Temple, the Executive Vice President of the University. My friend told us to drag our feet on the counteroffer as long as we could. So that's what we did and sure enough, six weeks later DeKalb County padlocked the property for non-payment of taxes. Mr. Temple immediately called First American Bank, in Birmingham—they held the first mortgage on the property—and bought the hotel for only $3.5 million dollars.

With the property in hand, our proposal was complete. The committee chose our site in Atlanta and they held a dinner to celebrate. The ACS invited Boisfeuillet Jones and me to this dinner. Everyone was in a good mood, and Boisfeuillet got caught up in the spirit of things.

"Do you think we ought to offer them moving expenses?" he asked me.

"Well," I said, "That would be awfully nice."

"What do you think? A million dollars?"

"That would be really nice."

"Well is that too much?"

"No, no, that would be fine."

So we announced that night that we were going to give them $1 million dollars.

The ACS invited William J. Todd, who was my executive assistant at the time, to be the project manager for the construction effort. He had graduated from Georgia Tech so he certainly had the background for such an undertaking. Well, it turned out that he was more than just qualified—construction finished on-time and under-budget!

During the planning stage of the project, the ACS had insisted that we build one extra floor on the building. The ACS figured that they would eventually grow into this space and felt that it would be better to have it ready than have to build it later on. An Atlanta foundation generously donated $1 million dollars to cover the cost of this additional floor.

This empty floor presented an excellent opportunity to the University. In the late 1980s Emory decided to open a new School of Public Health, which would fall under the umbrella of the Woodruff Health Sciences Center. At this time we had yet to secure funding for a building for the new school. I asked the foundation to pass their gift to the ACS through me, so that I might request a lease on the space when I presented the check. I signed a five year lease for the empty floor, providing the nascent school with a temporary home. This was a bit of a gamble; if we did not put up a new building by the end of those five years, the school would be homeless.

A School of Public Health was exactly the type of program to kick-start our relationship with the CDC. No other academic discipline lined up as well with the Center's mission. Opening a new school is no small task though. There would have to be committees, faculty searches, fundraising efforts, and of course bureaucratic jostling, but in 1990 we opened Emory's first new School in over seventy years.

For a long time we had had a good Public Health Program within the Medical School. Throughout the 1980s a number of people and events came together to push the program into a full-fledged school. The director of the program at the time was Dr. Eugene Gangarosa. In 1982, recently retired President Jimmy Carter and his wife Rosalynn founded The Carter Center as a part of Emory University. Dr. William Foege joined The Carter Center in 1986 as their Executive Director. He had previously served as the director of the CDC, from 1977 until 1983. He was also very interested in third-world health, as was President Carter. Through conversations with these men, among many others, I made up my mind that it was time to move the Public Health Program out of the medical school. I felt that a medical school and a robust public health program would have wholly different priorities. For the public health program to be successful, it would need its own budget

We asked Dr. Krause (the Dean of the Medical School), Dr. Foege, and the then current Director of the CDC, Dr. James Mason, to advise us on how to move forward. They brought in Dr. D. A. Henderson, the dean of the School of Public Health at Hopkins to consult. I thought that they would come back and propose turning the program into an independent division within the health sciences center. The Yerkes Primate Research Center holds this status. This affords the center the benefits of independence without the financial obligations of a full-fledged school.

Well they came back and told me that they could not pass up the opportunity to establish a new school. I asked them if they were sure, if they understood all that was involved, especially the taxes levied upon a school by the university. They said that even despite all the extra work and money involved, a new school seemed like the best plan. By this time the Public Health Masters program had already moved into the recently completed ACS building. Epidemiology and biostatistics moved over there with them. Dr. Ray Greenberg, a young doctor on the medical school faculty, was in charge of both of these programs. Dr. Greenberg and many of the public health people could feel the gravity beginning to exert its pull, all of them together in that far-flung building. But that was not all they felt—the clock was ticking.

We worked it out so that the CDC would furnish about one-hundred-and-fifty faculty members to the school at no charge. In turn, more of our graduates have gone on to work at the CDC than anywhere else.

I presented all of this to the Executive Fundraising Committee of the Board of Trustees of the university. I made a presentation and at the end of it, they asked me how I planned on funding the school. I told them that I had two or three prospects in mind. Mr. Rollins called me over to his chair and said, "Don't contact anyone else, just come and see me—this sounds like something I'd be interested in."

I talked with Mr. Rollins a couple of days later. He asked me to prepare a paper for him outlining what I would do if I had a School of Public Health. I asked Dr. Ray Greenberg, Chairman of the Department of Epidemiology, to help me draft something. We put it together, making sure to touch upon some topics that I knew Mr. Rollins was interested in. It was nothing too specific, but two or three faculty members took umbrage to the way we drafted the letter. They thought that I was attempting to direct what kind of research they would be doing.

"No, " I said to them, "I cannot imagine a major research facility that wouldn't be interested in cancer and Alzheimer's Disease *somewhere*. I've got to tell Mr. Rollins we're going to study Alzheimer's or we're not going to have any money for a building. That's just how it works."

With the funding seemingly taken care of we began to look for a dean. We formed a search committee and they ultimately recommended three candidates. Dr. Ray Greenberg was a full decade younger than the other two candidates. His youth appealed to me. I have always believed that it is important to bring people into your organization when they are young. Too often Emory has contented itself with hiring established individuals who have already made their mark. If bright people are brought in when they are still young, it is likely they will make their mark working with you, not someone else. Obviously the risk with youth is that their future is unknown. Emory, the gracious southern belle that she is, never likes to fire anyone. If you are not willing to fire someone, then the risk of hiring an unproven commodity only grows. In the end I decided that Dr. Greenberg was worth the risk.

He stayed with us for five years. From the very start he made a very fine dean. He did an outstanding job launching the school, but Ray had greater ambitions, and in 1995 he moved on to the Medical University of South Carolina, where he eventually became the president.

Before he left, the School of Public Health finally moved into a building of its own at 1518 Clifton Road. We dedicated the school's new home in February of 1995, only five years after Mr. Rollins had mentioned to me that funding a public health school was something that he would be interested in. A lot happened in the interim. Sadly, Mr. Rollins passed away in 1991. We had not yet begun construction on the new building, and I grew worried. I said nothing for about two weeks. And then I received a phone call from Mrs. Grace Rollins. To my great relief, she told me that she knew how much the School of Public Health meant to her husband; she would provide the funds as agreed. Construction began in 1993. We named the building the Grace Crum Rollins Public Health Building in honor of her incredible generosity during such a difficult period in her life. In recognition of the Rollins' contributions to the Public Health program, we named the nascent school, the Rollins School of Public Health.

I learned an important lesson building the Grace Crum Rollins School of Public Health Building. The site we initially selected was just down the street from the Rollins Research Building. That lesson I learned? Don't be too free to make changes just to get an agreement done. Well, we marked off the site with balloons, and the family drove up and down Clifton Road to look it over. They came to me to express their concerns that the new building would block the view of the Research Building. They asked if I could move two or three hundred yards toward the CDC.

I, in my naiveté, said, "Oh yes, of course, we'll move it up the hill a little farther."

What I learned, subsequently, was that we moved from a more or less ideal building site on to an outcropping of granite, which ultimately added $300,000 to the construction costs, money we were forced to cough up. After that, when someone made such a request, while I offered to explore the possibility, I never again said, "Oh yes," without going to the builders and the architects.

•◆•

With Dr. Greenberg on the way out we began a search for a new dean. My goal was to find someone a bit different than Ray. He had done an outstanding job and in a way, he validated my feelings about youth by leaving. He made his mark at Emory—he helped us launch the first new American School of Public Health in a half-century. Sure enough he was plucked away by an impressed institution that was ready to grant him greater responsibility. Anyway, Ray had guided us through Phase One— launching the school. Now we were about to enter Phase Two—growing the school. Dr. James Curran seemed like an excellent choice for this difficult task. He had a Masters of Public Health from Harvard and he had been working down the road at the CDC for years, leading their effort to identify AIDS in the early 1980s. Everyone agreed and we quickly brought Dr. Curran aboard. He has excelled since taking over in 1995—the young school is already one of the top ten ranked public health programs in the country. Under Dr. Curran's leadership they have expanded rapidly, building up one of the largest faculties on campus, while growing into the university's second greatest winner of grant dollars.

•◆•

However laborious it may have been, opening up a School of Public Health was probably the most exciting thing one could hope to do as a Vice President for Health Affairs in the 1980s. Public health was then and is now at the forefront of medicine, a field where important research has been done and will continue to be done throughout the twenty-first century. Flip through the pages of a newspaper and you'll read of the threat of biological terrorism and the risk of an Avian flu pandemic. Meanwhile

AIDS continues to ravage sub-Saharan Africa; and the epidemic threatens to spread to the massive urbanizing economies of the BRIC nations (Brazil, Russia, India and China). Thanks to its special relationship with the CDC, the faculty and students of the Rollins School will help fight these crucial battles.

I am very proud of our effort to open the Rollins School. Unfortunately, a couple of years before I was honored with this great responsibility, I had to close a school, which is certainly the most painful thing any university administrator ever has to do.

The Emory Dental School presented me with an administrative problem as soon as I took office. The school was running a deficit of about $2 million dollars a year. Students throughout the nation were disenchanted with the notion of a career in dentistry. Not as many people were applying to dental schools and a number of schools closed during the 1980s. We happened to be the first to close, but a few others followed our lead, while others shrank the size of their classes—in all, the equivalent of ten schools were shuttered. There was also the issue of the type of student whom the Emory Dental School was attracting. As the popularity of the dental school shrank, the size of the school became something of a liability. At its peak the school had been graduating about 180 students per year. By the time I took office they were having a hard time attracting that many new students each year. While the Medical School generally did not consider an applicant with less than a 3.5 undergraduate GPA, toward the end, you could make it into the Dental School next door with a *gentleman's C*. I felt that if we were going to lose $2 million dollars a year, I wanted to lose it on something that was a clear-cut plus for the university.

Prior to World War II, Emory had been the premier Dental School in the southeast. The states contiguous with Georgia—Florida, Alabama, Tennessee, and South Carolina—all contributed money to the School in order to reserve places for their students. After the war, one by one, each state announced its intention to open a local school of dentistry. In 1965, the State of Georgia approved plans for a public dental school. The state school opened two years later, at a cost of about a third the tuition of Emory. For twenty years the school grew, cannibalizing Emory's student base, which had already been in decline due to the establishment of the other southern state schools. I never thought of opposing the state's school, but the idea of having two schools in Georgia just did not make sense, so ours was going to have to go.

I heard grumblings from the alumni of the dental school both ways, but most came to me to ask me to close the school; they felt that the community could not absorb as many dentists as we were graduating every year. Once the decision to close the school was made public everyone rallied around the students, and some of the same people who privately supported my decision cast me as a villain. I can't say that I didn't expect this. I stood firm though—I knew the decision was the right one for the university. In 1984, the administration of the dental school informed the board that they were expecting the following year's incoming a class to have no better than a C+ average. There were ongoing budgetary squabbles between the school and the university over assessments and financial shortcomings. The Board of Trustees of the university agreed that the time had come to shutter the dental school. That year we did not accept an incoming class. We then took a series of steps to close the school in a way that was as fair and as delicate as possible.

We met with the students as soon as the announcement was made, in order to assure them that they would still be able to graduate from an accredited school, that we had every intention to operate for three more years. Now doing so meant committing ourselves to a serious expense, as members of the faculty were less than enthusiastic about staying with us, knowing that they would not have jobs in three years. Getting people to stand on the deck of a sinking ship, even during a controlled sinking, is not exactly an easy thing to do. I offered the faculty an extra year's pay if they remained with us until the school was closed. This amounted to a significant sum, but the action was one that we had to take. We rolled up the debt we took on, amortized it for a number of years, and slowly paid off the balance.

We had said that everyone would graduate from an accredited school. Whether that school was Emory was a decision we left to each student. If they opted to transfer to another school we provided assistance with the application process and financial compensation. If they had a scholarship or financial aid, we allowed them to take that money with them on to the new school. If they transferred to a city where the cost of living was higher than Atlanta's, we made up the difference in the cost of living. As we were going to operate the school for three more years, with a full faculty, I thought that these offers to the students who wished to leave were quite generous. The dean of the dental school during the closure was Dr. Ronnie Weathers. His cooperation and assistance were invaluable.

There were some elements of the school that we thought we could preserve. The oral pathology program was very good, as was the oral surgery program, and I arranged to have them subsumed into the medical school's pathology and surgery departments, respectively. The Dental School had a small endowment, and I decided that the fair and appropriate thing to do was to earmark those funds for the two programs that we retained.

This endowment would remain independent of the medical school's own endowment, so no one could claim that the medical school 'stole' the money.

By acting delicately, deliberately, and most of all fairly, I think now, with the benefit of hindsight, everyone involved would say that we acted appropriately throughout the long and sometimes painful process of closing the dental school.

•◆•

Crawford Long had been willed to Emory in the 1930s by Drs. Davis and Fisher and the hospital retained much of its independence for the next fifty years. While I was still the director of the clinic, the dean of the medical school asked me to regularize Crawford Long, which would mean finding a group of doctors down there who could qualify for clinical faculty appointments and establishing a Section of Medicine at The Emory Clinic (along with some others). Any attempt to integrate the hospital into the Emory Healthcare system would also have to involve a massive renovation project as the facilities at Crawford Long predated World War II. The integration went through, eventually, but the renovation project is an entirely different story.

There were many issues that had to be worked out in order to regularize Crawford Long Hospital. At Crawford Long, we did not control anesthesiology, radiology, pathology, or obstetrics—the so-called hospital based services—they were still in private hands. At the time, these services did not contribute any funds to the medical school. The dean asked me to see if I could work something out with these people so that they would voluntarily join The Emory Clinic. They did not want to do that and it took me about a year-and-a-half to figure something out. The departments of medicine and surgery were already organizing services to be run by the medical school.

The doctors at Crawford Long were not unanimously in favor of the integration plan. In the end the integration was good for every doctor at Crawford Long whom I had had to coerce into the clinic and into the clinical faculty status. Each one of them eventually told me it was the best thing that ever happened to his or her career. There were no lawsuits, but I certainly had scars to show for the fight. It took about two years to get everything done.

I can remember one particular evening, when Dr. Laney and I went down to Crawford Long to speak to the medical staff at their quarterly meeting. A young surgeon stood up at this meeting and asked Dr. Laney, "Why should we believe what you're saying tonight? You've never told us the truth before."

Now this was Dr. Laney—a Professor of Christian Ethics, former Dean of the Theology School, and the President of Emory University! Well Jim didn't know quite how to respond to an absurd accusation like that, and I only mention it to show how entrenched in their position some of the doctors at Crawford Long were back then. They saw integration as a threat to their income, and they were willing to lay everything on the line to preserve their earnings. Ironically, the integration into Emory did nothing but enhance the incomes of these doctors.

More Research

EMORY, AS I MENTIONED EARLIER, was not alone in its position as a research university in Georgia, even in metropolitan Atlanta. Soon after I assumed the dual position of Vice President for Health Affairs/Director of the Woodruff Health Sciences Center, I picked up on the strong desire among many for an increased level of cooperation between Emory University and the Georgia Institute of Technology. Repeatedly, at social functions, faculty and administrators from Georgia Tech would suggest to me various collaborative programs. It was obvious that each school had a significant level of admiration for the other, and that this admiration was in excess of what we held for any other institutions in the state.

On one such occasion, attended by the President of Georgia Tech, I suggested that we should set something up, or quit talking about it. Pressed for specifics, I proposed that Emory would put up a sum of money, which Georgia Tech would match. These funds would be available to pairs of investigators—an Emory medical scientist and a Georgia Tech engineer—who expressed a desire to work cooperatively on a bio-medical project. The fund would provide seed money for these pairs of investigators, but would not be available for independent investigators from each institution. I believe the initial commitment was $300,000 dollars from each institution.

Well, this really got the ball rolling. As we got closer to implementing the program, it was suggested that we outline a formal working arrangement to account for the legal complications of a partnership between a private university and a state school. I suggested, in the interest of time, that we look to the arrangement between Harvard Medical School and the Massachusetts Institute of Technology. I declared my willingness to accept their framework as an acceptable beginning, which we could modify to fit our unique situation any time in the future; Georgia Tech accepted this agreement. State and local politicians, as well as educational leaders, applauded this cooperation between our institutions.

Soon afterward, the Georgia Research Alliance launched as a public-private partnership of the state's large research institutions, corporations, and government. The alliance's mission is to use research to promote economic development. The GRA does not compete with the Georgia Board of Regents for educational funding. Today its member institutions are: Emory, Georgia Tech, the University of Georgia, Clark Atlanta, Georgia State, and the Medical College of Georgia.

The presidents of the six universities meet once a year to consider project and research requests from the participating institutions. In submitting Emory's proposals, I made it quite clear to our scientists that we should never receive more funds than Georgia Tech or the University of Georgia, and that if we saw the possibility of this occurring, we were to talk up proposals from the other institutions, or withdraw one of our applications. Though this may be the opposite of how you would expect us to compete for research dollars (after all, as I stated earlier, it was my goal to greatly increase our research grants), I had a good reason for taking this approach. I do believe that the public (and especially the state politicians and education administrators) would have taken umbrage at Emory, a private university, taking the greatest share of this pool of money. In this way we still received a steady, healthy stream of research dollars without offending anyone's sensibilities. The program has been a tremendous success for all involved:

To date, the Alliance has invested some $400 million, which has helped to attract more than 50 Eminent Scholars, leverage an additional $2 billion in federal and private funding, create more than 5,000 new technology jobs, generate some 120 new technology companies, and allow established Georgia companies to expand into new markets.

Over time, the cooperation between Emory and Georgia Tech has grown more and more sophisticated. In 1997, the two schools established a joint Department of Biomedical Engineering. The chairman of the department holds faculty appointments at both institutions. This department has benefited greatly from a $25 Million dollar gift from the Coulter Foundation made in honor of Wallace Coulter the Georgia Tech student who developed the Coulter Counter (used to perform a complete blood count, one of the most commonly performed diagnostic procedures in the world).

It is fitting that Emory and Georgia Tech have developed a close collaborative relationship in the field of engineering—Georgia Tech's first President, Isaac Hopkins was recruited from Emory, where he studied as an undergraduate and served as president and chair of the "Department of Toolcraft and Design." With Hopkins' departure, Emory's nascent technology program, which was initially housed in Hopkins' own home, was without a leader. And so, in 1889, the school ceded the field of engineering to Georgia Tech. Over 100 years later, they came back together, not in competition, but in cooperation.

An Ape Named Charlie

TIGHTENING OUR BONDS WITH THE CDC was not the only way we beefed up our research efforts in the 1980s. The Yerkes National Primate Research Center—one of the eight national NIH-funded primate research centers—has been located on Emory's campus since 1965. Functioning as an independent division of the health sciences center, it played an important role in our drive to expand our research efforts in the 1980s. As it was an independent division, the director of Yerkes reported directly to me (in my role as Vice President for Health Affairs). So, when Dr. Fred King—the longtime director of Yerkes—retired in 1994, it was my responsibility to assist in the recruitment of a new director. Around this time the National Primate Centers were changing their missions; formerly, the directors of the divisions had been Primatologists, and as such behavioral studies had been the focus of their research. I saw a rare opportunity to take advantage of this unique population by shifting the focus of the center's research to neurosciences and ophthalmology.

We appointed Dr. Mahlon Delong, Professor and Chair of Neurology, as the Chairman of the Search Committee. Assisting Dr. Delong were a number of outstanding faculty members. President Bill Clinton, who had recently taken office, had just appointed Dr. Judith Vydakitis as the Director of the Center for Research Resources at the National Institutes of Health. I was unsure of her politics, but the thought crossed my mind that perhaps she might insist upon a woman for the position. I did not care whether we selected a man or a woman for the position, but I did not want to appoint a female director—because of other considerations—if she were not the best candidate in the pool. While I had the authority to make the recommendation, Dr. Vydakitis had to concur in the appointment. Thus I made sure to include her in the search process from the beginning.

I notified Dr. Vydakitis of the upcoming search, and followed up with information on the chairman and members of the search committee. She responded in an appreciative manner. Once we selected a field of finalists some months later, I forwarded her their CVs. Soon I was ready to recommend a candidate; I contacted her office to ask for an appointment to discuss my plans directly with Dr. Vydakitis. She received me most graciously in her Washington office. I expressed my desire to appoint Dr. Thomas Insel of the National Institutes of Health to the directorship. Dr. Insel was an outstanding neurologist, and I felt he would lead a research effort with the change in emphasis that I desired. Dr. Vydakitis concurred in the offer I proposed to make to Dr. Insel.

That evening I entertained Dr. Insel and his wife at the Jockey Club at the Ritz Carlton in Georgetown. I made him a generous offer, which he quickly accepted. In determining what level of compensation I should offer Dr. Insel, I looked at his current income at NIH, along with the earnings of his wife, a local school teacher. I combined these two numbers, and then padded the sum with a bit for moving expenses. In this way, Mrs. Insel could retire if she wished, without any effect on their joint income, and their move to Atlanta could be done without any expenses incurred on the Insel's part.

Dr. Insel proved to be a very satisfactory and popular appointment. He served as the director of Yerkes for the better part of a decade; his tenure was marked by an increased emphasis on neuroscience and ophthalmologic research, with a particular focus on AIDS and vaccine research. He continues to serve as the Founding Director of the Center for Behavioral Neuroscience, an interdisciplinary research center that draws faculty and students from eight Atlanta colleges and universities. In 2002, Dr. Insel declared his desire to go back to the research laboratory on a full-time basis; he returned to Washington as the new Director of the National Institute of Mental Health.

Dr. Michael Johns, my successor as the Vice President for Health Affairs, appointed Dr. Stewart Zola to head up Yerkes; I hear that he has functioned brilliantly in that position.

•◆•

In the 1980s, the Atlanta Zoo came into some considerable difficulties. A rating organization had listed their facility as one of the poorest in the nation. Attendance was slumping, and several instances of inadequate or inappropriate animal care had been documented. Animals died under mysterious circumstances; others were sold off to circuses. The American Association of Zoological Parks and Aquariums denied the facility accreditation in 1984. A movement developed to privatize the zoo. The Atlanta Zoological society led the charge; they accomplished their mission with the acquiescence of local politicians.

The Friends of Zoo Atlanta—the new non-profit civic group formed to finance the zoo's operations—secured Dr. Terry Maple, a comparative psychologist at Georgia Tech, to lead the reorganized Zoo Atlanta. Dr. Maple expressed to me his interest in having Emory loan the Zoo some of the great ape families residing at Yerkes. The Zoo had become something of a black eye on Atlanta's civic conscious, and I was eager to do my part to help in its restoration. I met with Dr. Maple, Mr. Robert Holder of the Zoological Society, and Dr. King of Yerkes to work out an animal loan program.

Several families of great apes were loaned to Zoo Atlanta. These animals were made available without charge or restriction by Yerkes; but as federal property, Yerkes was to retain exclusive ownership and breeding rights to the apes. Further, Ford Motor Company agreed to contribute approximately $2 Million dollars to build a habitat for these animals, the Ford African Rainforest. Realizing that this new and improved habitat was superior to the conditions at Yerkes, and that the expenses for maintenance and routine care of these animals would be transferred to Zoo Atlanta, and quite cognizant of what a primate exhibit of this magnitude would mean to Atlanta and the viewing public, this arrangement proved to be a win-win situation for all involved. The primate exhibit became quite popular (it is one of the largest great ape collections in the United States) and greatly improved the reputation of Zoo Atlanta. In 1987, the zoo recovered its accreditation.

Later, we worked out a similar loan arrangement with Busch Gardens, in Florida. I visited their park, and was again convinced that better facilities and care could be provided for our animals in a more proper zoo environment than at Yerkes. These primates have been a big hit at Busch Gardens, just as they are at Zoo Atlanta.

A small animal hospital was subsequently constructed and named for my good friend, Dr. Mortimer Silberman, the Emory University Veterinarian. Dr. Silberman went on to serve as the Assistant VP for Governmental Affairs at the health sciences center. Dr. Silberman was chosen for this honor on account of his valuable services to the zoo, services he also provided to the private zoo assembled at the White Oak Plantation by the late Howard Gilman. For his various consulting activities and all-around expertise with large animals, Mort became known as "Super Vet," an honorary title in which he took great pride.

Up until the Yerkes animals joined the Zoo Atlanta population, the Zoo cared for only one great ape, Willie B. Willie B. had been named for Mayor William Hartsfield, a long-serving mayor for whom the airport is more famously named, for his tireless work in developing Atlanta into an international airport hub. Upon my retirement, the zoo named a small young male gorilla "Charlie," after me. When people would tell me what an honor this was, I joked that naming opportunities for a gorilla were somewhat limited. I seriously doubt if any of our politicians today would see the humor of naming a gorilla in their honor. Although I joked about it, I did consider it quite an accolade!

The Nell Hodgson Woodruff School of Nursing

THE NELL HODGSON WOODRUFF SCHOOL of Nursing was a vital division of the Woodruff Health Sciences Center when I became Vice President for Health Affairs. Although several private universities had decided to close their schools of nursing during this period, the role of Emory University School of Nursing had been officially reaffirmed as a division of our health sciences center.

However, the school was not without its challenges. Nationally, a shortage of nurses had developed, but the disparity between the tuition at a private university school of nursing and a public or hospital based school was quite significant. The starting salaries for graduates of private schools and other schools of nursing were essentially the same. I felt that increased financial assistance to the students at the Nell Hodgson Woodruff School of Nursing was quite in order. I therefore gave my full support to the NEAT program (Nursing Employment and Tuition). In return for a steady supply of trained nurses, Emory University Hospital, Crawford W. Long Hospital of Emory University, and several private hospitals in Atlanta provided scholarships to the school of nursing. The program placed the student nurses in the hospital providing the scholarship funds for as many electives and other rotations as possible, hopefully providing a nurse capable of assuming his or her responsibilities shortly after employment without additional training. The nursing student agreed to an appropriate period of employment at the sponsoring hospital, reducing nurse staff turnover and its associated costs. This program worked reasonably well until the outside participating hospitals entered competing hospital systems and health maintenance organizations.

In the 1980s the faculty of the school of nursing was very anxious to develop a Ph.D. program in nursing. Initially I was reluctant to approve this doctoral program, having some reservations about whether nursing offered a sufficient body of knowledge to be the basis of a Ph.D. degree. I preferred for the nurses interested in obtaining a Ph.D. to get the degree in a more formal discipline, i.e., a Ph.D. in physiology, a Ph.D. in chemistry. Medical schools did not offer a Ph.D. in medicine; would it be appropriate for our nursing school to offer such a Ph.D. in nursing? Ultimately, the faculty convinced me that our school would be at a disadvantage in faculty recruitment until such a program was instituted. I acquiesced, and over the next several years the school developed its Ph.D. program. Two students enrolled in this doctoral program focused on clinical research in 1999, well after my retirement. The dean and faculty of the school of nursing are quite proud of this program, and consider it to be most successful.

The other major challenge faced by the school during this period related to the planning and construction of a new and larger state-of-the-art building. These plans were developed by the school and submitted to the university for approval. All such building projects were presented to university administration for official approval before being placed on the fundraising list. Once placed on the officially approved list, fundraising could commence. Funds raised in this manner could ultimately be matched by the university. The spending rate of the university at that time was 4 1/2 % of the three year rolling average of the value of the endowment. One half of 1% of these monies was placed in a building account to provide these matching monies. It soon became apparent that fundraising for a building of this size and expense would prove to be quite difficult. The nursing school building on Asbury Circle had been constructed in 1968. Aware that Emory University Hospital needed additional space, I asked Mr. John Henry if he would be interested in acquiring the nursing school site and/or the building. His immediate answer was "yes, by all means."

An official appraisal followed, and subsequently Mr. Henry made an offer of approximately $7 million for the property. With this offer in hand, I suggested to the Dean of the Nursing School, Dr. Dyanne Affonso, that she approach the University for matching funds. This was done, and the matching funds were made available. There was some discussion of the irregularities involved, but no one wished to deny funding for this very worthwhile project. The school of nursing moved into its current beautiful building on Clifton Road in 2001 under the administration of Dean Marla Salmon.

Ada Fort had been Dean of the School of Nursing from 1951 to 1976. Dr. Edna Grexton was appointed dean in 1976, and served until 1984.

Shortly after my appointment as vice president, Dr. Grexton vacated the deanship of the school of nursing. A committee was appointed made up of faculty and alumni. I served as chairperson of the committee. Early in our deliberations, we made a list of candidates to be considered. Each committee member was furnished a complete C.V. on each candidate to be considered, and asked to rank the candidates in numerical order. The candidates with the highest rankings would be interviewed initially. At the next meeting of the search committee, it quickly became apparent that the most highly regarded candidate was Dr. Clair Martin. I then realized that I was the only person in the room who was aware that Dr. Clair Martin was a male. When I divulged that fact to the committee, the room became very quiet. I asked if it made any difference to them that Clair Martin was a man. All except one now took the position that it did not matter. One senior faculty member admitted that it did make a great deal of difference to her, and that she would withdraw her support for Dr. Martin. I told the committee that it made a great deal of difference to me as well, and that I was most reluctant to appoint a male dean to a school that had always had female deans, and that the university might object to one its few female deans being replaced by a male. I was soundly criticized for this, and told that the school should be allowed to have the dean of its choice, and that I would just have to face up to the criticism that this appointment might engender. I asked for a vote of the nursing school faculty before finalizing the appointment, and Dr. Martin received favorable votes from over ninety percent of the faculty. He was appointed in 1986, and served until 1992.

It had long been my desire to have the nursing division at Emory University Hospital and the Nell Hodgson Woodruff School of Nursing work cooperatively. In 1984, Ms. Mary Woody, a longtime colleague at Emory had just returned to the campus after a tour as the founding dean of the Auburn University School of Nursing (1979-84). Mary Woody was named Director of Nursing at Emory University Hospital and Associate Dean for the Nell Hodgson Woodruff School of Nursing. She worked very closely with Dean Martin in a cooperative and collegial manner which made it possible for nursing school faculty to maintain clinical practice, and for hospital nurses to participate in student teaching.

After Dr. Martin resigned the deanship in 1992, Dr. Dyanne Affonso was appointed dean and served until 1998. Dr. Affonso was a native of Hawaii, and had been very active in nursing research and was at the time one of the most heavily funded nursing researchers in the United States. Dr. Affonso served as dean for five years before Dr. Michael Johns appointed Dr. Marla Salmon to the deanship. Dr. Salmon proved to be an excellent appointment. Currently Dr. Linda A. McCauley serves as Dean of the Nell

Hodgson Woodruff School of Nursing, and initial signs indicate that this, too, will be an outstanding appointment.

The Woodruff family is intimately tied to the history and development of the school of nursing. When Emory University made known its desire to name the school after Mrs. Nell Woodruff, Mr. Robert Woodruff clearly understood the agenda, but he was pleased for Mrs. Woodruff to receive this recognition. She remained very active in the programs of the school of nursing. During their courtship, Nell Hodgson of Athens, Georgia, was a student nurse at an Athens hospital, and it is said that Mr. Robert Woodruff took the bus over to Athens each weekend to court Ms. Nell. Invariably he would board the bus holding a bouquet of roses. Someone commented that they would like to have a boyfriend who was so thoughtful. Mr. Woodruff joked that these roses were not for Nell. They were for her supervisor at the hospital so that she could get off duty for her date with him!

Initially, Mr. Woodruff provided a gift each year of some six figures to the Nell Hodgson Woodruff School for its endowment fund. One year, without his knowledge, the dean of the school of nursing, apparently with the permission of the Emory University president, used this annual gift to cover operating costs in the school rather than add it to the endowment as directed. Mr. Woodruff was quite upset, and terminated these annual gifts. Mrs. Woodruff participated in the groundbreaking for the building on Asbury Circle in 1965, and tragically died only five days later, apparently of a cerebral hemorrhage. I and many others believe that Mrs. Woodruff and her interest in nursing and the care of patients helped to determine that health sciences would ultimately become a (or the) major site of his philanthropy.

The Consolidation of Pediatric Health Care in Atlanta

BOTH DRS. ABBOTT AND LOGAN had been active for some time at the Egleston Children's Hospital located on the Emory campus. They had been performing closed cardiac surgery, but the hospital staff was unwilling to let us establish a pediatric open heart surgery program. They did permit us to bring the older children to the Emory University Hospital for surgery. We would watch over these children in the regular ICU for a limited period, and then we would return them to the pediatric facility. As we dropped the age of patients undergoing surgery toward newborns, it became increasingly difficult to justify this arrangement. I used to joke that I had arthritis of the knees and right elbow from kneeling and tipping my hat to the Egleston administration, trying to get them to agree to open heart surgery.

Eventually, the hospital relented. We recruited Dr. William Plauth from the Boston Children's Hospital to serve as our Chief Pediatric Cardiologist. Bill Plauth had been a friend and colleague at Hopkins. He served as the chief resident at the Harriet Lane Home for Invalid Children the same year that I was the Halsted resident in surgery. Our new program was successful almost from the start. Dr. William D. Logan and I participated in many of these pediatric cases, and on occasion Dr. Abbott served as the operating surgeon. By and large, the children of that era presented significantly less surgical risk than the older adults who had experienced congestive failure or other symptoms over a period of years.

There are few things more rewarding to a cardiac surgeon than to be able to correct or significantly ease the condition of a child with congenital heart disease. This is especially true when cyanotic heart disease can be significantly improved or completely corrected. The look on the parents' faces when they see a 'pink' child for the first time is an unforgettable experience.

•◆•

For years Emory University and the Henrietta Egleston Hospital for Children enjoyed the mutual benefits of institutional cooperation. Mr. Horace Sibley, an attorney with King and Spalding, was the chairman of the Egleston Board of Trustees in the early 1990s. Horace was very involved in bringing the Olympics to Atlanta in 1996, and he wished to restructure the Egleston Hospital and Board Administration before resigning, so that he could devote more time to the Olympic effort. The first step in this process involved an evaluation and position paper developed by McKinsey and Company. The McKinsey partner assigned to the project was Mr. Alan Gayer. He developed a very satisfactory vision statement for Egleston, the details of which pleased Emory University and the Trustees of Egleston Hospital.

Shortly after this work had been accomplished, Mr. Sibley called me and wished to know what I thought about appointing Alan Gayer as the CEO of the hospital. He was terribly impressed that Mr. Gayer was a young partner in McKinsey and Company, and that he had been a Rhodes Scholar. I did not question Mr. Gayer's abilities, but raised concern about asking a consultant to take over and manage executive responsibilities. I regarded then, and still regard, the appointment of a consultant to a high administrative position within the organization he has evaluated, as a classic error to be avoided at all cost. But Horace was very impressed with Mr. Gayer's credentials and the Vision Statement he had written. As CEO of the Woodruff Health Sciences Center I had to agree to this appointment, though the appointment had to originate from the Board of Egleston Hospital.

At that point, Mr. Sibley announced that he thought that Mr. Inman Allen would be an excellent replacement for him as Chairman of the Board. I questioned the wisdom of having these two positions filled simultaneously with new and inexperienced individuals, but Horace was quite convinced of the ability of both, and was anxious to accomplish these appointments before his resignation from the Board of Trustees.

Over the next several years, the details of the Vision Statement became somewhat blurred. Originally committed to the support of teaching and research, the hospital shifted its focus to the bottom line as healthcare grew more competitive. Mr. Allen settled into the position of Chairman of the Board and served in that capacity for a number of years.

•◆•

Mr. Gayer and Egleston Hospital encountered the harsh changes taking place in the pediatric medical marketplace as Health Maintenance Organizations arrived in the Atlanta area. The HMOs frequently pitted Egleston Hospital and the Scottish Rite Hospital for Invalid Children against each other. They bargained from a strong position—they could threaten to take their business to the other hospital if one of the hospitals did not agree to their terms. Each of the hospitals began to establish numerous out-patient clinics throughout the metropolitan area, and both undertook extensive and expensive publicity activities. I jokingly commented at one meeting that they reminded me of McDonalds and Burger King building a store on every corner and trying to convince the public that each of the brands was superior, when in point of fact there was very little difference in what was being offered by the two institutions.

When I had first arrived at Emory, two outstanding individuals directed the Medical Services at the Children's Hospital. Dr. Richard Blumberg was Chairman of the Department of Pediatrics at the Emory University School of Medicine, and the Section Head of Pediatrics in The Emory Clinic. Dr. Joseph Patterson was the Chief Physician of Egleston Hospital. There was some tension between these two positions, and I determined, later when it became my responsibility to be involved, that these two positions might be combined and thereby avoid any possible friction. When Dean James Glenn appointed Dr. George Brumley as Chairman of Pediatrics, I urged that he also be made the Chief Physician at Egleston Hospital. Dean Glenn took my advice and this was accomplished.

Dr. Brumley was a neonatologist, and dedicated to the academic mission of pediatrics. He had been an intensivist by training, and therefore did not draw referral patients into the hospital as Dr. Patterson had. Throughout his career, Dr. Patterson was regarded as the final authority on the diagnosis and treatment of sick children, and was an invaluable source of referral to the hospital from pediatricians throughout the state. When Dr. Brumley did not step up to fill this role, Egleston Hospital was disappointed and felt victimized by Emory University. Friction developed, which made Dr. Brumley's position quite difficult.

I was not at all involved in the administration of Scottish Rite Hospital, but I noted their progress in a difficult environment, and the CEO of that

Hospital, Dr. James Talley impressed me. In this setting, I received a phone call from the office of Mr. James B. Williams, who at the time was chairman of the Woodruff Health Sciences Center Board of Trustees, and also the Chairman of the Board of Trustees of the Woodruff Foundations. He had with him in the office Mr. Larry Gellerstedt, Jr., who had replaced Mr. Inman Allen as Chairman of the Board of Trustees of Egleston Hospital. They had talked about the competitive situation involving the two hospitals, and had wondered if it might be possible to forge a merger of the two institutions to the benefit of both, and the Atlanta community. They asked me to quietly undertake discussions with Dr. Talley and Scottish Rite Hospital. Since I was enthusiastic about this opportunity, I was pleased to undertake these discussions.

I made an appointment with Dr. Talley and drove out to the Scottish Rite Hospital. He received me graciously, but as soon as I brought up the question of a merger of the two hospitals, he quickly stated that he would never, under any circumstances, work for Mr. Alan Gayer. I chuckled, and told Dr. Talley I was a very busy person, and if I had thought that that was in the cards, that I would not have wasted my time in coming out to talk to him. This quieted him down, and we had very productive discussion about the advantages of a merger of the two hospitals into Children's Healthcare of Atlanta. I suggested that he would be a likely candidate for the top position in such a merger. Dr. Talley stated that though he felt the likelihood of a successful merger to be very small, he would discuss it with his Board of Trustees

He subsequently reported that the Board of Trustees, though also rather skeptical about a possible merger, had agreed that out of consideration and respect for me, they would explore the possibility. They retained a public relations firm to poll Atlanta civic leaders and philanthropists regarding their feelings on a merger of our two pediatric hospitals; this poll found that support for the merger within the community was almost unanimous.

As a result of my own actions, I now faced the prospect of a merger of the two pediatric hospitals without a significant relationship to the Emory University School of Medicine. This would have been the worst possible outcome of these discussions from the standpoint of the Emory Department of Pediatrics. Fortunately, others saw the need to guarantee the relationship between Emory and a merged hospital. The Woodruff Foundation strongly supported this relationship, and made it clear to those involved that a proper relationship with the Department of Pediatrics and the hospitals would benefit from the Foundation's financial support. Since Scottish Rite did not have a history of supporting an academic mission in their hospital, I suggested that the monies being spent on advertising could be diverted to the Department of Pediatrics without any noticeable budgetary affect.

I was not at all involved in the merger of these two hospitals, except to help plant the seed and offer encouragement. I did see the various health plans and HMOs pitting one hospital against the other, and I predicted that a merger was inevitable, and that it should be accomplished before the two institutions were impoverished by this competition. I further stated that the merged hospital entity could take a firm stand with the HMOs and they would have a very strong position in these negotiations so long as their charges were regarded as fair, and supported by the general public in Atlanta. As I anticipated, the new CEO of Children's Healthcare of Atlanta was Dr. James Talley. Mr. Alan Gayer graciously stepped aside and departed the scene with a golden parachute. Children's Healthcare has been very successful, and has fulfilled its responsibilities to the children of Atlanta and the surrounding area without any loss in public support and private philanthropy.

Services have been divided where appropriate, located to a specific hospital.

When consolidation was in order, reductions were made. The relationship between Children's Healthcare and the Emory University School of Medicine remains very satisfactory.

I consider the establishment of Children's Healthcare and the merger of Egleston and Scottish Rite Hospital to be among the most positive developments in Atlanta's recent history, and I have offered congratulations to all concerned in this bold and strategic merger.

The Changing Nature of the
Academic Health Sciences Center

As the Vice President for Health Affairs, I quickly discovered that the changing medical marketplace presented many difficulties for Academic health sciences centers.

First, there is the constant friction between the clinical enterprise and the research enterprise. We needed to expand the size and scope of the research enterprise, and I set that as my highest priority. The first building that we brought online was the Rollins Research Building. As I have discussed in other places, I brought the idea to increase our emphasis on research to the Board of Trustees in detail. They encouraged me to expand the research enterprise, but to do so without an adverse affect on the clinical enterprise. I stated that all of this would be very difficult to do, but that I would do my best.

Unfortunately, it is quite difficult to develop these two enterprises simultaneously. Recruitment is influenced by the type of individuals added to the faculty, and if one is expanding research, individuals with a primary interest in research are recruited as department chairmen and division chiefs. In the process of recruitment, it is almost an afterthought that individuals are queried about their interest in clinical medicine and their ability to run a multimillion dollar clinical enterprise. Within six months of an appointment, it would be clear that someone leaned in one direction or another, but there are a limited number of "Leonardo Da Vinci's" who can be superior in all aspects of academic work — clinical care, research, and teaching. It is therefore necessary to take the position that all of these activities are valuable, and the faculty member should be rewarded for excellence in any of these fields. The most difficult job was to reward teaching. Superior clinicians make money, and superior researchers achieve fame and increase grant funding, but superior teachers rarely achieve such easily recognizable rewards.

Whenever a clinician was proposed for promotion, there were frequently one or two basic science chairmen who would question all activities except bench research. In the back of their minds I am certain that some clinicians considered the researchers to be 'Rat Doctors.' To avoid this type of discussion, we settled on three tracks for the medical faculty. The Academic Track was for those individuals who were interested in clinical medicine, but who continued to perform meaningful research and were outstanding teachers. The Academic Track would be similar to the routine tracks in many medical schools. The Clinical Track was for those individuals who were active members of The Emory Clinic, who were capable of supporting themselves through their practice, and therefore did not require a tenured commitment of salary support by the School of Medicine. The Research Track drew individuals who were predominantly involved in laboratory research, and would provide grant funding once they were established, except for those times when they might require periodic support from the School of Medicine between funded grants.

Although I realized that other institutions had various ideas about the solution to these problems, I found that the multiple track approach was very helpful to me, and it seemed to avoid evaluation of a faculty member's career by someone totally disinterested in their area of activity.

As the notion of managed care developed, I anticipated less and less profitability from the clinic and the hospitals. At the same time, I was convinced the National Institutes of Health would provide an ever-increasing funding stream for research. Accordingly, we added to the research enterprise to take advantage of these increased funding opportunities, and developed the research teams necessary to compete effectively for Center Grants. Research funding has increased several fold in the past few years under my successor, Dr. Michael M. E. Johns, and more recently under Dr. Fred Sanfilippo. As predicted, the clinical enterprise struggled for several years after my departure, and has only recently returned to profitability of modest proportions. The Emory Clinic is no longer able to offer the medical school the type of financial support provided in my era. This is a simple reflection of the changed economics of modern healthcare.

Secondly, I realized that the departmental structure of the School of Medicine was even more rigid than I had supposed. Department chairmen, almost to a man or woman, were primarily interested in their departments— frustratingly, their own professional interests determined in large part their relationships and degree of cooperation with other departments.

Department chairmen cherished their authority, and rightly so. But this can carry over to an authoritarian control of clinical monies, which is quite counterproductive. As an example, the chairman of pediatrics at one point was overly aggressive in distributing monies from pediatric cardiology into other less profitable divisions of the department. Whenever clinical monies are divided arbitrarily, there

is resentment, and hostility will develop. In a relatively short period of time, a large segment of the division of pediatric cardiology resigned and set up a separate competitive practice within the Atlanta metropolitan area. This resulted in a rapid decrease in hospital census, and a decreased volume of cardiac surgery.

The Chairman of the Board of Trustees of the Henrietta Egleston Hospital for Children arranged a meeting with me. He felt it was imperative that I seek the return of the pediatric cardiologists who had left the system. He stated quite clearly that 1/3 of the revenues of the Hospital depended upon the heart services. I jokingly assured him that I was going to assist with the problem, but that I wished a few minutes just to enjoy having been told that the hospital could not survive without the heart program, when years before I had begged and pleaded with the hospital to allow us to begin open heart surgery in the first place.

I met with the disenchanted pediatric cardiologists, and asked them to prepare a paper for me outlining the type and number of personnel they needed, and the facilities that would be required to have the finest pediatric cardiac program that they could envision. They returned with a proposal that required several million dollars of funds, which the hospital somewhat reluctantly made available.

The pediatric cardiology program was reconstituted, but after this episode the board realized that the program was too vital to be left to the actions of any one department chairman. Accordingly, a Governing Board for the Pediatric Heart Center was developed that included the chairman of pediatrics, the chief of cardiovascular surgery, the chairman of anesthesiology, and the chairman of radiology. The various departments all had commitments to and vital interest in the success of the Pediatric Cardiology Program, and yet no one person would be in a position to inadvertently sabotage the effort. In the beginning I served as chairman of this Board, but as soon as it was determined that the Pediatric Heart Center was going to be extremely successful with this organizational structure, I stepped aside.

I had always insisted on a productivity factor in determining income at The Emory Clinic. Each year the section head or chairman, the partner and I would look over their productivity and determine proper compensation. In these discussions I acted as the ombudsman for the non-chairman partner. The formula used was so well known that in over a decade of experience there was no one who felt that any decision had been arbitrary; and I cannot recall a single episode of unpleasantness related to an individual's compensation from clinical activity. If money is arbitrarily shifted from one specialty to another, or from one individual to others in a department by the action of a chairman, this has an immediate negative effect on productivity, and in time results in the departure of the more productive clinicians. People who have large clinical practices have readily available opportunities in a metropolitan area like Atlanta. If an exodus begins, it will involve the best and brightest. The less productive partners will remain with you because they see very limited opportunities available to them in the outside world.

• ◆ •

The Board of Trustees once asked me if I pursued a more generous compensation for the partners of The Emory Clinic relative to certain academic institutions in our area. I readily admitted that such was the case. I used Duke University as an example for why I followed this policy. If a faculty member at Duke wishes to resign, he has a number of major life decisions to face—moving out of Durham, North Carolina, selling a home, relocating his children to other schools, asking his wife to accept a new circle of friends, and so on. If a faculty member who is a partner of The Emory Clinic wishes to resign, the next morning he only has the decision of turning right or turning left at the end of his driveway. He will take a position at one of the city's private hospitals, at increased compensation compared to the university. Therefore, we had to remain in a range sufficiently close to private practice to permit us to retain the best and brightest of our clinicians.

Dr. Rein Saral

I must state that from 1953 until the early 1990s, The Emory Clinic operated as a private partnership. Partnership was achieved after one to four years of work at the clinic. Each partner had an equal vote. The Administrative Committee, made up of the chairmen of the clinical departments of the medical school and section heads, managed the business of the clinic through monthly meetings. But each quarter there was a meeting of the full partnership at which time all actions taken by the Administrative Committee were to be ratified or rejected by the full partnership of the clinic. When it became necessary to establish Emory Healthcare, the system that involves our hospitals and The Emory Clinic, it became desirable for the clinic to become a non-profit foundation instead of remaining a for-profit partnership. A bi-product of this change was to greatly increase the authority of the chairmen and section heads, and to decrease the authority of The Emory Clinic Director. I realized in retrospect that I had always enjoyed the support of the rank and file. For a chairman or a group of chairmen to object to my articulated policies was usually deemed unwise.

Once the clinic became a non-profit foundation, the Administrative Committee became in essence a Board of Directors, and the clinic director felt that he reported to them, and was subject to their ultimate authority. This had the unintended effect of making the clinic director a person with great responsibility and very little personal authority. The hospitals also became larger and more productive components of the system. They are now the rather dominant partners. In adjusting to the changes taking place in the marketplace, the decision was made that Emory Healthcare should be placed under the authority of a businessman. As such, the day to day activities of the health system are now in the capable hands of an appropriate individual. The Executive Vice President for Health Affairs must relate to this new and evolving organizational structure.

I came to Emory in 1962, at the end of the first decade of the clinic's existence. We saw patients on referral from other physicians only. We were not involved in primary care, and certainly not in the routine follow-up of patients. Following their diagnosis and treatment at The Emory Clinic, patients were returned to their referring physicians for on-going care. With the advent of managed care, Academic health sciences centers have had to spend millions of dollars developing primary care programs. Doing so has put them in direct competition with the very doctors who had been our lifeblood. This redefining of the role of the Academic Health Center has not been particularly inspiring.

Leadership and Recruitment

RECRUITING IS THE VITAL FUNCTION of Senior Administration at an Academic health sciences center. Yet sometimes I feel we do not have a proper system. When a vacancy occurs, it is necessary to advertise in certain journals and periodicals. This usually means that the people who apply are frequently dissatisfied with their current position. Alternately, the technique of calling around the country to other institutions rarely results in a viable candidate, since it is unlikely that someone will be mentioned as a potential candidate if they are performing quite well where they are. The tendency is to recommend people who are unappreciated locally for academic performance, or indeed who may be regarded as 'trouble makers.' I have therefore favored the use of search firms in preparing a list of potential candidates rather than advertising and word of mouth from deans and chairmen.

I believe that we should go to the trouble to identify the next bright star in a department and not settle on a known entity who has acquired a senior status in another institution. Recruitment of such a senior person is invariably expensive, as you must duplicate all that he has accumulated over years at his other institution. In many cases, his or her best work has already been done. At any rate, we tend to recruit such individuals on the basis of some bit of outstanding scientific work or a very impressive bibliography. Their interest in clinical matters and their ability to operate a large business enterprise is routinely assumed, and discussions of the clinical enterprise take place almost as an afterthought. I look to Ray Greenberg and the success he had building up the School of Public Health as a powerful example of the alternative approach.

An overriding consideration in these matters is institutional culture. Most deans, chairmen and division heads are given the benefit of every doubt, and usually retained long after it is widely known that they are not going to succeed. Part of the anxiety involved in dismissing such senior individuals has to do with the perceived negative impact that this will have on recruiting future individuals in the same category. If indeed such hesitancy to dismiss a dean or chairman is the institutional culture, then recruitment has to be pursued quite carefully. The individuals considered are usually at the peak of their careers in a comparable institution. It is sort of like getting married without the possibility of divorce. If you know that the individual appointed is not going to be dismissed regardless of performance over the next several years, it is probably wise to recruit only known entities with established national reputations. As I said in an earlier chapter, this makes it rather hazardous to appoint young individuals who may be on the verge of outstanding work.

If an institution is going to select a youthful, rising star, the institution must also be prepared to make a mid-course correction if the appointment does not prove satisfactory. The two philosophies must be observed simultaneously. The institution must be prepared to relieve that individual rather promptly if the appointment does not work out. Overly conservative management of key appointments deprives the institution of youth and vigor, and limits senior appointments to known individuals with proven track records, who are at the peak of their careers. Such recruitment is expensive, and the results are often less than spectacular.

Coups and Colonels; Movie Stars and Figureheads

THE 1970S A SURGEON, DR. Eimar Delly De Araujo, who was also an officer in the Brazilian Navy, invited me to speak at the Brazilian College of Surgeons. This was during the time when the military controlled the government. When we landed in Rio de Janeiro the stewardess made an announcement, asking me to identify myself. I joked to my colleagues with whom I had made the trip, "Oh, we haven't even touched the ground and I'm in trouble already!"

A military officer was waiting for us on the tarmac in his car. He told me that we would have coffee while our luggage was handled. He took us to a beautiful little room and we had coffee and some sweet rolls. We then left for our hotel. As I had been invited by a member of the military, I was put up at the government-owned National Hotel, on the Copacabana Beach. I made four lectures over four days; it was a lot of work, but I enjoyed it very, very much.

I knew a patient of Dr. Warren's, Mrs. Antonio Frager, who lived in Brazil. Her family was involved in the local ship-building industry. She invited me to her house for a dinner attended by the Minister of Health and other important guests. She also made her car and her driver available to me during my visit to the country.

One night at the College there was an affair with samba music and dancers in ruffled dresses wearing massive wigs with fruit baskets on their heads and all the rest. Toward the end of the performance the lead dancer came up to our table, reached across the table, and invited me to dance. I politely declined. The president of the College of Surgeons said, 'Oh no, no, it is expected that you get up and dance.'

Well I got up and by the time I reached the stage I had already picked out the spot where I expected to collapse, in order to facilitate my resuscitation. She went to it and I decided, by God, I was going to match her samba for samba. They said I did well, but by the time it was over I was so tired I didn't know what was going on.

As the Director and CEO of the clinic I made contact with a number of interesting personalities—abroad and in Atlanta. I can still remember the day when my secretary called and said, "I think there is a crazy man on the telephone."

Somewhat amused I took the call and was greeted with an enthusiastic, "Charlie, baby, how you doin' man? I hear you're the guy that handles things in Atlanta."

I returned his friendly greeting and asked what I could do for him.

"Well," he said, "Richard Harris is in town and we need some cast insurance to cover him while he's making a movie. It would be quite helpful if you could see him, put your stethoscope on his head and certify him for this cast insurance. He's really in good health, and this should take only a few minutes of your time, and you can charge us two or three times what you charge for a normal physical examination. The only thing is, Richard will not come out to your office; he wants to be seen in his hotel suite."

I assured the caller that I would be pleased to arrange for someone to do the exam of Mr. Harris, as I was much too involved to personally take the time off to go down to the hotel. He expressed disappointment, but then said that he quite understood, and he would appreciate it if I would just send the proper individual. I called a cardiologist friend of mine, and he was happy to go down to the hotel that afternoon to give Richard Harris the basic examination that was necessary for the insurance. That night I was telling the kids about the interesting call, and Charlie asked me, "Dad, why didn't you go down and see Richard Harris?"

And I said, "Son, I'm afraid that was not to be. Richard Harris felt that he was too important to come out to the clinic, and I felt that I was too important to leave the clinic and go down to the hotel. These things unfortunately happen. I'm sure I would have enjoyed seeing him. You know he's one of my favorite actors."

He really was, and I did enjoy taking care of famous patients, especially those whom I admired, but I was never going to interrupt my clinical duties to partake in a little stargazing. Of course, there were many occasions when I could tend to a star.

In the late 1970s, Mel Ferrer was in Atlanta filming a movie and we made Emory's medical campus available to the shoot. I thought it was extremely gracious of Mr. Ferrer to call and thank me for making the site available. We had a very pleasant conversation, and I asked him if he had any dinner plans that evening. He said no, and I extended an invitation to him to have dinner with me at the Piedmont Driving Club, in Midtown. He accepted with enthusiasm, and I arranged for a car to pick him up and bring him to the Driving Club. We had dinner in the Tack Room of the Club, and he seemed to enjoy himself, and the other diners in the club seemed to enjoy checking us out. We spoke of his broken marriage with Audrey Hepburn, and his dissatisfaction with the movies then being made in Spain. He was particularly pleased that I had enjoyed and recalled the details of *Scaramouche*. Though our paths never crossed again, both of us enjoyed the evening.

I received a call from Washington asking if I would serve as one of the hosts for Mrs. Maria Pia Fanfani, wife of Amintore Fanfani, Prime Minister of Italy, who was on a visit to Atlanta. Mrs. Fanfani wished to visit Egleston Children's Hospital for a television opportunity so that her countrymen could witness some of her activities on her visit to the United States. She would be a guest for a dinner and then continue her travels. Mrs. Fanfani proved to be a very charming and beautiful lady, and I enjoyed her visit tremendously.

Some time afterward I was in Rome to attend an international cardiac surgery conference and to fulfill a commitment as a guest professor at the University of Rome. On my first night in Rome, Professor Balsano, chairman of the department of medicine, and Professor Marino, chairman of the department of surgery at the University of Rome, took me to dinner at the Hassler Hotel. The Hassler, at the top of the Spanish Steps, is one of the finest hotels in the world, and it has hosted countless VIPs, as well as this doctor from Attapulgus! After dinner, they led me down the Spanish Steps to an awaiting car, one walking on either side and holding me by the upper arm. We drove to St. Peter's Square, where the Bernini Columns stood out so beautifully in the vivid moonlight. The next day at the University, we entered a large conference room with a portrait prominently displayed on the wall at the end of the hall. I guessed that the individual must be Professor Pietro Valdoni; I asked my host if indeed it was his portrait. They immediately inquired enthusiastically if I knew Valdonni. I answered, not well, but I had met him on a visit to Johns Hopkins. From that moment, I was absolutely golden in their eyes. In Italy there is no greater surgical accolade than to operate upon a Pope, and this Professor Valdonni had done so some years previously.

Upon learning that I was in Rome, Maria Pia Fanfani placed a call through her secretary to invite me to dinner with her and her husband at the Palace; they mentioned that I should feel free to bring several of my colleagues with me if I so desired. I promptly invited Professors Balsano and Marino and their wives to join me. The ladies were particularly delighted by this invitation, as none had had the privilege of dining at the Palace previously. We had a delightful dinner, and I remember Mr. Fanfani telling me at the table that people were dining in this very room before the United States had been discovered! After dinner we retired to an adjacent drawing room for a musicale. It was an exciting experience, and I was glad to extend the hospitality offered to me to my Italian medical colleagues.

And there were other instances in which medical arrangements were made. When Jessica Tandy was filming *Driving Miss Daisy* on Lullwater Road, my street, she and her husband, Hume Cronyn, needed to be under the care of a proper cardiologist. Dr. Spencer King, of the clinic, was happy to make the necessary arrangements for their care. Fortunately, neither suffered from a cardiac episode. Both did extremely well, and enjoyed the attentions of Dr. King.

On those occasions when I was not called personally I always enjoyed making the facilities, including the suites at Emory University Hospital, available to our distinguished guests. When Carroll O'Connor filmed *In The Heat Of The Night* in Covington, Georgia, he became ill and was referred to Emory. Dr. Jeremy Swan, Mr. O'Connor's private physician in Los Angeles, called Dr. Willis Hurst to take charge of his medical care. Dr. Spencer King did a coronary arteriogram. Dr. Hurst referred Mr. O'Connor to Dr. Joseph Craver, one of our fine cardiac surgeons.

There were local celebrities as well. One of our most popular humorists was Georgia-born writer and comic Lewis Grizzard. Lewis suffered from a congenital heart defect, which caused him a number of problems. He required an aortic valve replacement, and his care was directed by Dr. Willis Hurst, who was well known and respected beyond Emory for his service to the country as President Lyndon Johnson's cardiologist.

Dr. Ellis Jones, my first 'number one draft pick,' operated on Lewis Grizzard initially. Lewis had a well documented problem with his dental care, and prior to surgery we discussed this with his private physician. He felt that he could finally get Lewis to agree to proper dental care, with the necessity of cardiac surgery; unfortunately he was unable to get Lewis into the dental chair in time. Lewis developed bacterial endocarditis on a trip to Russia, requiring that he be reoperated upon on his return to Atlanta. This time we insisted that he have his dental care prior to re-replacement of his valve. Nevertheless, his infectious complications persisted, requiring a third cardiac procedure, which Dr. Robert Guyton undertook as a last ditch measure. Ultimately Lewis succumbed to his complications.

Lewis' social history during these trials was rather interesting. After a thorough explanation of the need for cardiac surgery, he informed me that his priorities in life were his writing, his tennis, and his wife, in no particular order. I was somewhat taken aback by this statement, as I perceived these remarks to be painful for his wife, but he followed this up by asking her for a divorce shortly after we discharged him from the hospital. He stated that he felt he had a limited time to live, and so he wanted to be free to pursue a range of activities. He got his divorce, and he did not approach matrimony again until his very last days in the hospital. His fiancée was very keen on marrying him before he passed away, and though I doubted Lewis' enthusiasm for the ceremony, he acquiesced and they were married shortly before his death.

Interestingly, Lewis Grizzard documented some of his experiences during cardiac surgery in his book, *They Took My Heart Out, And Stomped That Sucker Flat!* He recounted the removal of his chest tube as one of the most painful experiences of the perioperative period. Now this is a detail of care always handled by cardiovascular surgery—either by the surgeon himself, the house staff, or on rare occasions an experienced physician's assistant. It is customary to administer an analgesic, allow adequate time to pass, and then return to the Intensive Care Unit to remove the chest tube. This results in minimal discomfort, and the procedure is rarely remembered the way Lewis focused on it in his book. Well, I checked and found to my consternation, that in his particular situation, someone from the anesthesiology staff who was serving as an intensivist at the time had removed the chest tube himself. I think his desire to participate directly in Lewis Grizzard's care caused this break in routine. Removal of the chest tube by a physician not routinely involved in the procedure probably led to the memorable discomfort that Grizzard experienced.

This is not uncommon. During my time at Walter Reed I witnessed this type of atypical care, delivered by individuals not functioning in a routine capacity. When President Eisenhower visited the hospital, guards had to be placed around his suite, because technicians were known to drop by from time to time, to obtain a urine sample, or perhaps even a sample of the president's blood.

In the early 1980s the prime minister of Thailand came to see Dr. Andreas Gruentzig. The CIA had contacted me and said that the prime minister needed to come to the United States for his heart treatment. They wanted to keep the trip very hush-hush; the last time the prime minister had left the country there had been an attempted coup. He also did not want the people of his country to know that he suffered from heart problems. They asked me if we would be willing to work under these circumstances. I said that we would be glad to see the prime minister.

It worked out that the CIA would fly him from Bangkok to Seattle, then on to Atlanta. He was supposed to arrive at Emory Hospital around two-thirty in the afternoon. Well, I got a page from the hospital at eleven in the morning saying that he was already there. I went over to the hospital and said to the CIA agent, "So you don't trust me.'

'Well,' he said, 'this is a routine matter, we always have guests arrive at a different hour than is published.'

Andreas saw him, as he was a candidate for angioplasty, not surgery. I was present to provide back up. The prime minister was very gracious—he stayed up in the Woodruff Suite—and on the last night of his visit he gave a wonderful Thai dinner for all of us who had helped take care of him. The next day he flew back to Thailand without anyone ever finding out that he had left the country. There would be no coup, that week at least.

As a result of this contact, the King's brother decided to come see us in Atlanta. He brought his niece, the Crown Princess with him. She was a delightful young lady. They invited me to visit them in Thailand, but of course I thought I was too busy to accept. Some years later I came to regret turning down such a nice invitation.

The Columbian president was another visitor we had during this period. When it became apparent that he needed to have heart surgery, his government appointed a commission of medical experts whom they asked to review the international situation and give him advice as to where he should go for treatment. To our great pleasure and honor, they recommended that he come to Emory to be evaluated by Dr. Willis Hurst, who determined that he needed coronary bypass surgery. The surgery was successful. During his visit, he invited me to fly to his country, and though the prospect of dove shooting down there was quite enticing (theirs is supposed to be some of the best in the world), I thought such a trip was not the safest proposition given the near-perpetual state of civil war in his country. He gave me a beautiful leather briefcase during his visit; unfortunately burglars broke into my home and made off with the briefcase before I ever had the opportunity to use it.

These kinds of visitors were a big deal to us back then. We were still vying for people from the southern United States to come to Emory as an alternative to Dr. DeBakey and Dr. Cooley in Houston. We were not interested in growing into the largest heart program—we were happy to leave that to Houston, the Mayo Clinic and the Cleveland Clinic—but we were striving to be one of the best.

All of our special patients were not foreigners or celebrities. Mr. Jack Whitehead was one of these cases. In 1982 he had made a $135 million dollar gift to MIT to set up the Whitehead Institute of Molecular Biology. A number of years later, the doctors at Massachusetts General informed him that he needed heart surgery. He conferred with his staff. He knew that he was in good hands at Mass. General, as his doctors were professors at Harvard, but he wanted his staff to make sure that he was in the *best* possible hands. They reported back to him about a week later. He repeated to me what they told him:

'Well chief, you're in good hands, there's no question about that, but if you're asking us if you're in the best possible hands, that's not so. There's a little hospital down in Atlanta that is regarded as absolutely the best.'

He asked me what I thought. We went over his situation and I said, "We'll be happy to see you. I think you need surgery. We don't know if we'll have to replace your aortic valve or not, but you've got to have several bypasses. We have a new instrument that helps us clear the calcium deposits in your valves with ultrasonic bombardment and it could be applicable to your case."

Dr. Ellis Jones saw him, and he did real well for him in the surgery. When Mr. Whitehead checked out he left me a note: He was sorry that he had already given away so much of his money. He was tied to MIT, but he would talk us up as best he could. He cut Emory a $100,000 dollar check as a token of appreciation.

We also took care of a number of local patients who enjoyed special relationships with the university. Mr. Robert Woodruff was very involved with the clinic and a number of us attended him, especially in his later years. Dr. Scarborough had cared for him up until the 1960s, before Dr. Herndon replaced him. When Dr. Herndon died, Dr. Christie took over this important and time-consuming task. Dr. Christie himself was not well and by the early 1980s many of the senior physicians at the clinic were looking after Mr. Woodruff.

Mr. Woodruff was more than a Coca-Cola president, more than a patron to Emory University—he was as much a leader of Atlanta as any politician in the 20th Century. As an Atlantan, you could judge how far you had climbed up the city's social ladder in the way you knew Mr. Woodruff.

The first thing was to meet him. Dr. Scarborough introduced me back when I was a young doctor in the early 1960s.

Eventually you ran into him about town enough times that he recognized you. This came for me after I became the director of the clinic.

He then invited you to his home.

307

After that you would get an annual Christmas card, always a print by Athos Menebone of a bird that had been sighted at Ichauway.

Another step up and you would receive a single red rose on your birthday—never a note, only a single red rose.

An invitation to lunch at the Coca-Cola headquarters on North Avenue came next. I remember he used to bring Cuban cigars with him. He would pass several to me, and say, "Put these in your pocket, Doc."

Eventually you got invited to lunch so often that you knew the daily menus.

Later, when he was deaf, he had me sit at his side and hand him little cards with information on his friends who were at the hospital. Even then, he always liked to lead the conversation.

Finally, if you made it to the top of the ladder you got the invitation to come down to Ichauway. I never made it that far before Mr. Woodruff passed away. He was ninety-five years old when he decided that it was time to die. He was down at Ichauway and he just quit eating and drinking. He quickly grew dehydrated. He was so weak that it took two people to get him out of bed. His staff put him on a plane and flew him up to Atlanta. The doctors all descended on him like you would imagine. They wanted to pump fluids into him, place a central venous pressure catheter, insert a catheter to measure his urinary output, and all other sorts of things. I could see what was going on. I asked everyone to leave me alone in his room with his niece, "Little" Nell Hodgson Watt.

"Nell," I said, "We can probably keep Mr. Woodruff alive a week or ten days in spite of his wishes. I don't feel comfortable pitting all this technology against him because he's the one who made it possible for us to have the technology. Now he wants to die and we're in here making sure he lives to next week."

Relieved, she told me that she agreed. We gave him a daily bottle of IV fluids and all the morphine he needed. A few days later he floated off peacefully.

As for Ichauway, once Mr. Joe Jones took over, he invited me and other Emory Clinic physicians down for several days each year. One year I was invited to join former mayor, Ivan Allen, Jr., for the first hunt of the season.

Mr. Woodruff's younger brother George left us differently, sowing a bit of controversy after he was gone. He was seriously ill at Emory Hospital when he called me.

"Doc," he said, "they're just torturing me. I can't take it anymore."

He broke down.

"Well what's wrong Mr. George?"

"I apparently don't have any veins. They come in here every morning and they stick me and stick me and stick me. They can't get blood. They can't get in the vein. That one will go away and someone else will come and they'll stick me and stick me and stick me. I just don't think I can stand it anymore."

I dropped what I was doing and ran over to the hospital. I told the nurse to get me a central venous catheter. I put it in through the jugular vein, often a site of last resort. I put in a three-way stop cock and taped up the site. I wrote on the tape: *all injections to be given here and all withdrawals to be taken here.*

I put my arm around him and said, "Mr. George, you've had your last needle stick."

I don't know if it was that or whatever it was, but he attached a codicil to his will—he had intended to give the university another $15 or $20 million dollars upon his death, but he changed it so that the money went directly to the health sciences center. He died at ninety-two.

I remember Dr. Laney said, half-seriously, "Some people will do anything for money!"

Mr. Jimmy Williams was there and he said, "Well no, the money's got to go to the Medical Center because Mr. Woodruff said so, and the Bank is the executor of his will."

There was also Mr. John Sibley, who died when he was 98. Mr. Sibley was a prominent Atlantan for much of the 20th Century. He served for a number of years as the Chairman of the Board of the Trust Company of Georgia (known today as SunTrust Bank). The bank has always had a close relationship with The Coca-Cola Company; the only written copy of the Coca-Cola formula is locked away in a SunTrust safe deposit box. Anyway, Mr. Sibley's second wife was a Christian Scientist, so she didn't use doctors at all.

She called me one day and said, "My husband John feels that he should have a physician of record. He's asked if you would be willing to be his doctor. Now, you know how I feel about doctors, so we're certainly not going to bother you unless he absolutely insists upon it."

I told her that it would be an honor to be Mr. Sibley's doctor.

I did not hear anything from them for a year or two. And then one rainy Saturday afternoon I got a call from a nurse.

"Dr. Hatcher," she said, "I've had your name and phone number as long as I've been working for Mr. Sibley and he's never wanted me to call you until today. A little while ago he said, 'Would you mind calling Dr. Hatcher for me? I think I need to see him.' I think that's significant."

"I think that's very significant. I'll be right out." I promptly called Dr.

Stephen Clements of the Emory Clinic Cardiology staff and asked if he could join me in the visit to Mr. Sibley. We arrived together and began our evaluation of Mr. Sibley.

He was dressed, lying on a chaise-lounge.

"How are you Mr. John?" we asked.

"Doctors, I just don't feel good."

"Oh, let's see what we can find out."

We sat down and went through a standard review of symptoms—headaches, nausea, pain in the chest, indigestion, trouble with bowels.

"No," he said, "I just don't feel good."

"Well, let us examine you and see what we can find."

As we began our examination, Mr. Sibley suddenly stopped breathing and his pulse became unpalpable. He was gone. Dr. Clements and I remained with the nurse and Mr. Sibley until his son arrived several minutes later.

Section Eight: A Happily Ever After Ending

A Personal Word

I am fortunate to have grown up in my little community with such excellent teachers, good friends, and encouraging parents. Taking care of patients was never a burden or a bother; it was a privilege. There is no greater compliment than someone placing their life in your hands.

Medicine will continue to be a wonderful profession. To all young doctors I say that if you entered the profession for the right reasons, you will enjoy your career and be extremely happy. I hope that applies to most of you.

I have indeed been blessed.

A Wonderful Remarriage

AT THE TIME OF MY divorce, I truly believed that I would never remarry. Ten years of bachelorhood followed, seeming to confirm this. Then I met Phyllis Gregory Slappey. Phyllis had also been divorced for approximately ten years, and like me had little interest in remarrying. We met and I quickly began to rethink my position on marriage.

It was in the summer of 1986 that I received a call from a cousin of mine in Bainbridge, Georgia. At that time I was spending quite a few weekends checking on my parents who were now in their eighties. My cousin felt that I should join the social activities in Bainbridge and attend some of their parties during these weekend trips. I demurred, saying that I didn't really know anyone in the group to date, and that I enjoyed spending this limited time with my parents. She countered by saying that she had someone she wanted me to meet, an interior designer from Tallahassee, Florida, who was assisting her with a new home. I was intrigued by her description of Phyllis, and accepted her invitation for dinner the following Saturday evening.

Earlier that evening I had called my hostess when it became apparent I could not get my parents squared away for the evening in time for the dinner. I asked if I may arrive in time for dessert and coffee, and she graciously accepted my late arrival. I arrived just as the group was finishing dinner.

Phyllis immediately impressed me. In the after dinner conversation I learned that she was raising her three children as a single parent. I also learned that she had B.A. and M.A. degrees from FSU, and was quite busy with her career as an interior designer, co-owner of a fabric shop in Tallahassee, and as a member of the faculty at FSU. The evening was delightful, and I made it quite apparent that I wished to see Phyllis again.

313

I returned to Atlanta the following Monday for an early morning regular meeting of the medical center senior staff. Immediately one of my administrative assistants asked if I felt alright.

"What do you mean", I asked.

"Well, you look somewhat upset. Dr. Hatcher".

I confessed that we were going to have to rethink a number of things. That I had met a lovely lady over the weekend that had made me think more kindly of remarriage. Later I learned that Phyllis had told her children that she had finally met a man she would consider marrying.

I called Phyllis for a date the following weekend, and soon was making regular weekend trips to Tallahassee. As my staff noticed my increasing interest in Phyllis, they began to offer suggestions on how an older man should court an attractive younger woman.

"Dr. Hatcher, you can't continue to let Richard drive you down to Tallahassee in your gray Fleetwood Cadillac. You must project more youth and vigor. You need a new car, and you must drive yourself.

"I do?"

"Yes Sir, you do, and we've taken the liberty of ordering you a new car. But don't be upset. Your accountant has approved our actions, and it will be at least a week or two before the car arrives."

"What kind of car do you think I need?"

"A Jaguar."

"A Jaguar! Well, what color did you order?"

"A red four-door van den plas sedan."

"Red!"

"It's not a bad red. It's called Bordeaux Red, and it's very nice; and your friend, Bob Hennessey, at Hennessy Cadillac-Jaguar says it's perfectly alright if you don't want the car when you see it. He can sell these new models as fast as he gets them."

Well, I purchased the car when it arrived, and I looked forward to driving it to see Phyllis the following weekend. We were planning to spend the weekend on Sea Island, Georgia. I arrived at Sea Island on time, but shortly thereafter received a telephone call from Phyllis' business partner informing me that she was on her way but would be delayed. I left the car parked in the driveway of the house we had rented on the Island. When finally she arrived, she seemed very happy to see me, but didn't mention the car at all. I waited for some time before I brought the subject up.

"What do you think of my new car?" I asked.

She looked at me inquisitively, "you're in a different car?"

"Yes".

The following Monday I called my young advisors up to my office. I told them not to bother giving me any more advice about courtship.

"You don't know a thing more than I do about women", I said. "You've spent my money, and she didn't even notice the new car!"

As we learned more about each other, we realized that we had grown up only about 12 miles apart, and we were both a part of the old shade tobacco culture of our area. Our families had been lifelong members of the Methodist Church, and had known each other, though I had not met Phyllis as a child. She once brought that up, and I jokingly commented that child abuse was frowned on, even in that era, and that we had not crossed paths with each other because of the difference in age. I was starting college when she entered the first grade. We did figure out the first time we knew for sure we were in the same place at the same time. I was attending a family wedding in Havana, Florida, and Phyllis was a little flower girl in the wedding. We could recall the event, because one of the groomsmen, a West Point Cadet, had passed out at the altar during the wedding, apparently the victim of excessive partying the night before. It was humorous, and somewhat embarrassing that a West Point Cadet in perfect physical condition had passed out during the ceremony when no other groomsmen had any difficulty at all! In fact, Phyllis knew many of my relatives in her area quite well.

It was regrettable that Phyllis' mother and father had passed away before we met. I would have hoped that they liked me, and sincerely believed that I would take proper care of Phyllis and her children. I came to know her two brothers, and they participated actively in our wedding activities. I was also very fortunate in that there were several occasions over the following months to invite Phyllis up to Atlanta. I was the honoree of the Atlanta Heart Ball that year, and invited her to be my guest. A number of special friends had been invited to sit at my table, and it was a wonderful time to introduce them to Phyllis. Similarly, I had been cited by an apparel group as one of the ten best dressed men in Atlanta, and I got a kick out of taking Phyllis to that affair where I received a plaque which still hangs in my closet at home.

In 1987 I served as President of the Society of Thoracic Surgeons, the largest national organization of thoracic and cardiovascular surgeons. The annual meeting that year was scheduled for Toronto, Canada, as the STS includes the Canadian as well as American surgeons. I invited Phyllis and my children to accompany me to Toronto to share in the social events and to be present for my Presidential Address.

The dean of the school of medicine had put together a trip to various medical facilities in China. The trip was to honor Dr. J. Willis Hurst upon his retirement as Chairman of the Department of Medicine. I asked Phyllis to accompany me, and was delighted when she accepted. We had a wonderful time on the trip to China. Because of my position as the CEO of the medical center, I was a guest of the Peoples Republic which resulted in a number of courtesies. I was very appreciative of all the efforts the Chinese made to please our group.

In Xian I was a guest at a luncheon for our group and the leadership of Xian University. There was a dumpling luncheon, a tradition the city is famous for, and I was presented with the first dumpling of each course. After I had commented favorably on this dumpling, the round was served to everyone else at the table. I suppose to protect himself, the chef had a habit of preparing an extra dumpling for the group. I believe there were twelve of us sitting at a round table, and I was repeatedly given the extra dumpling at each course. An American doctor sitting next to me leaned over and said, "if I have another dumpling, I'm going to die!" I looked at him somewhat askance, and said "don't you dare die. You have no right to die. If anyone is going to die, I'm going to die. I'm eating twice as many dumplings as everyone else!"

Another day the governor of the province sent his car to drive us out to the excavations of the Terra Cotta Army. As we entered the immaculate black Mercedes, the interpreter turned to me and said, "Professor Hatcher, Mr. Lee wanted you to know that he drove President Ford and President Carter when they visited in our country." I nodded and replied, "Well, please congratulate him on his promotion." All morning Mr. Lee was looking into his rearview mirror trying to determine what sort of passenger he had. I can only assume that he credited me as being the head of Interpole or the CIA, or some other cloak and dagger organization. While we entered the excavation site, Mr. Lee put on a pair of rubber boots, and retrieved a five gallon can from the trunk. He carefully washed the mud spattered vehicle for our return trip. I asked our interpreter why in the world he would do such a thing, and he replied, "Mr. Lee would not want you to enter a dirty vehicle. It will reflect poorly on his hospitality. I was very impressed by this unselfish attitude, and ended the day with increased respect for all of our Chinese hosts.

By this time, Phyllis and I were discussing marriage. She had three children. An older daughter was a senior at the University of Georgia, a son then living with his father in Colorado, and a younger daughter who had two more years of high school in Tallahassee. We both felt that it would be unfair to ask Holly to move to Atlanta as a high school senior. After looking around Atlanta, we decided that the Woodward Academy would be an ideal school for her. Woodward is a private institution known to appeal more to newcomers, and the increasing international community, than the old line Atlantans who perhaps favored the Westminster Schools or the Lovett Schools. Holly was a very cute and vivacious young girl who fit beautifully into the Woodward student body. Many of her fellow Woodward students have remained among her closest friends. They stay in frequent contact with one another, and are now raising their children together.

On a visit to Atlanta for one of our hospital balls, Phyllis came down when I was in the kitchen with Richard, my son Charlie, and two dogs. She was wearing a lovely blue dress, but I pretended to insist that she needed some kind of accessory to pick it up. She was somewhat distressed by my reaction to her outfit until I produced a diamond engagement ring and said, "Here, let's try this, I believe it will brighten up your outfit." We announced our engagement that evening, and set about making final wedding plans. Phyllis has reminded me on more than one occasion that I proposed to her in the kitchen in the presence of a mixed group and two dogs!

Dr. and Mrs. Charles Ross Hatcher, Jr.

Though her health was obviously failing by this time, my mother was delighted when I informed her of my intention to marry Phyllis. She and

Phyllis had bonded, and Phyllis immediately assumed a prominent role in my mother's care. Unfortunately, shortly thereafter, mother fell and broke her hip. During her convalescence and rehabilitation following the hip surgery, mother was a patient at Tallahassee Memorial Hospital on her last birthday. Phyllis and Holly combined to make the day very special for her. Mother died quietly in February, 1987, and was buried on Valentine's Day. I had never thought that my father could out live my mother by more than six months, and although he started dying the day he lost mother, he lasted for a little over a year. My parents were quite devoted after sixty years of marriage, one child, and life in a small village.

Phyllis and I were married in the Attapulgus Methodist Church. Both of her parents were deceased, and my mother had passed away the year before the ceremony, but my father was able to attend in a wheelchair. This was the last time he was to leave our home. After the wedding we had a small reception at the farm in Attapulgus for some of the immediate family and friends. That evening Phyllis had a much larger reception in Tallahassee, and after we returned to Atlanta we had a third reception at the Piedmont Driving Club to officially introduce Phyllis to my friends. My daughter, Marian, had married her beau, George Thorpe, Jr., in 1987, the year before our wedding, and it was so nice to have Phyllis a part of that occasion. I had known and admired both of George's parents for many years. Unfortunately, George, Sr. had died of a heart attack before the 1987 wedding, but his mother, Sally, participated in the wedding activities and added her delightful presence to each event. Sally was very kind and helpful to Marian and George, Jr., and lived a very active life into her 90's. Marian and George are living in Washington, Georgia where Marian has inherited property from her mother and her grandparents. George is retired now. They both enjoy bridge and travel, and George plays golf almost daily.

Charles, III, had courted Leslie Williges, a New Jersey native, while they were students at Duke University. Charles is very fond of Leslie's parents. Dorothy and George Williges, and has enjoyed fitting into her larger family. Charles, III has pursued a career in banking and Leslie was associated for 20 years with INVESCO. They have three lovely and active children, Charles, IV, Caroline and Catherine. They have spent their married life in Atlanta, and it is a special pleasure to have them live within a mile of our home. Again, Phyllis was most helpful with the wedding of my son, as she had been with the marriage of my daughter. I always say that, although we got married later in life, Phyllis was with me and a great help to me in most of the major events of my life-- the deaths of both of my parents, the marriages of both of my children, and the many special events during my career.

While visiting Sea Island, Georgia in the months before we were married, I had been invited to White Oak Plantation, an animal preserve and center of pleasure belonging to Mr. Howard Gilman of the Gilman Lumber Company in St. Mary's, Georgia. White Oak was actively involved in the care and breeding of threatened species of African wildlife. On the day of that visit on a tour by John and Vanessa Lucas, who were in charge of the animal programs at White Oak, we were shown a young cheetah cub whose mother had died shortly after his birth. Humans had raised him until he was old enough to return to the colony of cheetahs. Because of his early contact with loving humans, he split away from the pack that day and came over to be petted by Phyllis. I was standing by her, and John Lucas got a wonderful picture of Phyllis showing great delight in playing with the cheetah cub. I determined on that spot that I would take her on an African Safari for our honeymoon.

John Lucas, who made annual trips to Africa to enhance the animal population at White Oak, advised me and put me in touch with the proper agents for a safari in Kenya. All arrangements were made on a personal basis. John Alexander, a retired British army officer served as our guide. He has remained in Kenya, and was quite familiar with wildlife as the former Director of the Aberdeers Game Preserve. John had been informed that we wanted a personal honeymoon safari just for the two of us, and with every convenience. I made suggestions for our menu, and ordered the wine and scotches in advance. We left on Swiss Airways to recuperate at the Baur Au Lac in Zurich, Switzerland, and then flew on to Nairobi, Kenya. The safari began at the Norfolk Hotel in Nairobi, followed by a week at the Masai Mara, a week at Aberdeers Reserve, and finally a week in the Samburu. In the bush we had delightful accommodations. A large tent for sleeping and relaxation, a bath tent with adequate amounts of hot water, and a dining tent with china and crystal, silver candelabras, and a generator capable of making almost unlimited amounts of ice.

Between relocations of the safari convoy to each of the three preserves, we stayed initially at the home of an old settler on Lake Navasha. The Mount Kenya Safari Club assigned us a cottage that belonged to William Holden. After the Samburu excursion we had planned to rest at the Intercontinental Hotel in Mombasa. Unfortunately, someone had broken a water main the week before, and we had no running water at the hotel, so we quickly disembarked by train for Nairobi, and the return home. All in all, a very delightful honeymoon! The trip to Kenya still ranks as our favorite of the many trips we have taken together -- perhaps because of that honeymoon flavor. I am certain we would have returned to Kenya, but the following year John Alexander was hacked to death in his bed in Nanuki.

In 1989 - 90 we expanded and renovated our home in Atlanta, giving Phyllis the opportunity to design a home in which she felt comfortable. Similarly, our guest house was rebuilt. The old bachelor pad disappeared as Phyllis restored and enhanced the original design of the house which had been built in 1928, and which I had purchased in 1963. To accomplish this renovation and expansion, Phyllis and I moved out of the house to a nearby condo. In all, the project took 16 months, but our architect and builder won a national prize the following year in the category of renovation of an older structure.

Four years later we conducted a similar renovation and expansion of our family home on the farm in Attapulgus. Again Phyllis was able to use her talents and skill to enhance the design of the home. The original family home on that site was built by my grandparents in the 1890's. My parents essentially replaced this structure in 1950. We still enjoy the country getaways to Attapulgus all year, and quail hunting in season.

Andrea graduated from the University of Georgia and moved to Atlanta to be near her mother. She is a delightful young lady, and although she has had many suitors of whom Phyllis and I were quite fond, Andrea has not yet chosen to accept their proposals of marriage, and enjoys her life as a single girl, and has developed a successful career as a jewelry designer.

Some years after our marriage, Phyllis was delighted when her son, Tom, asked if he might return to live with her in Atlanta. He transferred from Colorado State University to Auburn University, where he graduated and married his college sweetheart, Kari Riley from Birmingham, Alabama. Kari, like Phyllis, took her college degree in Interior Design, and she and Phyllis enjoy discussing their projects with one another. Tom and Kari have one son named Michael Henry who is a total delight. Kari has proved to be a wonderful mother, and we are all impressed by the way she is raising Michael. Only recently, Tom and his family have returned to Colorado where he is starting a franchise ice business, and enjoying the many pleasures of the outdoors of that delightful area.

My beautiful wife, Phyllis Hatcher

Holly initially attended Randolph Macon Women's College in Virginia, and subsequently transferred and graduated from Georgia State University. Holly married a Dutch South African who had attended and graduated from Emory University, Hjalmar Pompe Van Meerdervoort. Hjalmar has been quite successful in the orthopedic medical appliances field, and has worked several years in Europe, based in Amsterdam. Several years ago Holly and Hjalmar returned to the states and lived in northern New Jersey near the headquarters of Hjalmar's company. Most recently they have returned to Atlanta, and they, too, have purchased a home not far from us. Holly and Hjalmar are busy raising two active and energetic little girls,

Amalia and Olivia. Phyllis enjoys her role as grandmother as much as anything in her life.

Phyllis and I moved our church membership to Peachtree Road United Methodist Church where the pastor and his wife, Don and Mary Ellen Harp, and several of our closest friends urged us to become members of their church family. This lovely church has met our needs for a church home, and Phyllis is an active and treasured member of the Alter Guild and the Flower Guild. In all likelihood, Peachtree Road will be my final church home.

All in all a wonderful later life for two people who never intended to remarry. Phyllis and I will celebrate our 21st anniversary this year, and I love her very much.

Out of the Operating Room

DURING MY PERIOD AS ACTING VP for Health Affairs at Emory I had felt like the job was at most a one day a week responsibility. Dr. Laney had said that that would change as soon as I permanently replaced Dr. Herndon, and he was right about that. In those first couple of years as VP I tried to continue to do a few cases a week but it quickly became apparent that this was an untenable arrangement. There would be times that I would be scrubbing in, getting ready to operate, and all the while my assistants would be asking me to sign off on important business decisions. Half-seriously I said to them, 'Let's not do this when the decisions are over matters costing more than $1 million dollars.'

My schedule also caused a lot of conflicts. A lot of people with valuable time were clustered at the meetings I now attended on a regular basis. If I got a call from a nurse saying, for example, that someone had bled 200 CC's in the last hour, if I did not excuse myself and leave I was not being a very good doctor; if I did do that then I was not being fair to the deans and chairmen I left in the lurch.

After about two years of this I knew that it was time to give up surgery. I looked in the mirror every morning of my professional career; the first day that I doubted that I could operate as well as or better than anybody else was the day that I quit. Taking care of patients was never a burden or a bother; it was a privilege. There is no greater compliment than someone placing their life in your hands. But there is also no greater responsibility, so however much I longed to remain in the OR, when I knew it was time to quit, I did not hesitate for a moment. There was not an ounce of regret in my decision, only unhappiness that time had passed by so quickly.

In the late 1980s, I steadily reduced my clinical practice as I devoted myself more and more to my academic administrative duties. A single event would help me bring to a close my years in the operating room.

I had been referred a middle-aged male with multi-vessel coronary artery disease and a very low ejection fraction. He was a professional clown and very eager to return to his activities, parades and shows where he worked in the Emmett Kelly tradition entertaining children along the parade route. After thorough evaluation, I concluded that his ventricular function was too poor to permit survival with surgery, and that the benefits of surgery even if successful would be quite limited. After much discussion among the patient, his wife, his cardiologist and me, it was determined that surgery would be deferred, and that he would be placed on maximum medical therapy for at least six months to see if his cardiac function and exercise tolerance would improve.

Unfortunately, he returned in six months very depressed, and his wife stated that he continued to be incapable of his clown activities and that she couldn't stand to see him in the emotional state he was in. They both urged me strongly to attempt surgery, assuring me that they realized the risk involved. I really did not want to operate on him, but ultimately I acquiesced and surgery was scheduled. In the operating room the procedure went well, and we were able to wean him from cardiopulmonary bypass without tremendous difficulty. But early in the postoperative period he experienced ventricular fibrillation and could not be successfully resuscitated. With heavy heart I made the walk down to the cardiac surgery waiting room to speak with his wife. The waiting room was filled with his little clown friends in full makeup and costumes. They had arrived early that morning to keep his wife company, and hopefully cheer up his family. When I told them that he had not survived, they broke into tears and expressions of grief which were hard for me to handle. I, too, shed a few tears when his wife thanked me for giving him the chance at recovery by performing the operation he desired so strongly. After I left that special little group, I realized I could no longer take that degree of emotional trauma. I knew then that that procedure would be my last personal effort in cardiac surgery, and it was. From that day on I referred all surgical cases sent to me on to my colleagues.

Fifty percent of all the cardiac surgery performed in the United States is done by people under the age of fifty; when you get to be in your sixties your hand-eye coordination is simply not what it used to be. Standing at the operating table all day, every day, can get to be a bit much when you are sixty years old. I love surgery, but I always knew that it was something I would not be able to do forever. This is something that I understood from my earliest days as a medical school student working during the summer down at the Archbold Hospital in Thomasville. In my Presidential Address to the Society of Thoracic Surgeons, entitled *There is Life Outside the Operating Room*, I spoke on the roles that doctors can fulfill after a career in surgery.

I felt that it had been helpful to be a white-coat Vice President for those first couple of years. I sensed what the doctors were going through in a way that someone who ensconced himself upstairs in an executive suite could not have felt. If you isolate yourself, you cannot know what is truly going on in the hospital. If you do have some patients, you make your rounds and you are in the OR, and by virtue of simply being out and about on the floor you feel the pulse of the place. The doctors see you as one of them and they are not afraid to bring you trouble. Now some people do not want to hear about any trouble, but I think that this is the best approach. Even after retiring from surgery, I still took care of many of the trustees and university administrators. Whenever anyone got sick they called me, as I was still a doctor. I would arrange for them to see the proper physician or physicians and help explain to them their medical problems as best I could.

By the time I moved upstairs permanently I had more than enough on my desk to keep me busy. When I longed to be in the operating room I would say to myself, *Well, would it be better for me to do this operation, or would it be better for me to work out the deal here to build four new operating rooms, or add another hospital, or build a new Emory-Crawford Long.*

Eventually one realizes that you're playing a different ballgame. I often made the analogy that as a surgeon I had been a master carpenter, but the day came when I wanted to build more buildings and do more things, and to do that I had to form a construction company. There are some things that you just cannot do as an individual. What I enjoyed most about 'running the construction company' was the ability to *get things done.*

Of course I am a bit biased, but I did feel like authority was in the right hands. I had so much to overcome as a young surgeon—the administrators and some of the older doctors were obstacles instead of the helping hands I had expected them to be. I was determined that I was going to be a facilitator, helping our young doctors, and for this reason I took great pleasure in administering the clinic and then the entire health sciences center.

• ◆ •

Throughout my term as vice president, I had insisted that everybody offer me their resignation when they reached their sixty-fifth birthday. I felt that I would be quite a hypocrite to ignore my own advice. When I announced my retirement plans just before my sixty-fifth birthday, my friends in the administration and on the Board told me, again and again, that no one had even discussed my retirement, and that I should be in no hurry to leave. To this I said, "If no one has brought it up yet, then my timing is perfect." I wished to avoid being seen as an older obstructionist, not willing to depart the scene.

I felt ready to move on. It was time for some new blood. The nature of Healthcare in America was changing dramatically, as HMOs were beginning to dominate the landscape. Thankfully, I personally never had to deal with the HMOs all that much. On one occasion an HMO representative came to my office to try and sign me up for a contract. I told them that I would be glad to do their surgery, but that I wasn't going to start off by offering them discounted fees.

"We're going to concentrate the surgery over here. We can give you 500 cases!"

"Well, I'll tell you what I can do. You give me the 500 cases and next year we'll talk about a nice reduction. I'm perfectly willing to do that but I'm not discounting my fee on the first case when I don't know if you're going to send me anything."

"Well, we're terribly sorry, but we won't be able to work anything out."

I laughed and I said, "Lot's of luck then."

"What do you mean?"

"Lot's of luck going around Atlanta to the CEO's of these companies trying to sell them your HMO product—you're going to have to tell them that I'm not available if they have problems. Now you can avoid me and let's see how far you get."

That took care of that rather quickly.

Some of the other surgeons in the section joked that I will one day be introduced at Cardiac Surgery meetings as the last living surgeon who never accepted an HMO fee.

What is the solution? Though it is a long, difficult conversation, and one for a very different book, I do believe that some type of government-funded Universal Healthcare is the solution to many of the problems facing the modern medical profession. As the government already pays for so much, through Medicare, Medicaid, and extensive research funding, I do not believe the change would be as radical as some claim.

As a young man I had entered a learned profession, and I retired from a highly competitive business. In the early days of my practice before Medicare and Medicaid, we had made reasonable charges to our paying patients, and treated our charity cases for free. This contribution to society by physicians resulted in prestige and the respect and admiration of society. In order for physicians to accept these government initiatives, they were seduced by the promise of "payment of usual and customary fees." The new programs were to have little change in the practice of medicine. Older people experiencing difficulty in the payment of medical bills would be covered by Medicare. Initially, organized medicine resisted even this attempt at socialization. I felt at the time that it would have been much better if we, of organized medicine, had gone to the government and stated the problems we were noticing with our older patients, and assisted in the development of a program for their care. I was content to participate in the care of Medicare patients.

Medicaid, however, was a different matter. At the time Medicaid was being introduced, I deplored the profession's willingness to accept payment for our charity care. But again, the concept that physicians were about to be paid for all care they rendered indigent patients proved to be politically irresistible. Soon physicians were charging for everything they did, and many were itemizing the various components that went into routine care in order to enhance their payments. Throughout the '70s and '80s the cost of Medicare and Medicaid, though high, were fiscally tolerable. The medical payment system overheated, and physician income rose significantly. But then, with an aging population and tremendous expansion in medical technology, the cost of the health care system became unmanageable, and Congress and the American public chose not to create a single payer system or a system with well defined government controls. The political decision was made to open up the health care system to competition as a means of controlling costs. Some systems in our society do not lend themselves well to unbridled competition. There are many who feel that the airline industry is an example of a questionable system where there perhaps should be a role for government regulation. We are moving toward a system with only a few national carriers, hubs and large airports without service to smaller towns and cities, but the public remains enthralled with the concepts of private enterprise and the reality of reduced fees due to unsustainable competition. There is very little advocacy for return of a limited role of government regulation in this industry.

The health care system may well be another system that does not lend itself extremely well to unbridled competition. Many start-up HMO's have lowered fees to unsustainable levels, in order to build market share in a community. The failure of many of these health maintenance organizations is therefore inevitable, but in the interim prior to bankruptcy, many draw legitimate patients from stronger HMO's. The basic flaw in a "successful"

HMO is that profitability is related to decreasing the service provided. At the present, neither patients nor physicians are happy with the health care system. The government has spent an enormous amount of the public treasury to solve this problem, but a successful solution remains a prospect for the distant future. Electric power would not lend itself well to unbridled competition. Fortunately, it is regulated as a public utility. Though power companies remain in private hands, the fees that affect their customers must be approved by commissions or boards. I believe most people are satisfied with this public utility concept, and I believe we will move in that direction with our health care system. In the early days of my practice, my income was the average of fees received from private patients and charity work done without compensation. Today, health maintenance organizations offer payment at a reduced level for all their subscribers. So, in effect, physicians no longer contribute their services to indigent patients, but have become "low cost providers." Physician income would be quite similar with either means of payment, but physicians would feel much better about the role they play in society.

In recent years, improved medical therapy and interventional cardiology have reduced the number of patients undergoing cardiac surgery. Many types of heart disease continue to be treated appropriately with surgery, but the ability of the residency programs in cardiothoracic surgery to continue to attract the best and brightest is unclear. I have often said that I could have enjoyed a career in other professional fields, or a business, but if I were going to be a physician, I have been exactly the type of physician I would have hoped to be. Perhaps my colleagues and I did become physicians and cardiac surgeons in the golden era. Only time will tell.

Portrait of Dr. Charles Ross Hatcher, Jr.

Medicine will continue to be a wonderful profession. To all young doctors I say that if you entered the profession for the right reasons, you will enjoy your career and be extremely happy. I hope that applies to most of you.

Following my announcement, at the next Annual Meeting of the Board of Trustees of Emory University I received the proverbial "Gold Watch." Actually, they presented to me a handsome and classically simple gold Patek Philippe watch, with a black alligator band. This was the only watch I could imagine that would cause me to put aside my gold Rolex, which my parents had given me upon graduation from medical school some 50 years previously.

The multiple retirement affairs were quite flattering, but even more significant was the prompt establishment of the Charles Ross Hatcher, Jr. Distinguished Professorship. I was asked where I would prefer the chair to be located, in cardiac surgery or in health sciences center Administration. I chose cardiac surgery, and it was agreed that the professor and chief of the division of cardiothoracic surgery in the department of surgery of the School of Medicine would always hold this chair; and since it was further assumed that such an individual was unlikely to need personal income augmented by the chair, it was directed that the income from the chair be contributed to the research program at the Carlyle Fraser Heart Center at Crawford Long Hospital of Emory University. A proviso was added that if circumstances changed to the extent that the chair was needed in support of the professor and chief of cardiothoracic surgery, such arrangements could be made with approval by the chairman of the department of surgery and the dean of the school of medicine. I was honored that two of my close friends provided the financial backing for the chair, so as to avoid a fund-raising effort. Additional unsolicited gifts have been made to the chair so that the core was significantly enhanced in the near term.

The Rollins School of Public Health established the Charles R. Hatcher Jr. Award of Excellence, which is given annually to a professional within the health sciences center who deserves recognition for lifetime achievement in improving public health. I was named the first recipient. The annual presentation of this award is the highlight of my year. Phyllis and I make a point of attending the presentations and the receptions that follow.

I treasure each award I have been given, but none more than the Lettie Pate Whitehead Evans Award, which I received in 2007 for contributions to Emory University Hospital. Coming ten years after my retirement, this award means a great deal to me.

Each time I took on a new position—as chief of the section, director of the clinic, and the vice president for Health Affairs—I first served in an acting role. By announcing my retirement so early along, I hoped to avoid this situation. I found that it took about eighteen months to recruit, select, and move a replacement to Atlanta. When I announced my retirement I said, 'One minute to midnight I'll be in charge, one minute after midnight he or she will be in charge.'

A search committee was established to select my successor. The search concluded by the beginning of 1996, with the selection of Dr. Michael M.E. Johns, the dean of the Johns Hopkins University School of Medicine. Dr. Johns would assume his responsibilities on July 1, 1996.

In order to facilitate this transfer of authority, I dispatched one of my colleagues to Baltimore to check on the facilities that Dr. Johns had available to him at Hopkins, including some possible photographs and measurements. I had spent none of the money available to me for my personal office in the Woodruff Health Sciences Center Administration Building, and therefore had funds available to prepare a suitable suite for Dr. Johns. We decided that the suite was to be elegant but not ostentatious, and should compare favorably with the facilities he had enjoyed at Johns Hopkins.

The Emory Clinic had added some new administrative space that year, and they presented me with a suite, which they made available to me *in perpetuity*. I questioned the wisdom of that type of commitment. I warned the administration that they could not possibly offer facilities like that to retiring faculty, and that I was hesitant to set such a precedent. This was greeted by laughter, and they said, "We are not setting a precedent of making an office available to retired physicians, we are making this office available to you, and we do not anticipate that there are a lot of people who are going to come over here and complain that they didn't get an office but Charlie Hatcher was furnished one."

I was grateful and flattered, and ultimately accepted the clinic's offer. I moved over to my new quarters in April of 1996, which gave us three months to prepare Dr. Johns' suite in the Administrative Building.

The university asked me to remain on as a senior consultant to the president of the university and the university Board of Trustees. In this role I offered advice whenever it was sought, but I made a point to never volunteer advice to Dr. Johns. Further, I certainly refrained from ever publicly questioning a decision he made. If you really love an organization, you want it to succeed after you depart. Therefore, you should do what you can to give your successor every opportunity for success. Though it is hard to demure after leading for so long, often the best thing you can say is nothing at all.

In 2000, I retired completely, feeling that my continued presence was no longer necessary. I still maintain the office so graciously provided by the clinic. Mrs. Ruth Fincher, long-time Executive Administrative Assistant to me and to President James T. Laney, now retired from Emory University, still comes in as needed to help with my correspondence and my university activities—mainly patient referrals and fundraising.

Over the several months that followed my retirement announcement, I was given a grand series of farewell parties and events, beginning with small gatherings given by individual trustees. I was honored to speak at the Annual Board of Trustees meeting in November, 1995. In January, my partners in cardiothoracic surgery hosted a party for me at the annual meeting of the Society of Thoracic Surgeons at Disney World, in Lake Buena Vista, Florida. Subsequently, the American Cancer Society honored me for my contribution to their very successful move to Atlanta. A host of other celebratory events followed.

One of the most enjoyable events which honored my retirement was a dinner organized by my close friend and colleague, Dr. Mort Silberman. Mr. Howard Gilman, the owner of White Oak Plantation, had suggested to Dr. Silberman that he invite a number of guests with whom I had shared the White Oak experience over the years. Howard had suggested that the dinner be held in his home on the St. Mary's River at White Oak, although he would be in New York at the time, and could not attend.

Dr. Mort Silberman and Dr. Charles Hatcher

We had a thoroughly delightful evening, and following a splendid dinner the group presented me with a Merkel Side by Side 20 gauge quail gun. I still enjoy using this gun and thinking of the many delightful days I spent among this group as a guest of White Oak Plantation, and I miss Dr. Silberman more than I would have thought possible.

I had been prepared for feelings of abandonment, and had always said that if you stay at a university long enough, you will always leave with a broken heart. For reasons unfathomable to me, I was spared that fate, and retired with the affection and good wishes of my colleagues.

Atlanta and Emory:
Everything Changes

HEALTHCARE WAS CHANGING, AS WAS Emory. How far had Atlanta and Emory progressed in the preceding decades? When I arrived at Emory in 1962, Emory University was a regional school nestled in the suburbs of Atlanta. Over the next several decades Emory expanded from this regional institution to take its place in the first rank of American research universities. In many ways, this development and image paralleled those of Atlanta. Emory University was fortunate to have outstanding leadership during these years, and was the recipient of several very, very sizable gifts from Mr. Robert Woodruff and several of his foundations. More recently significant gifts have been provided by Mr. and Mrs. O. Wayne Rollins and the Rollins family and foundation. During the 1980's and early 1990's Emory University profited significantly from its close relationship to The Coca-Cola Company. With the success of The Coca-Cola Company came a greatly increased endowment. At one point, the Emory endowment ranked sixth or seventh in the nation, and was the only school to attain this rank located on the losing side in the Civil War. Of late, Emory University has experienced deterioration of its financial position, similar to other major institutions. The medical campus has grown tremendously, and is no longer recognizable compared to its appearance in 1962.

My good friend, President Laney, had left the University in 1993 to become the Ambassador to South Korea. The old administrators of the clinic who had been my elders when I first arrived were all gone. It seemed time to follow them out the door. As for the cardiac surgery section, I knew that it was in good hands, already under Dr. Guyton's care for quite a few years by this time.

Atlanta had changed too, the skyscrapers taller, the highways wider, the airport busier, and the suburbs seeming to stretch on beyond the horizon. Was *The New South* that *Atlanta Constitution* managing editor Henry Grady had championed during Reconstruction finally a reality? The upcoming 1996 Olympics seemed to confirm Atlanta's ascendance as a cosmopolitan, international city.

Atlanta had been undergoing tremendous changes when I first arrived. Whites controlled the City government– the mayor, the Council, the police chief, the judges, Grady Hospital, etc. etc. The situation has gradually shifted to the opposite of this. This has benefited Atlanta already, and I believe that the city is banking some very good things for the future. Atlanta is seen as a place where blacks have an opportunity to succeed. Black doctors, lawyers, architects – they are all drawn here, and the central power in the black community is shifting because of that, from the preachers in the pulpit to the professionals in their offices. These professionals look at financial matters with different eyes, just as I looked at dollars and cents differently than my academic-minded friends across Clifton Road.

It was inevitable that the political structure was going to change from white-dominated to black-dominated. And so, it was important that this happened in a way that would benefit everyone. Atlanta had always been a city where the local business interests played a large role in civic life, often working to smooth over the racial tensions that exploded into violence in so many other Southern cities. Men like Mr. Robert Woodruff, doing simple things such as quickly requesting tickets to a dinner in celebration of Martin Luther King's Nobel Peace Prize, let it be known that it was now quite alright to embrace the black community as they took on a very different role than they had after years of slavery.

Ivan Allen served as Atlanta's penultimate white mayor. He was the typical white patrician, Savannah born, to an old family. He was just enlightened. He was the first Southern mayor to integrate the school system (in 1961), though he caught a good bit of flack for that. He was the mayor when Martin Luther King was assassinated. Mr. Woodruff, aware of the explosive situation, called him, and offered up whatever funds would be necessary to arrange the funeral in a way that would prevent things from getting out of control. There were riots in many cities, and though the actual funeral was in Atlanta, I don't believe a single violent incident occurred here.

Sam Massell served for four years, following Ivan Allen. He was a great businessman, and he forged a coalition with many of the black leaders, which helped bridge the change to the new black-dominated city government. Sam Massell continues to play that role today, as the unofficial leader of the Buckhead district.

Maynard Jackson served as Sam Massell's Vice Mayor, before winning a runoff election to him for the Mayor's office. While serving his first term, he was married to his first wife, Bunny. Her mother developed a heart problem, and her doctors decided that she was a candidate for a pacemaker. She came to see me, and I put the pacemaker in. The orderly who came to pick her up for the operating room had a son who had recently been elected the Mayor of Chapel Hill, North Carolina. I was making rounds and stopped the House Staff in the hall to say "you're looking at the impossible dream. If when they were young anybody had told this nice old black woman that her son-in-law would be the Mayor of Atlanta, and this man that his son would be the Mayor of Chapel Hill, North Carolina, they would have thought you were crazy. This is a new era."

Maynard was a good man to serve as Atlanta's first black mayor. He faced pressure to work for the benefit of the black community, as well as pressures from the business community. He balanced the demands of both constituencies, handling the job so well that he returned to serve a third term in the early 90s.

Andrew Young, a veteran of the Civil Rights Movement served as President Carter's Ambassador to the United Nations. After a stint there, he came home. He had impeccable religious credentials, winning him the trust of citizens of various stripes. He curried support in the white community, especially from Mr. Charles Loudermilk of Aaron's Rents, and he won his way to the Mayor's office, where he served for two terms. He encouraged business investment, and brought the Democratic Convention to the city in 1988, surely a sign, in the wake of the GOP's 'Southern Strategy,' that Atlanta was moving forward on its own path.

I say that Atlanta was moving forward on its own path, because the city has always had an interesting dynamic with the state of Georgia. Though it is the state Capitol, many in the rest of the state view it warily, as a liberal, and perhaps even alien city. As such, I believe that my time in the North helped ease my transition to life in Atlanta, from a small southwest Georgia town like Attapulgus. When I arrived though, Atlanta was more like a big town than a small city, and Emory was a cozy regional school. But of course, over the next three decades Atlanta grew into an international city and Emory into a leading research center of some prominence.

I think if you look for a particular time when I realized that Atlanta had become something else, it was the early 1980s, right around the time I became Vice President of Health Affairs. The international terminal expansion opened, as did CNN. These two events, both seemingly insignificant, have come to define Atlanta a quarter century later.

In all of this, Mr. Woodruff was always there, guiding the city from his unique position outside of the city government. More than just contributing vast sums of money, he brought together leaders representing the city's largest companies, institutions, and social groups at weekly 'power lunches.' Though this unique position meant he was probably more powerful than any other person in the city, mayors included. Importantly, he always worked with the government, never against it. Mr. Woodruff was friends with Mayors William B. Hartsfield, Ivan Allen and Sam Massell, and worked very closely with them, but even later, as he neared the end of his life, he assisted Mayors Jackson and Young.

Unfortunately we ran out of good guys in 1994; in that year we come to Mayor Bill Campbell. He betrayed the public trust, and indeed he went off to Federal prison on tax evasion charges after facing indictments on charges of racketeering, bribery, and wire fraud. I can remember that lawyer friends of mine quit doing business with the City altogether during those years. Thankfully Mayor Shirley Franklin, Atlanta's first black female mayor, has cleaned up many of the messes she was left with, assuring Atlanta's continued growth, evolution, and success.

What had changed? Had *The city too busy to hate* simply swept its problems under the rug or had a new order emerged? At first glance it would seem that the problems of the past had been alleviated, if not overcome. Our schools had been integrated. The City Government including the Mayor's office came to be dominated by African-Americans. Our cultural institutions bloomed, thanks in large part to the generosity of Mr. Woodruff. When people look back upon the civil rights era they see that Atlanta was the birthplace of the movement.

Perhaps more so than anything else, Atlanta has always strived to be a commercial center and by that measure the city has succeeded—more Fortune 500 companies call Atlanta home than almost any other city in America, Coca-Cola is a global icon, and CNN broadcasts out from Atlanta to the world.

Have things really changed so much? In popular lore, Sherman burned the city to the ground. In reality there was little here to burn. Much of the world knows Atlanta only from *Gone With the Wind*, but in truth Atlanta had little to do with the antebellum South. The violent conflicts that broke out in many southern cities during the civil rights era never truly erupted here. The past Atlanta had supposedly shed itself of, never truly existed. At the same time, our proud boosters have always spoken of a present that is never quite here yet. So what is left is an idea of Atlanta.

The proper question would then be: whose idea of Atlanta now defined the city in the popular consciousness? Was Atlanta the odd city, 'South of the North, yet North of the South,' as W.E.B. Du Bois wrote in *The Souls of Black Folk*? Was it still Margaret Mitchell's romanticized *Old South*? Or was Atlanta *The City Too Busy to Hate*, the smoothed over, commerce enabling détente pitched by the boosters of Forward Atlanta? Perhaps landlocked Atlanta had become the placeless center of a new interconnected world—carried there by CNN during their unprecedented (though now commonplace) coverage of the Gulf War in 1990.

While everyone debated whether or not the Olympics confirmed that Atlanta had become an *international city*, no one bothered to ask what qualified a locale as an international city in the first place. Certainly having the busiest airport in the world must count for something, even if over half of the passengers are merely passing through to somewhere else. A MARTA rail expansion and a new international concourse both opened in time for the games. Perhaps name recognition is what is important. If CNN's ascendance put Atlanta in the daily conversation, then the Olympics planted the name—and a new idea of—Atlanta in the minds of billions.

During the Games I served as Honorary Co-chair of the Olympic Medical Support Group. My co-chair was Dr. Clinton Warner, Chairman of the Board of Trustees of Morehouse School of Medicine. Emory-Crawford Long Hospital, in Midtown, was close to the Olympic Village, and it handled many of the athletes during the Games. We chose Dr. John Cantwell, who had trained under Willis Hurst, and who worked primarily out of Georgia Baptist Hospital, to oversee the Medical Support Group. He specialized in exercise medicine and he did a fine job. We worked with him to line up a team of volunteers. Meanwhile Emory-Crawford Long readied its facilities for the temporary influx of international visitors.

The End of a Career

WE COME NOW TO THE end of a long and most pleasant career. The division of cardiothoracic surgery continues to be staffed with a group of excellent surgeons in spite of the fact that several of the oldest members of the group have retired. Case volume and variety remains excellent, and the resident staff remains of the highest caliber. The economics of the current medical marketplace has taken a toll on the financial resources of the division, but the necessary adjustments in income have been accepted without fragmentation of the division.

Surgical activities are increasingly concentrated at the Carlyle Fraser Heart Center at Emory-Crawford Long Hospital, and future plans call for new construction to house this center and research activities. I am confident that the leadership of the Woodruff Health Sciences Center is on target, and will permit the continuation of a very productive cardiothoracic surgical service.

The Emory Clinic is no longer the dynamic and productive partnership which existed for the forty years after its organization in 1953. In the days of for-profit partnership, The Emory Clinic was very entrepreneurial, and the clinic was a vital and expanding component of the health sciences center. I joined the clinic when there were less than 50 partners in the organization. I retired from the clinic when the membership totaled 850 members. In the early 1990's, in order to partner with Emory University Hospital and Emory-Crawford Long Hospital in the development of Emory Healthcare, it had been necessary for the clinic to become a non-profit foundation. The Emory Clinic continues to be populated with outstanding medical specialists and renders the finest possible health care to the patients of all our hospitals. However, there is a perceived diminution in physician input by clinic physicians in Emory Healthcare, and the clinic now functions more like a practice plan for the school of medicine than as a vital, separate component of the health sciences center on a par with the schools and hospitals. Only time will tell if these changes represent real progress, but they have been necessary adaptations to changes in the greater medical environment.

In 2007, my successor, Dr. Michael M. E. Johns, retired from the health sciences center, and became Chancellor of Emory University. His successor as Executive Vice President for Health Affairs, Director of the Woodruff Health Sciences Center and Chairman of Emory Healthcare was Dr. Fred Sanfilippo. Dr. Sanfilippo and associates have put forward an expansion and modernization plan for the health sciences center. The plan will cost well in excess of one billion dollars. Emory University is currently involved in a major capital campaign to reach the goal of $1.6 billion, over half of which has been raised to date. These monies will insure the continued growth and development of all components of the Woodruff Health Sciences Center, and insure Emory University's position as a premiere institution in the south. I am very proud of what has been accomplished by the school of medicine, the Rollins School of Public Health, and the Nell Hodgson Woodruff School of Nursing, as well as Emory University Hospital, Emory-Crawford Long Hospital and The Emory Clinic, plus our system of major affiliates. Over the past 45 years, it has been my privilege and pleasure to provide leadership to the Division of Cardiothoracic Surgery, The Emory Clinic, and the Robert W. Woodruff Health Sciences Center. I stand down with confidence in our leadership and the faculties and staff of our schools and hospitals. Personally, I am pleased to retire without ever having a malpractice suit, and I am personally unaware of any patient who would not be pleased to have me participate in their care should proper circumstances arise.

Presentation of the Woodruff Medal
Dr. Michael M.E. Johns, Mr. James B. Williams,
Dr. Charles Hatcher, Dr. William Chace

On July 1st, 1996—eighteen days before the Opening Ceremonies of the Olympics—I stepped down from my position at Emory. I continued to advise, but with each passing day, I stepped further and further away from the institution that had been my home for my entire professional life. I had been at Emory University for forty-five years, and I enjoyed all of the roles I was fortunate enough to play. I wore many hats, and it is unlikely that anyone could have enjoyed their positions of leadership more than I had.

As I departed, I recalled a statement made to me by President James Laney, in regards to my unique position of authority. "Charles," he said, "Emory University has been extremely fortunate to have you, but we must see that we never have another like you!" I understood what he meant. Things have changed, perhaps more than I ever thought possible.

Several years ago I attended my high school reunion. During the evening I was approached by a classmate who has had a distinguished career as an engineer based on the Island of St. Croix. Without warning, he stated simply, "Charles, you have been blessed." I attempted to mention how fortunate we were to grow up in our little community with such excellent teachers. He shook his head, "I'm not talking about that. I'm talking about you. You have been truly blessed in your life." I could only agree with his assessment. I have indeed been blessed.